LIFE SPAN

LIFE SPAN

Values and Life-Extending Technologies

Edited by **Robert M. Veatch**

Published in San Francisco by **Harper & Row, Publishers**

NEW YORK   HAGERSTOWN   SAN FRANCISCO   LONDON

FIRST EDITION

Designed by Jim Mennick

Library of Congress Cataloging in Publication Data

Main entry under title:
LIFE SPAN.
 Bibliography: p. 289.
 Includes index.
 1. Medical innovations—Moral and religious aspects. 2. Longevity—Moral and religious aspects. 3. Medical innovations—Social aspects. 4. Longevity—Social aspects. 5. Life and death, Power over. I. Veatch, Robert M. II. Institute of Society, Ethics and the Life Sciences. [DNLM: 1. Ethics, Medical—Essays. 2. Aging—Essays. 3. Death—Essays. 4. Longevity—Essays. 5. Life expectancy—Essays. 6. Life support care—Essays. WT104.3 L722]
 R725.5.L54   1978   301.24'3   78-3354
 ISBN 0–06–250908–X

79 80 81 82 83 10 9 8 7 6 5 4 3 2 1

Contents

List of Contributors

MARSHALL BREGER, B.Phil. (Oxford), J.D., is Associate Professor of Law at State University of New York Law School in Buffalo, New York.

DANIEL CALLAHAN, Ph.D., is Director of the Institute of Society, Ethics and the Life Sciences. His books include *The Tyranny of Survival* and *Abortion: Law, Choice and Morality;* he is editor of *The American Population Debate* and other books. He is a member of the Institute of Medicine, National Academy of Sciences.

JAMES F. CHILDRESS, Ph.D., is Joseph P. Kennedy, Sr., Professor of Christian Ethics at the Kennedy Institute, Center for Bioethics, Georgetown University. He is co-editor of *Secularization and the Protestant Prospect* and author of *Civil Disobedience and Political Obligation: A Study in Christian Social Ethics.* He is coauthor of a forthcoming volume entitled *Principles of Biomedical Ethics.*

H. TRISTRAM ENGELHARDT, Jr., M.D., Ph.D., is Rosemary Kennedy Professor of the Philosophy of Medicine at the Kennedy Institute, Center for Bioethics, Georgetown University. He is author of *Mind-Body: A Categorical Relation* and *Medical Ethics,* translator of *The Structures of the Life World,* by Alfred Shutz and Thomas Luckmann, and a contributor to *Death Inside Out.*

EDMUND L. ERDE, Ph.D., is Assistant Professor of the Philosophy of

Medicine, Department of Preventive Medicine and Community Health, University of Texas Medical Branch, Galveston. He has taught at Trinity University in San Antonio, Texas, and is a member of The Institute for the Medical Humanities. He is author of *Philosophy and Psycho-Linguistics* and contributor of "Free Will and Determinism" and "Philosophy of Medicine" (with H. Tristram Engelhardt, Jr.) in the *Encyclopedia of Bioethics.*

HERBERT GERJUOY, Ph.D., is Senior Staff Scientist at The Futures Group of Glastonbury, Connecticut. He is coauthor of *Life-Extending Technologies: A Technology Assessment,* also derived from the study on which the present volume reports, and a contributor to *Working with Older Americans.*

RICHARD A. KALISH, Ph.D., is presently a Faculty Member in Residence at the California School of Professional Psychology at Berkeley. He has taught at the Graduate Theological Union and the School of Public Health at U.C.L.A. He is coauthor with David K. Reynolds of *Death and Ethnicity: A Psychocultural Study* and with Lillian Dangott of *A Time to Enjoy: The Pleasures of Aging;* and author of *Late Adulthood: Perspectives on Human Development* and *The Later Years,* among others.

LAURENCE B. MCCULLOUGH, Ph.D., is Assistant Professor and Head of the Department of Humanities in Medicine, College of Medicine, Texas A & M University. He is co-editor of *Implications of History and Ethics to Medicine—Veterinary and Human.*

ROBERT S. MORISON, M.D., a Visiting Professor at the Massachusetts Institute of Technology, was Director of Medical and Natural Sciences at the Rockefeller Foundation in New York City and later Richard J. Schwartz Professor of Science and Society at Cornell University. He has written and lectured extensively on science, medicine, and social policy, and contributed the essay "Dying" to *Life, Death, and Medicine.*

ROBERT J. PARKER, Ph.D., is Math-Science Coordinator of the E.S.A.A. Teacher Training Program for the New York City Board of Education. He was formerly a researcher at the Roche Institute of Molecular Biology, where he published articles on gerontological research.

FRANK E. REYNOLDS, Ph.D., has done field work in Thailand, has served as a visiting professor at Stanford and Notre Dame, and is now Chairman of the History of Religions Department and Associate Professor of Buddhist Studies at the University of Chicago. He is author of *A Guide to the Buddhist Religion*, coauthor of *The Two Wheels of Dhamma*, and co-editor of *The Biographical Process* and *Religious Encounters with Death*.

ROBERT M. VEATCH, Ph.D., is Senior Associate at the Institute of Society, Ethics and the Life Sciences and is staff director of its Death and Dying Group. He is author of *Death, Dying, and the Biological Revolution, Case Studies in Medical Ethics*, and *Value-freedom in Science and Technology*, and is co-editor of *Death Inside Out* and other books.

Research Group Members and Consultants Participating in the Study

HARRY S. ABRAM, M.D., Professor of Psychiatry, Vanderbilt University.

ARTHUR CAPLAN, Ph.D., Research Associate in Ethics, Institute of Society, Ethics and the Life Sciences.

ERIC CASSELL, M.D., Clinical Professor of Public Health, Cornell University Medical School.

JOAN CASSELL, Ph.D., Center for Policy Research, New York City.

SAMUEL GOROVITZ, Ph.D., Chairman, Department of Philosophy, University of Maryland.

CLARK C. HAVIGHURST, LL.B., Duke University Law School.

MORRIS KAPLAN, LL.B., Legal Aid Society, New York City.

RICHARD A. MCCORMICK, S.T.D., Kennedy Institute, Center for Bioethics, Georgetown University, Washington, D.C.

WILLIAM F. MAY, Ph.D., Professor of Religious Studies, University of Indiana.

WILLIAM RUDDICK, Ph.D., Philosophy Department, New York University.

MARK SIEGLER, M.D., Department of Medicine, University of Chicago.

ROBERT E. STEVENSON, Ph.D., General Manager, Frederick Cancer Research Center, Maryland.

THEODORE TSUKAHARA, Jr., Ph.D., Manager, Operations Analysis, Products Division, Atlantic Richfield Company.

Preface

People have been intrigued, as long as history has been recorded, by the dream of extending life, and the twentieth-century person is no exception. Something is different now, however. For the first time, society may see those dreams come true. In this century alone life expectancy at birth in the United States has increased by twenty-four years. Techniques now on the horizon will not only continue to eliminate premature death from accident and disease, but will potentially change the length of the normal, full life span. Drugs, genetic interventions, and life-style changes may, within the lifetimes of some people living today, add twenty, thirty, or forty years to the life span. Although these interventions are in a very early stage of research and development, and most specialists in the field believe that significant clinical applications are still many years away, one drug already on the market for other purposes was found in preliminary laboratory tests to increase the life span of mice by 25 percent. Millions of dollars of government funds are directed to research on the mechanisms of aging. Private pharmaceutical companies and research centers are vigorously pursuing scientific breakthroughs whose social impact will be phenomenal. Our notions of work and leisure, the family, education, and normal health will be uprooted. The Social Security Administration, as now constituted, will be unworkable.

The existing and foreseeable technologies for increasing life expectancy and/or life span are numerous and problematic. Research and development are currently underway on technologies to cure specific diseases, replace failing organs with artificial prostheses, develop capacities to regenerate natural tissues, control environmental factors having an impact on health, and modify the basic processes of aging. Choosing to develop and use some or all of these technologies will depend in part on technical, scientific, and economic considerations. Learning what is technically possible at present and in the future is important for developing an informed policy.

Yet the critical choices will also depend on societal, individual, and group values, and our sense of ethical rights and responsibilities, for it is impossible to choose among technological options without resorting to a set of ethical and other values. This book, developed by the Research Group on Death and Dying of the Institute of Society, Ethics and the Life Sciences (The Hastings Center), is devoted to an analysis of these basic values and an examination of their implications for alternative life-extending policy options.

Early on, the members of the research group realized that several different types of technologies have the potential of extending life expectancy. Furthermore, two types of life extension are envisioned. First, life can be extended by intervening to change its course within the normal span, by focusing on diseases that cause premature death. Throughout this volume we refer to this type as changes in life expectancy, meaning the average number of years of life remaining at any given age. The increases in life expectancy at birth that we have seen in the modern period result from an increase in the percentage of people who live out the normal life span. If the percentage of people alive at a given age is graphed, as life expectancy increases the curve looks more squared off (see Figure 1.2, page 6). For this reason we refer to the technologies that extend life expectancy within the normal life span as "curve-squaring" ones.

Today we anticipate another set of technologies that have the potential of extending the normal human life span itself. By "life span" we mean the normal maximum age to which people will live if disease, accident, or other intervention does not bring about a premature death.

Consultants in the project agreed that in general terms—at least at the first stage of analysis—there were two distinct kinds of technological interventions. One group of technologies has curve-squaring as its principal effect while the other has life span changes as its primary effect.

The technologies themselves are extremely complex. The curve-squaring technologies are those that change the course of specific diseases: cardiovascular and cerebrovascular disease, and cancer. The interventions include prevention, better diagnosis, and treatment. Other curve-squaring technologies include nonbiological prostheses, such as the artificial kidney and artificial heart, and interventions that improve the environment.

Life-span-extending technologies are of a different sort; they are technologies, such as dietary control or supplementation, that alter cellular aging processes; that alter aging of organ and tissue systems, such as the reticuloendothelial system (which rids the body of debris); that alter aging induced by systems, such as hormone-induced aging; and technologies that have the potential of regenerating tissues of the body. A general summary of the state of the art is provided in the first chapter.

Collaborating with the Research Group on Death and Dying was the Futures Group, a research firm specializing in future-oriented policy analysis. Together the groups conducted a study of the policy questions raised by the development of life-extending technologies. The work was done originally to assist the National Science Foundation in planning investments in research and development of the technologies. The Futures Group was responsible for the technological and economic forecasting; their report to the NSF filled six volumes. The Hastings Center's responsibility was the assessment of the ethical and other value choices that will have to be made by our society as these technologies are studied and developed. This book is the result of that study. People who want detailed technical accounts of the technologies will have to turn to other sources in the scientific literature. The objective here is not to provide technical documentation, but to explore the ethical and other value issues raised by the possibility that these technologies will change human life expectancy and life span. As a background for the discussion that follows, however, the initial chapter provides a survey of the technologies under consideration.

The second chapter is a report presented as a rough consensus of the analysis conducted by the group. It is an adaptation drawn from the work of the group and is meant to summarize general areas of agreement. The group was purposely highly diverse. It is safe to say that not every member of the group concurs with every statement, even in the chapter summarizing the group's work. Chapter 2 is the result of eighteen months of work by the Research Group, criticizing the drafts of the background papers, interacting with staff and consultants, probing the impacts of alternative policy choices, and revising earlier versions of the report draft. Chapter 3, however, is a set of guidelines that were debated at length by the group and approved as recommendations of the group as a whole.

The Research Group on Death and Dying, an interdisciplinary research team of lawyers, philosophers, theologians, social scientists, and physicians, has, over the past six years, explored the social, ethical, and public policy dimensions of its field. For the present book the Research Group commissioned a series of background studies by its members and by consultants. Chapters 4 to 13 are made up of those background studies. They represent the views of the individual authors.

The objective is not to provide answers to the questions of values; individual members of the Hastings Center Research Group and the group as a whole have more or less firm opinions but no definitive expertise. Our task is to outline the major alternatives and the implications of each for policy choices that must be made regarding life-extending technologies.

We want to acknowledge the close collaborative relationship with Theodore Gordon and Herbert Gerjuoy of the Futures Group and the support of George Johnson and his colleagues at the National Science Foundation. A collaborative effort as complex as this one is sometimes as difficult as it is rewarding. Their spirit of cooperation made our task much easier. The Hastings Center is itself a complex collaborative effort. The members of the Research Group on Death and Dying and consultants to the group for this project, together with the staff of the Center, worked through draft after draft in numerous meetings. Special acknowledgment is due to Patricia Pierce, Nancy Taylor, Ira Singer, Ned Arnold, Barbara Ryan, Ernest Tai, and Allyn Perry for their efforts in the preparation of the book.

ROBERT M. VEATCH

I

LIFE-EXTENDING
TECHNOLOGIES

1

Life-Span Extension:
The State of the Art

ROBERT J. PARKER and HERBERT GERJUOY

This chapter provides an overall picture of the state of the art of life-span extension and a general frame of reference within which to consider the array of procedures that have been reported by researchers and theorists. It presents key information about each of the main approaches to life extension and the most significant life-span extension reported for each.

A great many of changes in normal bodily functioning and structure are age-dependent. As an individual gets older, the flow of waste products in the kidneys first increases and then decreases; the spinal column first becomes longer and then shortens somewhat with the erosion of the cartilage that separates successive vertebrae. Basal metabolic rate, cardiac output, maximum breathing capacity, nerve conduction velocity, and vital capacity of the lungs all decline with age (see Figure 1.1). Because such bodily processes and the structures that underlie them are intensely interconnected and mutually dependent, it is not surprising that various theorists have seized on particular age-related changes as fundamental, and attempted to show that they lead to most, if not all, the others. Each sees the problem from his own standpoint, like the group of blind men seeking to describe an elephant, each of whom felt a part and

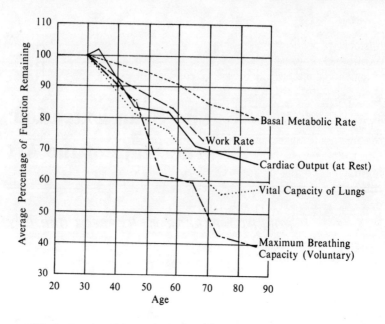

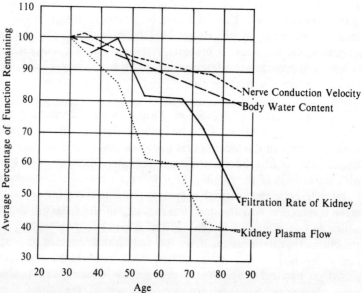

SOURCE: H. T. Blumenthal and A. W. Berns, "Autoimmunity and Aging," in *Advances in Gerontological Research,* vol. 1, ed. B. L. Strehler (New York: Academic Press, 1964), p. 292.

Figure 1.1 Degeneration of Bodily Functions with Age

mistook it for the whole. Theorists of aging are somewhat more sophisticated, however, each arguing that the portion he has fixed on is not the whole but the master or fundamental part. The result has been a number of different theories of aging.

Theories of aging may be either biomedical or nonbiomedical. The latter class includes psychological and social theories. Within the former we distinguish between theories that attribute aging to intracellular processes and those that attribute it to processes involving tissues, organs, or organ systems, i.e., to the action of groups of cells rather than to events within cells. Among the intracellular theories, some focus on the cell nucleus and others on those portions of the cell exterior to the nucleus (including the cell surface membrane and the cytoplasm).

DEFINITIONS AND DISTINCTIONS

Throughout this volume the terms *life span* and *life expectancy* are used to denote two different things. *Life span* refers to the maximum age to which a people lives, and *life expectancy* refers to their average length of life. To illustrate the difference, in a species in which half the members died at age 50 but the other half lived to 100, the life span would be 100 years, and life expectancy 75.

Thus, life span means the number of years an individual may be expected to live, provided no vicissitudes intervene to cut his life short. The notion of life span implies that if an individual lives long enough, eventually something happens to the body's functioning apparatus that makes longer life impossible; this process is built into the system from birth—or, more precisely, from conception—so that, if nothing causes earlier death, the terminal process assuredly sets the upper limit to survival. It does not imply that all individuals have the same life span or that each individual life span is determined by the same process.

As shown in Figure 1.2, there are in general two classes of life-extending technologies: those that increase the likelihood that the individual will complete the span and those that extend the span. We are mainly concerned with span extension here, techniques for which are reviewed below.

Technologies that extend individual survival within the span have been called *survival curve-squaring*. The curve referred to dis-

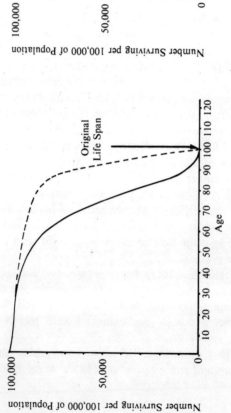

Original Life Span

Effect of Life-span-extending Technologies

Age

Number Surviving per 100,000 of Population

100,000

50,000

0

10 20 30 40 50 60 70 80 90 100 110 120

Original Life Span

Effect of Curve-squaring Technologies

Age

Number Surviving per 100,000 of Population

100,000

50,000

0

10 20 30 40 50 60 70 80 90 100 110 120

Figure 1.2

plays the proportion of persons surviving past birth to a given age. If everyone were to live until some fixed age, say 70, and then die, the survival curve would be a step function, remaining at 1.00 until age 70 and then stepping down to 0.00.

On the other hand, there are technologies whose principal effect is to extend life span. They may be expected not to make the survival curve more rectangular, but to stretch it out. If, for example, it were possible to transform people at every age so that they were physiologically like persons half their age, we would expect the survival curve to be like the present curve, but with the horizontal axis doubled.

It is hard to conceive of a purely curve-squaring technology that would not have some effect on life span, and vice versa. For example, any process that tended to square the survival curve by eliminating death due to heart disease might also be expected to extend life span in individuals whose aging is due partly to reduced oxygen and nutrient supply to tissues because of failing cardiac function.

PROGRAMMED AND ENTROPIC AGING

The notion of life span suggests that death is due to some sort of positive program; that it is the culmination of a bodily metamorphosis termed aging. Some feel, however, that aging is an entropic process, due, for example, to cumulative wear and tear or to the accumulation of insoluble waste products.

IMMORTALIST, INCREMENTALIST, AND MELIORIST
APPROACHES TO LIFE EXTENSION

Efforts to extend life span may be called *immortalist.* Curve-squaring efforts may be called *incrementalist,* since they seek to eliminate those causes of death that are traditional targets of medical or socio-medical research—identifiable disease processes, accidents, and suicide. The third or *meliorist* approach attempts to improve the quality of life of individuals, particularly the elderly, without necessarily changing mortality except as a secondary effect.

This tripartite division of technologies is based less on theory than on the points of view of researchers. Some proponents of life-span-extending technologies argue, for example, that it will scarcely be necessary to eliminate the diseases of old age, if persons can be kept from getting old. They argue that prevention is the best approach to such diseases as hardening of the arteries, and that the best preventive approach is to prevent aging itself. They point out that in the past twenty years enormous concentrations of resources have been directed toward the prevention and cure of the degenerative diseases with relatively little of value to show. Recent medical advances have primarily been in improved methods of sustaining life at the end stages of degenerative diseases. With this strategy, the cost of intervention increases rapidly as its effectiveness diminishes—the sicker the patient, the greater the resources needed, but the slimmer the chances for success. Those whose goal is to keep people from getting old argue that the basic processes underlying the decline in physical and mental functions with advancing age are also responsible for the increasing incidence of degenerative disease among the elderly. Therefore, the prospect of substantially extending both life expectancy and life span is likely to depend on the ability to counteract or reverse these aging processes.

Incrementalists argue, however, that step-by-step research has been the one successful path to medical achievement. They point to the many serendipitous benefits to general health that have flowed from progress in dealing with narrowly defined ailments. Improving circulation by conquering disease, for example, eliminates this source not only of mortality but also of morbidity, giving us a population of older persons who are effectively younger. They also argue that such incremental advances contribute greatly to achievement of meliorist goals, since poor quality of life among the elderly is partly due to the fragility of that life, and to the many disabilities to which it is subject.

Finally, the meliorists argue that improving the life situation of older persons will increase their resistance to the vicissitudes that cause death before the completed life span, and indeed will increase the span. They argue, for example, that cancer and heart disease have substantial psychosomatic components and that the incidence will be lower among old people who live in pleasant surroundings. General satisfaction it with one's life situation may also be an important factor in the rate of aging.

APPROACHES TO SPAN EXTENSION

DIET

Over the past forty years researchers have, through severe dietary restriction, produced significant life-span extensions in laboratory animals. This was first done in 1935 by C. M. McCay in research on Sprague-Dawley rats, a standardized laboratory-bred strain. The life span of the males was increased from 933 to 1323 days, that of the females from 1117 to 1456 days.[1] This experiment was repeated in B. N. Berg's laboratory at Columbia University in 1960,[2] in A. J. Carlson's laboratory at the University of Chicago in 1946,[3] and most extensively by Morris Ross at the Institute for Cancer Research in Philadelphia, in ongoing research begun in 1965. Ross's work over a two-decade period produced rats that lived in excess of 1600 days and experienced many other health benefits. The incidence of disease was sharply lower, and disease occurred at a much later time in life than in the control animals. Varying the diet produced different degrees of life-span extension.[4] The diet with the smallest amount of sugar contained thirty-four percent sugar, a regimen that would be disastrous for humans but that provided the easiest way to satisfy caloric needs in the rat.

In McCay's initial work, it was not found possible to extend the life span of the rat once adulthood had been reached. Ross, however, significantly extended the life span by starting the dietary restrictions at 300 and 365 days of age. Rats that had been eating twenty grams of food a day were restricted to eight grams, and their life span was significantly increased. Decreasing the allotment to ten grams a day increased the life span even more—to nearly a year greater than that of the controls. The incidence of cancer was also dramatically reduced in these animals.

Application to Humans. Actuarial tables indicate that the life span of underweight people may be fifteen to twenty years greater than that of the overweight. A moderately slow decline in food consumption to a final level that is two-thirds of the amount normally consumed, supplemented with vitamins and minerals, is certainly feasible in humans, and would undoubtedly produce the largest life-span increase that could be expected from any presently known interventions. For persons "without an ounce of fat on the

body," reducing food intake by thirty-three percent might of course
be fatal. It might be more reasonable for such a person to aim for a
twenty percent reduction, with "stops" at five, ten, and fifteen percent.

A diet has been set up by Dr. Pritikin, of the Longevity Research Institute in Santa Barbara, California, with life-span extension as its goal. Another is being established by Chadd Everone as
part of his Life Extension and Control of Aging Program. It will be
individuated to the unique dietary needs of each participant by a
computer, in order to maximize the diet's nutritional benefits.

Tryptophan-Deficient Diet.   Paul Segall and Pacta Timiras
have maintained rats on diets grossly deficient in tryptophan, an
amino acid thought essential to human life. While many became
very ill and died, those rats that survived lived surprisingly long
lives.[5] Tryptophan deficiency has extended the duration of litter-
bearing capacity by eleven months and increased life expectancy by
four and a half months. This may, however, be mainly a variation of
dietary restriction, since the elimination of tryptophan produces a
retardation in growth which nearly parallels the effects of severe dietary restriction described by McCay and Ross. Because dietary restriction has produced the only significant increase in life span, this
procedure should be studied as a means of understanding how dietary restrictions affect aging. It is not practical, however, for humans to live on a tryptophan-deficient diet, because the deficiency
produces severe illness (e.g., serious defects in brain function), or
even death.

Vitamins and Minerals.   A minimum level of vitamins is essential to ordinary longevity in humans; in addition, wheat germ
supplement has been found by McCay to produce a twenty-one percent increase in the life expectancy of female rats.[6] Pantothemic
acid, a B vitamin, has also produced extensions of life span in laboratory animals, and so it would seem that increases in vitamins and
mineral supplements might be investigated as a means of prolonging
human life. It is likely that the amount and type of vitamin supplementation that will maximize longevity will vary from individual to
individual.

NUCLEIC ACID

Nucleic acid therapy has increased the life expectancy and life
span of white mice in at least two laboratories. The largest increase

in life expectancy is seventeen percent for female mice, reported by T. B. Robertson, a researcher in Australia. He also reported a 100-day increase in the life span of the male mouse.[7] T. S. Gardner achieved a life-span extension of about two-thirds of this amount using one-tenth of the dose of nucleic acid Robertson used.[8] Gardner's dose, extrapolated to humans, would be five and a half grams of nucleic acid a day—an amount which could certainly be tested in humans. Since nucleic acid therapy produces many other beneficial effects, such as improvement of the immune system and of the memory, this is one of the first therapies that might be investigated systematically.

Dr. Benjamin Frank has written four books on nucleic acid therapy, parts of which describe administration to humans.[9] There is some evidence that it improves memory.[10] The original rationale behind investigating the effects of nucleic acids was probably the expectation that they would increase the body's nucleotides, which could improve protein synthesis. The increase in nucleotides might explain the increase in immune function found following nucleic acid treatment[11] and could make available more ATP, a substance essential to many interactions in the body. A fairly exhaustive review of the benefits and possible mechanisms of nucleic acid therapy has been written by Saul Kent for *Geriatrics* magazine.[12]

LOWERING BODY TEMPERATURE

John Maynard-Smith was able to extend the life span of the fruit fly by lowering body temperature;[13] Roy Walford and R. K. Liu have attained similar results with the annual fish *Cynolebias belotti*. In one experiment the life span of the fish increased by seventy-six percent. The fish grew faster at the lower temperature, indicating that the temperature-related deceleration of the rate of aging was probably not due to a general metabolic slowdown. Walford believes that lowering body temperature increases life expectancy by slowing the increase of auto-immune phenomena, i.e., allergy or sensitivity to one's own tissues, especially during the latter half of life.[14] He is currently trying to prolong the life span of mice through intraperitoneal injections of drugs that produce mild hypothermia. Robert Myers at Purdue University has increased the life span of monkeys by manipulating the "thermostat" in the hypothalamus, and Barnett Rosenberg of Michigan State University has achieved similar results with a drug that lowers the temperature a few degrees in rats. R. T. Balmer of the University of Wisconsin is presently following up these leads.[15]

CORRECTING OR PREVENTING FAILURE
OF THE IMMUNE MECHANISM

It is thought by some (Walford, among others) that the central factor in aging is the progressive failure of the immune mechanisms which provide the organism with a sort of primitive stimulus-response capability. On the stimulus side, immune mechanisms enable the organism to distinguish its own cells, cellular products, and cellular components from foreign materials that might disrupt bodily functioning. Such foreign materials include pathogenic microorganisms and their products, cancer cells, pathogenic viruses, and various toxins. With any recognition system, questions of signal-to-noise ratio can be important. It is not hard to invent a model which has the reticuloendothelial system, that bodily system which governs immunity and allergy, gradually losing its capacity to distinguish friend from foe due to accumulation of noise in the sentinel program that evaluates the immunological password of a possible foe. At the response end, the immune system must seek to neutralize a vast variety of foreign substances. Here, too, there is obviously sensitivity to noise which may disturb the way the system's response is modulated according to the nature of the stimulus.

In the near future, several agents thought to improve various aspects of the immune system will be tested clinically, in the hope that they may turn out to be useful in increasing immune competence. Thus far, none of the interventions specifically designed to improve the immune system has increased survival, but many procedures have been devised which improve the immune system significantly.[16] These should be studied to determine their potential to increase the life span.

CELLULAR THERAPY

Placental cells and extracts have been used extensively on humans in Europe and Russia, with many reported benefits. The human placenta is very rich in B vitamins, particularly pantothenic acid (an antioxidant that has been used to produce moderate increases in survival as noted above).

GEROVITAL

Gerovital H_3, a solution containing procaine hydrochloride, a widely used local anesthetic, has significantly extended the life expectancy and span of not particularly long-lived rats in at least two laboratories. Procaine hydrochloride inhibits MAO, which is responsible for the breakdown of dopamine, norepinephrine, and serotonin—in the brain. These are all substances involved in the brain's control of the level of excitability of various of its sections. Inhibition of MAO activity might result in better functioning of certain neurons are particularly plentiful.

Gerovital is the most popular antiaging drug of all time. Given to hundreds of thousands of patients since Romanian physician Ana Aslan first discovered its supposed benefits in treating the elderly, it has been alleged to alleviate or reverse the symptoms of virtually every affliction of the aged. Aslan began her research in 1951, at the Bucharest Institute of Geriatrics. In her fifteen-year open-longitudinal study (i.e., one in which new cases were added as they became available), Aslan tested several chemotherapeutic agents in three groups of elderly patients.[17] One group received procaine, the second, vitamin E, and the third (which served as a control group), an extract of the pineal gland near the center of the brain. (The pineal gland corresponds to the centrally located third eye in certain species.) The mortality rate was fifteen percent for the control group, ten percent for the vitamin E group, and only five percent for the procaine group. However, these data are not only scanty and incomplete but also apparently inconsistent with earlier reports of the same study. Moreover, the studies have been criticized as being uncontrolled and too subjective in their findings. In six of eight double-blind control studies (i.e., studies in which both the patients and those treating them are unaware of whether the drug or a neutral placebo is being administered) conducted in the United States and the United Kingdom in the early 1960s, no benefits were reported for procaine-treated patients; two other studies reported only slight benefits in psychologic and cognitive functions of procaine-treated patients. These later studies, however, did not use the trace additives in their procaine preparation as that Aslan used.[18]

HORMONAL APPROACHES

A final major group of theories views the aging process as essentially hormonal. One important theory sees the hypothalamus, that portion of the brain concerned primarily with emotions and basic biological urges such as hunger, as secreting important hormones that mediate the aging process. At the laboratories of the University of California School of Medicine, Paul Segall has hypothesized that the aging-inducing effects of the hypothalamus hormone require tryptophan in the diet of the organism, probably because it is an essential precursor of the age-causing hormone.

The Pituitary.   Early studies have shown that whole pituitary extract can prolong the life span of old rats. W. Donner Denckla of Harvard has suggested that the pituitary gland produces a decreasing-oxygen-consumption factor (DECO) that actually programs dying.[19] Extending life span would mean defeating the action of DECO, perhaps by developing an immunological or chemical antagonist. Denckla hypothesizes that DECO interferes with the functioning of the thyroid. Although he has yet to isolate this factor, he has presented substantial evidence for its existence and suggested that the human life span might be prolonged by eliminating, reducing, or modifying its release.

It has also been suggested that oxytocin, an extract of the posterior pituitary gland, may have an impact on life expectancy.[20] It is generally agreed that the aging process is associated with a redistribution of salt and water, in particular with increases in water turnover and loss, and a decrease in urinary salt content. The use of posterior pituitary powder on rats by S. M. and C. L. Friedman resulted in an increase in life expectancy and partial alleviation of the above symptoms. Vasopressin (a hormone that increases blood pressure), the assumed active factor, was also tested but did not increase the life span.[21]

M. Bodanszky, repeating the experiment on Sprague-Dawley rats, also obtained an increase in life expectancy (see note 20). He guessed the active factor to be oxytocin, and obtained a modest but not quite significant increase in survival using the milk ejection hormone. If oxytocin is the pituitary factor responsible for the effect, its mode of action is not known.

Thyroid Hormones.   Some researchers have begun to suspect that there is genuine hypothyroidism with old age. Because the span of acceptable values of thyroid function is so great, it is difficult to establish the onset of hypothyroidism with age. Broda Barnes has reported the beneficial effects of thyroid hormones in older persons and there is a growing body of evidence that many aged individuals experience a mild form of hypothyroidism. The symptoms include slightly lower than normal body temperature, tendency to fatigue and sluggishness, some edema (possibly in the face), poor circulation, and lower metabolic rate. These symptoms can be removed by a moderate regimen of thyroid hormone therapy—a quarter to half grain daily, and never more than one grain—under strict supervision of a physician. Dr. Barnes found his therapy very helpful in preventing recurrence of heart attacks; in a total of 2,000 patients over a twenty-year period, he saw only four cases of recurrent heart attack among those receiving thyroid therapy, or a rate of two per 1,000 patients. In a study conducted in Framingham, Massachusetts, 5,000 heart patients were encouraged to eliminate cholesterol from their diet, stop cigarette smoking, exercise, and reduce stress in an effort to avoid a second heart attack. Over a twenty-year period, 600 patients suffered a second attack—an average of 120 per 1,000 patients, a rate sixty times that seen by Dr. Barnes.[22]

No increase in life span has been reported with the use of thyroid hormones, but it is possible that their use may, in certain instances, improve the quality of life for people aged fifty and over.

In 1904, M. A. Lorand, noticing similarities between hypothyroidism and senescence, gave thyroid hormones to many elderly patients and eliminated the symptoms of hypothyroidism. At the turn of the century there was a flurry of interest in thyroid hormones as the possible elixir of youth, but all the patients eventually died, as did the interest in the hormones.[23]

Steroids. Steroids are the class of substances which includes the sex hormones and hormones involved in the body's response to stress. Large increases in the life expectancy of a particularly short-lived strain of mouse have been produced by prednisolone, a major steroid.[24] One of the most outstanding results of dietary restriction on weaning animals is the pronounced growth-inhibiting effect of prednisolone. Corticosteroids, those steroids primarily involved in response to stress, have a similar growth-inhibiting effect, and rats treated for several weeks remained healthy despite the reduced rate of growth. Although the growth-inhibition is not permanent, it is interesting to study the effects of the continuous administration of this type of steroid over the entire life span. Steroids of the cortisol type might be useful tools with which to investigate the relationship between the rate of growth and certain age changes in metabolism. The negative feeling about long-term use of steroids makes it unlikely that adequate clinical trials of prednisolone will be done on humans.

L-DOPA

L-dopa in much larger dosages than are used in humans for the treatment of Parkinson's disease has significantly increased the life expectancy of male Swiss Webster albino mice.[25] L-dopa is the immediate precursor of dopamine, which in turn is the immediate precursor of norepinephrine. Its administration might increase the chances for better functioning of the dopaminergic and cholinergic neurons in the brain. Inadequate functioning of the brain is undoubtedly incompatible with continued good health into old age.

Because of persistent reports that prolonged use of L-dopa produces nausea, cardiac irregularities, depression, and other bad side effects in humans, it is unlikely that life-span-extension trials on humans will be attempted in the near future.

CORRECTING AND PREVENTING CELLULAR
BIOCHEMICAL ERRORS

An alternative to the theory of cellular programming is the theory that aging results from an intra- or extra-cellular biochemical breakdown in the cell's ability to reproduce itself. It has been proposed by Johan Bjorksten, director of the Bjorksten Research Foundation in Madison, Wisconsin,[26] that cross-linkages in DNA and other molecules may be the primary cause of many aging processes. Cross-linkage is the inadvertent coupling of two molecules caused by the accumulation of free radicals or other, less common, sources of excessive chemical energy in the cell, in such a way that they cannot carry out their normal functions.

Accumulation of Free Radicals and Abnormal Oxidation.
Free radicals are very energetic molecular fragments generally produced by a high energy event in the cellular protoplasm outside the cell nucleus. They may be related to X-rays or to any sort of ener-

getic radiation. Once formed, they tend under most circumstances to be sources of positive feedback for abnormal metabolic processes and to participate in reactions whose products are also likely to be highly energetic and physiologically destructive. Free radicals constitute a kind of poison whose direct interference with cellular metabolism is much greater than such relatively inert agents as deuterium or lipofuscin.

As serious as free radicals may be in the cytoplasm, the most dangerous consequences arise when they form in special structures such as the ribosomes or nuclear genetic material. By adding a considerable amount of noise to the genetic record they may be responsible for mutations that could kill a cell or prevent its growth and replication.

Free radical reactions which are everywhere in living systems have been implicated in the degradation of such systems. They may be diminished by the proper administration of an antioxidant drug which is a free radical scavenger.[27]

Several theorists have stressed the importance of abnormal oxidation processes in the progressive loss of cellular function. The process is similar to the way in which fats such as butter become rancid. In the cell membrane and cytoplasm, important metabolic and immunological components are primarily lipid in nature, and therefore liable to this kind of oxidative attack. Thus, progressive oxidation of fatty components of the cell membrane may explain why older cells are more vulnerable to attack by the body's own immunological defenses. Antioxidants may slow aging by absorbing excess oxidizing capabilities. It has been suggested that when oxidation reactions go wrong, free radicals are formed. Therefore, antioxidants may be particularly important antiaging compounds.

D. Harman has been trying to slow the aging process by inhibiting deleterious free radical reactions with dietary antioxidants. He has identified certain compounds (2-mercaptoethylamine hydrochloride, for example) that extend the survival of mice between thirteen and forty-five percent. Another antioxidant, ethoxyquin, was tested by Alex Comfort. He found a twenty percent increase in life span over the control group for an experimental group of mice.[28] Vitamins E and C are natural antioxidants, and some experiments indicate that their use increases life span and life expectancy. While some *in vitro* experiments have produced analogous results, others have had negative outcomes. The role of antioxidants may be the inhibition of certain harmful environmental or nutritional factors which cause control animals to show suboptimal survival rates.

Free radical reactions alter certain molecules (such as collagen, elastin, and DNA), break down some organic sugars (mucopolysaccharides), cause accumulation of inert materials that may be harmful (lipofuscin), and change membrane characteristics due to lipid peroxidation, a process in which fatty constituents of cells undergo a change, due to reaction with oxygen, similar to the change in stored fats or oils which become rancid. If they contribute to the degradation of biological systems, it might be possible by acceptable, practical dietary regulation to increase the life span by decreasing their level by means of antioxidants. Life-span extension has been reported for most of the following chemicals: butylated hydroxtoluene (see note 27), ethoxyquin (see note 28), nordihydroguaiaretic acid, cysteine, vitamin E (see note 27), and pantothenic acid.[29]

A large segment of the United States population, exposed to antioxidants in the form of spoilage retardants, are unwitting participants in what may be the largest life-extension experiment ever performed on humans. While there is evidence that certain food additives have deleterious effects, there is no proof that all are harmful or that life expectancy has been shortened by all additives. Moreover, it appears that the incidence of some stomach cancers has decreased as a result of BHT, which is put in bread to prevent spoilage. It may be time to test antioxidants on humans in a systematic way.

Membrane Damage.   Lysosomes, pockets of fluid in the central part of every animal cell, contain potent digestive enzymes that break down nutrients and various components within the cell, and are then renewed by protein synthesis. When functioning properly, the lysosome releases its enzymes at the rate necessary to "clean up" the cell. When the lysosomal membrane is defective, the enzymes leak out at an uncontrolled rate which can lead to cell damage or death. Aging processes may reflect the accumulated consequences of membrane breakdown within cells. The lysosomal membrane is particularly sensitive to damage by lipid peroxidation and other free radical reactions associated with normal cell metabolism. Leakage of hydrolytic enzymes through damaged lysosomal membranes into the cytoplasm, the nucleus, and extracellular spaces has been thought by many scientists to produce the kind of damage to DNA, cellular machinery, and extracellular proteins which is variously postulated to underlie aging.

In addition to antioxidants which can neutralize some free radical reactions, there is a class of compounds with diethylaminoethyl (DEAE) or dimethylaminoethyl (DMAE) moieties (major portions of their molecules), which can have membrane-stabilizing effects.[30]

Prominent among membrane-stabilizing agents which have been tested extensively on laboratory animals and insects is centrophenoxine, which has a DMAE moiety. Richard Hochschild of the University of California used centrophenoxine on Swiss Webster albino mice and produced a fifteen percent increase in life expectancy and a twenty-six percent increase in life span, from twenty-six to thirty-three months of age (see note 32). Unfortunately, because the maximum life span for the rat in the laboratory is at least forty months, the findings are ambiguous.

Compounds with DEAE and DMAE moieties have been tested in many labs for life-span extension and for improvement in general well-being (see note 32).[31] Centrophenoxine has also been found to reduce the amount of lipofuscin in guinea-pig neurons[32] and the nervous system of old rats.[33] A large clinical trial of the chemical seems warranted.

Application to Humans.   Centrophenoxine has been used in Europe with some effectiveness in treating problems of old age such as depression and loss of memory and mental acuity. Despite many reports of its use on humans, there is no definitive report of any increase in life span.[34]

LOSS OF TISSUE ELASTICITY

Some theorists have emphasized the increasing stiffness of connective tissue with increasing chronological age and account for it by pointing to progressive changes in the long molecules that form the backbone of connective tissue fibers. This process, very similar to the one by which rubber becomes brittle and inelastic, is caused by cross-connecting sulfur bonds that reduce the capacity of the long molecules to slip past each other. Many of the effects of aging can be shown to be consequences of loss of tissue elasticity.

Aging of mammals is associated with profound changes in the elastic properties of fibrous connective tissue proteins. In collagen, the fibrous component of tendons and other connective tissue, where the changes have been studied most thoroughly, the age-related increase in rigidity has been ascribed to the formation of intermolecular cross links. The types of cross links, and arguments that altered connective tissue can explain many of the debilities and diseases of aging, have been described in an article by R. P. Kohn.[35] In order to prevent the formation of cross links, it will be necessary to study the long-term effects of certain nitriles which produce the generalized connective tissue defects of lathyrism. Not all cross links are deleterious, however, and in removing undesirable ones by use of a nonspecific agent, such as BAPN, necessary structural cross links might also be removed.

LIPOFUSCIN ACCUMULATION

Species that have a shorter life span have a proportionally more rapid accumulation of the pigment lipofuscin in the cells; in most mammalian species, when the animal is halfway between birth and completion of the species life span, whether long or short, the concentration of lipofuscin is roughly the same. Since lipofuscin is not subject to metabolism, it tends to lie inside the cells as an inert included material, but in amounts that hardly interfere with cellular functioning. While it is not yet clear whether the accumulation of lipofuscin in aging cells is harmful, the accumulation of a closely related substance, ceroid, has been linked to neuron degeneration and death. There have been several reports that the accumulation of lipofuscin in neurons can be reversed by the drug centrophenoxine.[36] In experiments by Kalidas Nandy and Bourne at Emory University, this drug produced a notable diminution of pigmentation in most parts of the central nervous system (see note 34).

ALTERING THE AGING PROGRAM

The research of Leonard Hayflick and others suggests that a cellular program may be responsible for the process of aging.[37] Hayflick observed that human diploid fibroblasts—which are so-called WI-38 cells derived from a human embryonic lung—have a finite reproductive capacity which allows one to predict the growth, senescence, and death of an *in vitro* cell population. In Hayflick's experiments this reproductive limit has been shown to be approximately fifty population doublings.[38] When adult cells, which have presumably already experienced a number of doublings, are cultured in the same way, they undergo markedly fewer doublings than do the embryonic cells. This strengthens the argument for a natural limit to the reproductive process, and this limit seems to be fixed by the cell itself. That is, a cellular component appears to program the aging of the organism.

The next question addressed by Hayflick was whether this "program" is contained in the nucleus or the cytoplasm of the cell. In his research, cytoplasm was separated from the nucleus of both young and old WI-38 cells and fused to other whole cells. The resulting heteroplasmons were then cultured (that is, cultures were made and allowed to proliferate in the following combinations: young cytoplasm/young cell, young cytoplasm/old cell, old cytoplasm/young cell, and old cytoplasm/old cell). Hayflick says of these experiments, "In no cases were young cytoplasts able to rejuvenate old cells. This implies that cellular senescence is not a result of the selective depletion of any cytoplasmic component over time. . . . The fact that a significant number of old cytoplast/young cell heteroplasmons grew as well as young cytoplast/young cell controls suggests that old cytoplasm is not able to age young cells. These results thus imply that the control of cellular senescence is a nuclear rather than a cytoplasmic function."[39]

There has been considerable controversy over the interpretation of these experimental results, and it remains an open question whether this apparent limit of fifty population doublings of human cells cultured *in vitro* represents a real limitation on human cell mitosis *in vivo*. Some research suggests that peroxidative damage is a major contributor to the finite mitosis demonstrated in Hayflick's limit.[40] It is possible, however, that some genetic or other program in the nucleus of human mitotic cells determines human senescence and death. If this is the case, it has a number of implications for various aspects of life-extension research.

Presumably the existence of such a cellular program—a biological clock—means that the cell could be reprogrammed for an indefinite number of reproductions. It would only be necessary to find the precise nature of the program and a way of superseding it. This is obviously possible, since germ cells exhibit this kind of immortality.

In addition, Hayflick's limit suggests ways of controlling cancer and certain viral infections. Neoplastic cells and some virus-modified human cells demonstrate the opposite reproductive capacity from normal human cells; they seem to be capable of indefinite population doublings. Understanding the cellular program which induces senescence could also lead to controlling the unlimited growth of cancer and virus-modified cells. An understanding of programmed aging may suggest ways to regenerate postmitotic cells, such as those in the central nervous system, which have been damaged by accident or disease.

CONCLUSION

Our understanding of the aging process is expanding rapidly. It is too early to say we have mastered the mechanisms of aging or that a treatment for the problems of aging is available. Aging may be programmed in genetic material of the species; it may be the result of accumulated errors at the cellular level or a hormonal phenomenon produced by the biochemical regulatory endocrine organs of the body—the pituitary or the hypothalamus.

It is clear from this survey of the potential interventions of the aging process that have been tested in animals and man that research will proceed. Experimental regimens of drug, diet, and lifestyle will be tested even while basic research continues to seek the fundamental mechanisms of aging. Breakthroughs in extending life span and life expectancy seem to be on the horizon, if not for this generation then for its successors.

NOTES

1. C. M. McCay, "Chemical and Pathological Changes in Aging and after Retarded Growth," *Journal of Nutrition* 18 (1935): 15–25; C. M. McCay, "Experimental Prolongation of the Life Span," *New York Academy of Medicine* 32 (1956): 91–101; C. M. McCay et al., "The Effect of Retarded Growth Upon the Length of Life Span and upon the Ultimate Body Size," *Journal of Nutrition* 10 (1935): 63–79; C. M. McCay et al., "Retarded Growth, Life Span, Ultimate Body Size and Age Changes in the Albino Rat after Feeding Diets Restricted in Calories," *Journal of Nutrition* 18 (1939): 1–13; C. M. McCay et al., "Growth, Ageing, Chronic Diseases, and Life Span in Rats," *Archives of Biochemistry* 2 (1943): 469–479.

2. B. N. Berg, "Nutrition and Longevity in the Rat," *Journal of Nutrition* 71 (1960): 242–254; B. N. Berg and H. S. Simms, "Nutrition and Longevity in the Rat," *Journal of Nutrition* 71 (1960): 255–263; B. N. Berg and H. S. Simms, "Nutrition and Longevity in the Rat," *Journal of Nutrition* 64 (1961): 23–32.

3. A. J. Carlson and F. Hoelzel, "Apparent Prolongation of the Life Span of Rats by Intermittent Fasting," *Journal of Nutrition* 31 (1946): 363–375.

4. M. H. Ross, "Aging, Nutrition and Hepatic Enzyme Activity Patterns in the Rat," *Journal of Nutrition* 97, supplement 1 (1969): 563–602; M. H. Ross, "Length of Life and Caloric Intake," *American Journal of Clinical Nutrition* 25 (1972): 834–838; M. H. Ross, "Length of Life and Nutrition in the Rat," *Journal of Nutrition* 75 (1977): 197–210; M. H. Ross, "Dietary Behavior and Longevity," *Nutrition Review* 35 (1977): 257–265; M. H. Ross and Gerrit Bras, "Tumor Incidence Patterns and Nutrition in the Rat," *Journal of Nutrition* 87 (1965): 245–260.

5. P. E. Segall and P. S. Timiras, "Age-Related Changes in Thermoregulatory Capacity of Tryptophan-Deficient Rats," *Federation Proceedings* 34 (1975): 83–85; P. E. Segall and S. Timiras, "Patho-physiologic Findings after Chronic Tryptophan Deficiency in Rats: A Model for Delayed Growth and Aging," *Mechanisms of Ageing and Development* 5 (1976): 109–124.

6. A. F. Morgan, "Vitamins and Senescence," *Scientific Monthly* 52 (1941): 416–421; H. C. Sherman, "Vitamin A in Relation to Aging and to Length of Life," *Proceedings of the National Academy of Science* 31 (1945): 107–116; H. G. Paul and M. T. Paul, "The Relation of Vitamin A Intake to Length of Life, Growth, Tooth Structure and Eye Condition," *Journal of Nutrition* 31 (1946): 67–78.

7. T. B. Robertson, "On the Influence of Nucleic Acids of Various Origin upon the Growth and Longevity of the White Mouse," *Australian Journal of Experimental Biology and Medical Science* 5 (1928): 69–88; T. B. Robertson et al., "A Comparison of the Utilization of Nucleic Acids of Animal and Vegetable Origin," *Australian Journal of Experimental Biology and Medical Science* 4 (1927): 125–150; T. B. Robertson et al., "The Influence and Intermittent Starvation Plus Nucleic Acid on the Growth and Longevity of the White Mouse," *Australian Journal of Experimental Biology and Medical Science* 12 (1934): 33–45.

8. T. S. Gardner, "The Effect of Yeast Nucleic Acid on the Survival Time of 600 Day Old Albino Mice," *Journal of Gerontology* 1 (1946): 445–452; T. S. Gardner and F. B. Forbes, "The Effect of Sodium Thiocyanate and Yeast Nucleic Acid on the Survival Time of 700 Day Old Albino Mice," *Journal of Gerontology* 1 (1946): 453–456; T. S. Gardner, "The Possible Roles of Oral Yeast Ribonucleic Acid (Y-RNA) in Geriatrics and Gerontology," *Gerontologia* 7 (1963): 109–117.

9. B. S. Frank, *Nucleic Acid, Nutrition and Therapy* (New York: Bantam, 1977).

10. K. Wolff, "Treatment of Memory Defects in Geriatric Patients," *International Journal of Neuropsychiatry* 1 (1965): 216–219.

11. W. Braun et al., "Synthetic Polynucleatides as Restorers of Antibody Formation Capacities in Aged Mice," *Journal of the Reticuloendothelial Society* 7 (1970): 418.

12. S. Kent, "Can Nucleic Acid Therapy Reverse the Degenerative Processes of Aging?," *Geriatrics* 32, no. 10 (1977): 130–136.

13. J. Maynard-Smith, "Review Lecture on Senescence: I. The Causes of Aging," *Proceedings of the Royal Society*, series B 157 (1962): 125–127.

14. K. E. Cheney and R. L. Walford, "Immune Function and Dysfunction in Relation to Aging," *Life Sciences* 14 (1974): 2075–2084; R. K. Liu and R. L. Walford, "The Effect of Lowered Body Temperature on Lifespan and Immune and Non-Immune Processes," *Gerontologia* 18 (1972): 363–388; R. K. Liu and R. L. Walford, "Mid-Life Temperature-Transfer Effects on Life-Spans of Annual Fish," *Journal of Gerontology* 30, no. 2 (1975): 129–131; R. L. Walford, *The Immunologic Theory of Aging* (Copenhagen: Munksgaard, 1969); R. L. Walford, "The Immunologic Theory of Aging: Current Status," *Federal Proceedings* 33 (1974): 2020–2027; R. L. Walford et al., "Alterations in Soluble/Insoluble Collagen Ratios in the Annual Fish *Cyndebias Bellotti*, in Relation to Age and Environmental Temperature," *Experimental Gerontology* 4 (1969): 103–109.

15. R. T. Balmer, "Entropy and Metabolism—A Macroscopic View of Aging." Report produced as part of grant no. RO1 AG 00498–01 given by the National Institute on Aging to the University of Wisconsin School of Engineering and Applied Sciences.

16. D. Metcalf et al., "Influence of the Spleen and Thymus on Immune Responses in Ageing Mice," *Clinical and Experimental Immunology* 2 (1966): 109–120; P. G. Rigby, "The Effect of 'Exogerous' RNA on the Improvement of Syngener Tumor Immunity," *Cancer Research* 31 (1971): 3–4; Fabris et al., "Lymphocytes, Hormones and Aging," *Nature* 240 (1972): 557–559; R. L. Walford et al., "Longterm Dietary Restriction and Immune Function in Mice: Response to Sheep Red Blood Cells and to Mitogenic Agents," *Mechanisms of Ageing and Development* 2 (1973): 447–454; P. Meredith et al., "Age-Related Changes in the Cellular Immune Response of Lymph Node and Thymus Cells in Long-Lived Mice," *Cell Immunology* 18 (1975): 324–330; P. Meredith, M. Gerbase-De-Lima, and R. L. Walford, "Age-Related Changes in the PHA: con A Stimulatory Ratios of Cells from Spleens of a Long-Lived Mouse Strain," *Experimental Gerontology* 10 (1975): 247–250; K. Hirokawa et al., "Restoration of Impaired Immune Functions in Aging Animals," *Clinical Immunology and Immunopathology* 5 (1976): 371–376; Y. H. Pilch et al., "Immunotherapy of Cancer with 'Immune' RNA," *American Journal of Surgery* 132 (1976): 631–637; S. Kent, "Why Does Humor Immunity Decline with Age?," *Geriatrics* 32, no. 2 (1977): 107–120; S. Kent, "Immunoengineering May Increase Longevity," *Geriatrics* 32, no. 6 (1972): 107–110; S. Kent, "Can Drugs Increase the Immune Response?," *Geriatrics* 32, no. 7 (1977): 101–112; E. G. Bliznokov, "Immunological Senescence in Mice and Its Reversal by Coenzyme Q_{10}," *Mechanisms of Ageing and Development* 7 (1978): 189–197.

17. A. Aslan et al., "Long-Term Treatment with Procaine (Gerovital H3) in Albino Rats," *Journal of Gerontology* 20 (1965): 1–8.

18. See Herbert Bailey, *CH₃: Will It Keep You Young Longer?* (New York: Bantam, 1977).

19. W. Donner Denckla, "Role of the Pituitary and Thyroid Glands in the Decline of Minimal O_2 Consumption with Age," *Journal of Clinical Investigation* (Febru-

ary 1974): 572–581. See also Caleb Finck, "Neuroendocrinology of Aging: A View of an Emerging Era," *BioScience* (October 1975).

20. M. Bodanszky and S. L. Engel, "Oxytocin and the Life-Span of Male Rats," *Nature* 210 (1966): 751.

21. S. M. Friedman and C. L. Friedman, "Effect of Posterior Pituitary Extract on the Life-Span of Old Rats," *Nature* 200 (1963): 237–238; S. M. Friedman and C. L. Friedman, "Prolonged Treatment with Posterior Pituitary Powder in Aged Rats," *Experimental Gerontology* 1 (1964): 37–48; S. M. Friedman et al., "Prolongation of Lifespan in the Old Rat by Adrenal and Neurophypophyseal Hormones," *Gerontologia* 11 (1965): 129–140.

22. B. O. Barnes and C. W. Barnes, *Solved: The Riddle of Heart Attack* (Fort Collins, Col.: Abner Press, 1976).

23. M. A. Lorand, "Some Considerations on the Causes of Senility," *Clinical Practices in Social Biology* 57 (1904): 500–502.

24. D. Bellamy, *Experimental Gerontology* 3 (1968): 327–333.

25. G. D. Cotzias et al., "Prolongation of the Life-Span in Mice Adapted to Large Amounts of L-Dopa," *Proceedings of the National Academy of Sciences* 71, no. 2 (1974): 2466–2469.

26. J. Bjorksten, "The Crosslinkage Theory of Aging," *Finska Kemistsamfundet Meddelanden* 80, (1971): 23–38; J. Bjorksten, "Approaches and Prospects for the Control of Age-Dependent Deterioration," *Annals of the New York Academy of Sciences* 184 (June 1971): 95–102.

27. D. Harman, "Aging: A Theory Based on Free Radical and Radiation Chemistry," *Journal of Gerontology* 11 (1956): 298–300; D. Harman, "Prolongation of the Normal Life Span by Radiation Protection Chemicals," *Journal of Gerontology* 12 (1957): 257–263; D. Harman, "Free Radical Theory of Aging: Effect of Free Radical Reaction Inhibitors on the Mortality Rate of Male LAF_1 Mice," *Journal of Gerontology* 23 (1968): 476–482; D. Harman, "Free Radical Theory of Aging: Effect of Free Radical Inhibitors on the Life Span of Male LAF_1 Mice—Second Experiment," *Gerontologist* 8, no. 13 (1968); D. Harman, "Prolongation of Life: Role of Free Radical Reactions in Aging," *Journal of the American Geriatric Society* 17 (1969): 721–735; D. Harman, "Free Radical Theory of Aging: Dietary Implications," *American Journal of Clinical Nutrition* 25 (1972): 839–843.

28. *Dietary Antioxidants and Effects on Aging*, Monsanto Technical Abstract no. 6; F. S. LaBella, "The Effect of Chronic Dietary Lathyrogen on Rat Survival," *The Gerontologist* 8, no. 3 (1968), p. 13; A. Comfort et al., "Effect of Ethoxyquin on the Longevity of C3H Mice," *Nature* 229 (1971): 254–255; Monsanto Report no. 6 on Current Technology, "Santquin Antioxident: Can It Actually Slow the Process of Aging?," *Scientific American* 235, no. 7 (1976): 104–105.

29. N. P. Buu-Hoi et al., "Action Retardante de l'Acide Nordihydroguaiaretique sur le Vieillissement chez le Rat," *Comptes Rendus des Seances de la Societê de Biologie et de Ses Filiales* 153 (1959): 1180–1183; S. Oeriu and E. Vochitu, "The Effect of the Administration of Compounds Which Contain Sulfhydryl Groups on the Survival Rates of Mice, Rats, and Guinea Pigs," *Journal of Gerontology* 20 (1965): 417–419; S. Oeriu et al., "Changes in Thiol Enzyme Activity, As Occurring in the Aged Body under the Influence of Folicysteine Adminis-

tration," *Gerontologia* 11 (1965): 222–225; T. S. Gardner, "The Use of Drosophila Melanogaster As a Screening Agent for Longevity Factors," *Journal of Gerontology* 3 (1948): 1–13; R. B. Pealtan and P. J. Williams, "Effect of Pantothenic Acid on the Longevity of Mice," *Proceedings of the Society of Experimental Biology and Medicine* 99 (1958): 632–633.

30. R. Hochschild, "Effects of Membrane Stabilizing Drugs on Mortality in Drosophila Melanogaster," *Experimental Gerontology* 8 (1973): 177–183; R. Hochschild, "Effect of Dimethylaminoethanol on the Life Span of Senile Male A/J Mice," *Experimental Gerontology* 8 (1973): 185–191; R. Hochschild, "Effects of Various Drugs on Longevity in Female C57BL/6J Mice," *Gerontologia* 19 (1973): 271–280.

31. M. Hasen et al., "Age-Associated Changes in the Hypothalamus of the Guinea Pig: Effect of Dimethylaminoethyl p-chlorophenoxyacetate. An Electron Microscopic and Histochemical Study," *Experimental Gerontology* 9 (1974): 153–159; S. Kent, "Solving the Riddle of Lipofuscin's Origin My Uncover Clues to the Aging Process," *Geriatrics* 31, no. 5 (1976): 128–137; D. Harman, "Aging: A Theory Based on Free Radical and Radiation Chemistry," *Journal of Gerontology* 11 (1956): 298–300; D. Harman, "Prolongation of the Normal Life Span by Radiation Protection Chemicals," *Journal of Gerontology* 12 (1957): 257–263; D. Harman, "Free Radical Theory of Aging: Effect of Free Radical Reaction Inhibitors on the Mortality Rate of Male LAF_1 Mice," *Journal of Gerontology* 23 (1968): 476–482; D. Harman, "Free Radical Theory of Aging: Effect of Free Radical Inhibitors on the Life Span of Male LAF_1 Mice—Second Experiment," *Gerontologist* 8, no. 13 (1968); D. Harman, "Prolongation of Life: Role of Free Radical Reactions in Aging," *Journal of the American Geriatric Society* 17 (1969): 721–735; D. Harman, "Free Radical Theory of Aging: Dietary Implications," *American Journal of Clinical Nutrition* 25 (1972): 839–843.

32. K. Nandy and G. H. Boume, "Effect of Centrophenoxine on the Lipofuscin Pigments in the Neusopes of Senile Guinea-Pigs," *Nature* 210 (1966): 313–314.

33. S. Riga and D. Riga, "Effect of Centrophenoxine on the Lipofusin Pigments in the Nervous System of Old Rats," *Brain Research* 72 (1974): 265–275.

34. H. Destren, "Essai Clinique de la Centrophenoxine in Geriatrie," *La Press Medicale* 69 (1961): 1999–2001.

35. R. P. Kohn, "Human Aging and Disease," *Journal of Clinical Diseases* 16 (1963): 5–21.

36. P. Gordon, "Free Radicals and the Dying Process," in *Theoretical Aspects of Aging*, ed. M. Rockstein (New York: Academic Press, 1974).

37. L. Hayflick, "The Cell Biology of Human Aging," *New England Journal of Medicine* 295 (1976): 1302–1308.

38. L. Hayflick, "The Limited *In Vitro* Lifetime of Human Diploid Cell Strains," *Experimental Cell Research* 37 (1965): 614–636.

39. W. E. Wright and L. Hayflick, "The Effect of Cytoplasmic Hybridization on *In Vitro* Cellular Senescence," *Proceedings of the 10th International Congress of Gerontology* (Jerusalem: 1975): 67.

40. D. Deamer and J. Gonzales, "Autofluorescent Structures in Cultured WI-38 Cells," *Archives of Biochemistry and Biophysics* 165 (1974): 421–426.

II

VALUES AND GUIDELINES

2

Values and Life-Extending Technologies

THE HASTINGS CENTER RESEARCH GROUP*

The ideal of extending life—even to the point of immortality—has throughout history been looked upon as a good. In the Judeo-Christian tradition, death is interpreted as the wages of sin, punishment for man's evil; yet, man has traditionally seen that avoidance of death can exact a great price. Socrates is reported by Xenophon to have observed:

> If my years are prolonged, I know that the frailties of old age will inevitably be realized.... Perhaps God in his kindness is taking my part and securing me the opportunity of ending my life not only in season but also in the way that is easiest.

In short, some extensions of life come at Faustian cost. In this chapter, we examine that price—the social, ethical, and other implications of life-extending technologies.

Americans are publicly committed in the Declaration of Inde-

---

* This chapter represents a rough consensus of the analysis done by The Hastings Center Research Group and is intended to summarize general areas of agreement. Because of the intentionally diverse nature of the Research Group, not every member would concur with every conclusion.

pendence and the Preamble to the Constitution to the pursuit of happiness and the promotion of the general welfare, or to producing social goods and the good life. The same commitment leads us to debate, in government and voluntary organizations, which goods and which life-styles are worth pursuing. This discussion has direct relevance to choices among policies concerning life-extending technologies. Thus the questions: "What is a natural or appropriate death?" and "Is there such a thing as a good death?" Related are questions of the relative values of preventing suffering and death, and of medical well-being as part of general welfare.

Whether we view aging as the result of cellular changes or as a process encompassing all levels of bodily organization also influences our choices. Can aging be reduced to a set of atomic or molecular processes, or does it have properties arising from the entire person as an integrated system not reducible to isolated parts? What values are assumed by either an integrated or a reductionist view? The family, work, leisure, value patterns themselves—we must ask how we value them and how alternative policies will affect them.

It is not enough to determine what things are, or should be, valued. If we assume that various people value different things and that we lack the resources to satisfy everyone, then questions of rights and responsibilities follow, especially in the area of justice. Policies serving the general welfare may exclude certain members of society; what is realizable may not be equitable. We explore varying views on this issue and the value accorded to lives by contending schools of thought. Competing claims of the elderly and the young, present and future generations, the seriously ill and the relatively healthy, the "socially useful" and the "less useful" receive attention.

The general welfare and/or individual good may also be compromised when they conflict with freedom or individual self-determination. Conceivably we could extend life expectancy or life span by curtailing the freedom to consume unhealthy foods or to engage in dangerous activities. On the other hand, in order to preserve freedom, we may adopt policies that sacrifice the goal of extending life, especially if citizens or groups differ as to its importance.

Other problems involve knowledge and uncertainty. We consider the duty of insurance firms to disclose changes in life expectancy if they could be used in determining insurance rates. We take up the matter of increase or decrease in certainty about our futures and the implications for policies of these changes. Finally, we explore suicide and euthanasia; alternative life-extension policies have implications for our attitudes and actions regarding these modes of terminating life.

ILLNESS, DEATH, AND CULTURAL VALUES

WHAT IS A NATURAL OR APPROPRIATE DEATH?

Among the basic questions underlying alternative life-extending technologies are those regarding the value of life itself and the definition of its loss, which we call death. There has been much philosophical and legal debate about human death.[1] What is crucial here is not a precise definition, but our image of death and the importance accorded to combating particular deaths. The Hastings Center Research Group has discerned three basic images, each with policy implications; probably no one holds any of these views in its extreme form, but they are useful as models for evaluating policies.

The Biological Approach. Death can be viewed as biologically natural and timely if it comes when a life span is complete. Traditionally we spoke of a life span as three score years and ten, but now we are beginning to think of a higher biological maximum, perhaps as much as one hundred years. Life, in this view, has a fixed limit, and death occurs when the "biological clock" runs down, the DNA program runs out, or cell mutations increase until "the whole system" collapses; only premature or artificially delayed deaths are unnatural.

There is serious confusion over the term *natural*. It can be used descriptively, meaning biological or statistically normal, or prescriptively, meaning good or appropriate. In the second sense, to call a death "natural" is to call it good. Again, some ethical traditions determine goodness or rightness on the basis of biological or statistical naturalness. One could find a particular death natural in this sense and still subject to deferment through technology.[2]

In simpler times, deaths were divided into those that were premature or adventitious,[3,4] that is, caused by infectious disease, accident, or homicide, and those that were brought about by natural causes. We combated the former. Now it has become necessary to ask if we should not combat the latter as well.

Several schools of thought in contemporary America hold that man has tampered too much with biological processes. This idea is found among traditional groups (including some natural law thinkers), the "counterculture," conservative religious bodies, and among respected scholars in philosophy and theology.[5] According to this pervasive view, man extends beyond reasonable limits and trespasses on God's creative design if he tries to modify human procreation and the natural course of life.

Carried to an extreme, this position implies that no medical interventions are ever acceptable. Nevertheless, the view that nature is to be respected is an important one and policy decision makers should be careful to consider this perspective.

The implications of the biological image of death seem clear. To adherents of its extreme form, no treatment for specific diseases, no organ replacements, and no life-span increasing methods are acceptable. To those who believe that some deaths are biologically natural, curve-squaring might be acceptable, but life-span extension is unethical. Biological age, according to this view, is the critical determinant of social policy; the goal is to make death biologically timely.

The Personal Approach.   A second school of thought is that deaths are good or appropriate on the basis of personal or social, as well as biological, timeliness. A good death is consistent with a particular and reasonable life plan and set of values.[6] Some deaths are natural and others not, but the critical variable is not simply age. New criteria are introduced: Life plan and obligations, physical and mental impact of the death, and social perception of death.

Daniel Callahan has suggested four criteria (discussed in greater detail in Chapter 7) for a natural or appropriate death: one's lifework has been accomplished; one's moral obligations to those for whom one has had responsibility have been discharged; the death will not seem to others an offense to sense or sensibility or tempt others to despair and rage at human existence; and the process of dying is not marked by unbearable and degrading pain.

This image of a good death is more subjective and, for policy purposes, more difficult to use than the biological approach. How should society handle people with unrealistic life plans or no plans at all? How do we compare the elderly who believe they will never fulfill their obligations to their offspring with those who consider their obligations fulfilled when their children are grown? The notion of offending sense and sensibility has subjective dimensions. These questions lead to a qualification of reasonableness: Death is more acceptable if a reasonable life plan and reasonable obligations have been completed, and if it does not offend a reasonable person's sense and sensibility.

With this qualification established, Callahan's criteria can help in forming judgments. First, priority for curve-squaring over life-extending technologies is implied. The provision of "reasonable time" focuses attention on premature or unexpected deaths; death in the prime of life or in childhood is the worst sort.

Second, death with unbearable and degrading pain and death that offends sensibility take high priority, even if it occurs at or beyond the natural life span. No technologies that extend life while increasing pain and suffering are acceptable.

Third, if plans and obligations change with the extension of the life span, some life-span technologies would be valuable.

The Utopian Approach. A third view rejects the notion of natural or acceptable death; the very concept is a temporary aberration in history. Before the fifteenth century, no death was natural; each was caused by some supernatural force. Now we learn from the pathologist that every death has a medical cause. Once that cause is known, a challenge is raised to conduct the research necessary to intervene and overpower it. This view is radically different from the first. With this, no death is natural, good, or acceptable; all death is external to human nature and evil. Immortality is the goal, although it is understood that it will not be realized. Man is responsible for his internal and external environment; to fulfill his character, he should use his intellect and technological skills to make life better and longer. To fail to act, when one can, is to be irresponsible.

This view has been articulated by numerous authorities. In biology and medicine, such authors as Joseph Fletcher,[7] Robert Sinsheimer,[8] and Joshua Lederberg[9] have defended the legitimacy and importance of genetic intervention. In the area of controlling specific diseases and styles and patterns of dying, many authors have defended the view that death is evil. Some want to move forcefully to develop the technologies to conquer certain forms of dying;[10] others see death as evil but are willing to accept it as the only appropriate course.[11] Still others want to modify the trajectory of dying, but accept that certain deaths should not be combated for the present.[12]

Many would argue that certain deaths are more acceptable than others. The criteria for this view may be similar to those mentioned previously. If a death can be delayed and modified, for example, only by the expenditure of great resources, other claims on those resources may take precedence.

This third image of death—actually a rejection of it—accepts fully the legitimacy of efforts to extend the life span, but shares reservations about priorities and just resource allocation. All deaths are evil but some more than others and thus deserving of higher priority. Since public resources will be used to develop technologies, claims for them will have to compete with other claims on grounds of justice, the general welfare, and other basic values.

PREVENTION OF DEATH VS. PREVENTION OF SUFFERING

A crucial judgment that will have to be made concerns the relative value of preventing death as opposed to preventing suffering.[13] Among those who agree on the evil of death, there is disagreement about the price we should pay to combat it.

Life as an Absolute Value. One school holds that life has absolute value and that our public policy goal should be its maximum extension at any price. It follows that death is an absolute offense. This view is probably as untenable as the extremes noted previously. It would direct resources to areas such as food, shelter, national defense, the arts, or other scientific pursuits only insofar as they contribute to life extension. Presumably we ought to choose life-extending technologies that add the most total years of life, through treatment of diseases, tissue regeneration, artificial prostheses, environmental changes, or antiaging research. Possibly diseases of infants and children should get highest priority, since overcoming deaths in the young would add more years for each life saved. If the costs per youthful life saved were great, however, other age groups might take priority.

A modified version is more tenable: Life is of great value; preserving life has an extreme claim on us, and we should pay a great price in money, effort, pain, and suffering to preserve it. Several groups in modern Western history have taken this view. Physicians often claim a special duty to preserve life, in justifying the extremes to which they go to provide life-prolonging treatment. Francis Bacon long ago observed that the physician has three duties:[14]

First the preservation of health, second the cure of disease, and third the prolongation of life.

Then he added,

(The) third part of medicine regarding the prolongation of life: this is a new part, and deficient, although the most noble of all.

Orthodox Judaism[15] and Roman Catholic moral theology[16] give special weight to the value of preserving life. In mainstream Catholic thought, the commitment to preserving life is tempered; no one is morally obliged to accept an extraordinary medical treatment, that is, a treatment that involves a grave burden or is useless given the circumstances of persons, places, times, and cultures.[17]

Right-to-life groups, which have organized primarily around the issue of abortion, are also interested in the moral duty to preserve life. Their members, who represent Protestant, Jewish, and secular traditions, as well as the Roman Catholic, deviate from traditional Catholic thought; some of them explicitly oppose decisions to stop preserving a life that is marked by pain and suffering. Preservation of life takes precedence over prevention of suffering.

The Quality-of-Life Position. At the other extreme is the view that only quality of life counts. A life that is not of sufficient quality is not worth living. Pain, suffering, or other adverse qualities justify ending life, especially if the individual consents or terminates his life himself. Holders of this view respond very differently to proposals for life-extending technologies, both those aimed at treating specific diseases and those aimed at extending the life span. Any increase in survival at the cost of significantly increased suffering or decreased quality of life is not worth the price. Given their depressant effect on life quality, kidney machines and artificial organs have either low priority or absolute disutility. Antiaging techniques that extend life but increase social dependence, feelings of uselessness, or senility should not be developed. The critical issue is not whether the technology squares the curve or extends the life span, but whether it increases or decreases the quality of life.

Among these thinkers, too, there are disagreements and contradictions. Some warn that quality-of-life judgments, especially if made by people other than one whose life is under consideration, are dangerous. In response, some proponents of quality-of-life assessments are willing to give weight to personal judgments of pain and suffering.

It is unlikely that many people would give absolute preference to preventing death or preventing suffering; policy planners must guard against techniques and objectives that focus exclusively on one or the other. Cost-benefit analyses measuring cost per life saved, cost per year of additional life, and similar assessments would therefore be inadequate and risky, because they would exclude consideration of other factors such as suffering. Attempts to quantify pain and suffering and to develop objective comparisons of suffering and death have been unsuccessful, yet intuitive or more formal comparisons must be made. The result of efforts to incorporate measures of suffering may be that life-extending technologies will have lower priority than those designed to reduce morbidity, especially in diseases with high morbidity but low mortality, such as arthritis. In the end, the most reasonable policy may be one that establishes an appropriate balance between these goals.

MEDICAL WELL-BEING VS. GENERAL WELL-BEING

Since prevention of death and prevention of suffering are relative not only to each other but to other goods associated with well-being, policy makers have to measure health goals against nonmedical objectives in the society.

In 1975 we spent an unprecedented 8.3 percent of our gross national product on health care—up 41 percent from the 1965 level of 5.9 percent.[18] Life-extending technologies and other interventions, taken singly, are usually found to be valuable. Yet each is purchased at a cost to some other health sphere or to another area.

Perhaps the best way to improve health is to focus on social improvements distinct from health care.[19] Better diet or housing, for example, may improve health more than health care can. Many believe that health and health care deserve no more public policy priority than they now receive; compared with other national social and political objectives, 8.3 percent seems right. Such a judgment depends, of course, on the evaluation of health and other social goods and the likelihood of investment benefits in various areas.

Claims for other human goods may help us discriminate among life-extending technologies. Usually the higher the value placed on other goods, the greater the tendency to choose technologies having social as well as life-extending payoffs. Environmental interventions that have aesthetic and economic benefits in addition to health benefits might get higher priority even if their health impacts are less than other life-extending technologies. Certain technologies related to diet (for example, the McCay effect, in which diet is radically controlled) may extend life at the expense of aesthetic pleasures. Some disease-preventing technologies may decrease personal happiness—antismoking campaigns, changes in fertility patterns, and physical fitness campaigns are examples.

There are two schools of thought regarding competition among social goods. One argues that social welfare problems are best managed by giving unspecified monies (or other generalized medium) for discretionary use rather than giving targeted welfare goods such as food stamps, housing subsidies, or health care. Individuals then use their resources to buy the things most valuable to them, thus maximizing the utility of the economic investment.

A second school argues for targeted funds, but the reasoning takes two forms. One group holds that the government should distribute the specific welfare benefits it believes will do the most good—that is, the experts should make the choice. The other argues that not all needs and desires have an equal claim on society. The priority of goods that are really rights—basic food, shelter, and medical care—should be elevated. Targeted welfare programs should be adopted because some items are basic and citizens have a right to them. This might justify the priority of life-extending technologies and other health care interventions over and above other welfare measures.

THE CONCEPTS OF ILLNESS AND DISEASE

In recent decades the medical profession has incorporated larger and larger segments of variant or deviant human function and behavior into the domain of medical interest and concern. At the same time, there has been sustained criticism of the traditional medical model of disease and illness as organic dysfunction induced by a specifiable causal insult to or infection of the body. "Caring, not curing" is the rallying cry for numbers of critics of current medical conceptions of illness and disease. Moreover, recognition of the impact of sociological, cultural, and other value factors has forced a drastic reassessment of medical and societal understanding of illness and disease.

There is a close relationship between these concepts and our choice of life-extending technologies. Research on life extension affects societal and medical perceptions of illness and disease, and these perceptions affect our choices.

A classification of current medical interpretations of illness and disease is necessary here. Broadly speaking, there are five major contemporary approaches.

The Physical-Organic Conception.   Illness and disease are synonymous terms in this view for organic dysfunction or abnormalities induced by specific invasive agents. A. L. Caplan[20] suggests five criteria relevant to this conception. Disease or illness is seen as: (1) being an organic state or process that produces discomfort or suffering, (2) possessing specific precipitating causes or circumstances, (3) manifesting a clear-cut pattern of sequential organic changes leading to disorder or dysfunction (an etiology), (4) resulting in observable symptoms or manifestations, and (5) excluding nonnatural or human interventions (such as poisoning, gunshot wounds, stabbings). Advocates of this view see it as value-free, admitting of an objective and rational analysis in light of purely scientific knowledge.

The Holistic Conception.   Many physicians argue that medicine's heightened awareness of the psychological and social setting of illness and disease has forced a new look at holistic or humanistic concepts, which view people as complex entities not simply as bodies with organic dysfunctions. Physicians must care for the needs of the person as a human being; the medical profession must learn to help afflicted persons to cope, and lessen the emphasis on curing organic disease.

The Dualistic Conception.   A third view accepts the validity of the organic model but emphasizes that many problems are psychosocial rather than organic.[21] It draws a sharp distinction between disease and psychosocial problems and excludes mental and social maladjustments from the medical domain. Deviant or abnormal behavior with no specifiable organic cause is simply not a matter of medical expertise and dependency on medical solutions in these cases should be broken.

The Value-Laden Conception.   Authors such as D. Mechanic,[22] P. Sedgwick,[23] and H. Fabrega[24] have pushed the critique one step further, arguing that these notions contain implicit and explicit value judgments, and that organic and holistic conceptions are closely tied to the cultural and social values held by physicians and patients at a given time. They adduce anthropological and sociological evidence that an "organic disease" in one culture (for example, smallpox in American society) is something else in another society (smallpox as a sign from the gods, unrelated to medical treatment among Hindus).

The Iatrogenic (or Doctor-Induced) Conception.   There has been a strong attack recently by authors such as Ivan Illich[25] and H. Jack Geiger[26] on the basic concepts of medicine; "health," "treatment," and "disease" are held to be meaningless jargon created solely for their economic value, to keep the public dependent on medical professionals. Illich has been particularly vehement in discrediting all four of the previously discussed conceptions. He claims that they are politically useful and exploitative and used to justify the existence of the medical profession; he advocates dissolution of the profession and a return to a free market, laissez-faire approach to human suffering and treatment.

There are close relationships between these conceptions and choices among life-extending technologies. The physical-organic conception is compatible with artificial prostheses and tissue regeneration, as well as with specific disease interventions and life-span increase technologies. It does not support all interventions equally, but focuses on those cases where a relatively simple physical-organic relationship exists between disease-causing agents and the resulting disease and, in the case of life-span increase technologies, on biochemical and genetic theories of aging. Replacement prostheses such as artificial kidneys and hearts are particularly attractive to holders of the physical-organic model.

There is currently a shift away from the physical-organic conception and toward other, more complex interpretations involving psychosocial components. The contemporary infatuation with holistic theories suggests the growing importance of environmental and life-style approaches to the extension of life expectancy. These approaches include environmental interventions to reduce carcinogens, life-style change campaigns to reduce myocardial disease, and life-span interventions such as lifelong dietary programs and the like. Strategies such as environmental engineering can be expected to grow in importance if current philosophical attitudes persist.

Since much of the criticism of traditional organic models is fueled by a concern for mental and physical health, the emphasis on organic intervention may be paralleled by concern for improvements in social and psychological skills and techniques. Caring for the quality of life may become a major part of medicine and allied professions. If psychosocial and value-oriented conceptions of disease continue to influence medical practitioners, technologies providing control of broader segments of human behavior, mental abnormality, and cultural capacities may be favored over simple amelioration of organic dysfunctions and disorders.

The dualistic conception, which separates organic from psychosocial elements, and the conception that emphasizes the value-laden character of judgments about disease and illness, both indicate that for some life-threatening situations, value choices are central. Because they are, these choices should be left to the public and not to scientific experts. These conceptions are likely to have impact, not directly on the choice among life-extending technologies, but on the method of making that choice. Social movements are demanding more lay and consumer participation in the policy decision-making process. Since the fundamental issues are those of life-style, choice tolerance is appropriate, and when governmental decisions must be made, as in the allocation of resources, democratic procedures are called for. The choice between life-span increasing technology and artificial prosthesis technology is, according to this view, a matter not of scientific judgment but of public discretion.

Neither will recent emphasis on the iatrogenic interpretation lead to clear preference for one life-extending technology. With this view, a generalized resistance to all technologies is likely. This view has an affinity with the one that accepts many if not all deaths as natural, and sees danger in tampering with man's biochemical and social environment.

We should anticipate that the choice of life-extending technologies will have an impact on our conception of health and illness. Both curve-squaring and life-span increase technologies that extend physical life without maintaining mental and physical vitality can be expected to cause a shift toward conceptions that are not limited to life preservation per se. More concern with the holistic and valuational dimensions may emerge, reinforcing models that encompass quality-of-life considerations, adaptability, behavioral deviancy, acculturation, and coping. Success in a particular technology may have an impact far beyond the medical sciences. Social, life-style, and environmental technologies could, if successful, add significantly to the momentum of the more holistic and social models. Government organization that separates health from housing, employment, nutrition, education, and labor could become implausible and lead to a breakdown of the present isolated health research bureaucracy. Of course, failure in such technological efforts would reinforce the iatrogenic interpretation of illness.

IS AGING A DISEASE?

A great deal of confusion surrounds the question of whether aging should be viewed as a disease. Labelling any state or condition a "disease" not only affects the attitude and actions of the medical and scientific community but also carries social, cultural, and economic implications.

The attitude that aging is a natural, normal part of human existence is plainly prevalent in contemporary medicine. Medical texts never refer to aging, in itself, as a disease, but concentrate on diseases such as pneumonia, cancer, and atherosclerosis that accompany it. Current research in life-extending technology is forcing a change in this attitude. It indicates ways of manipulating biological processes and intervening in environmental and behavioral events that force the medical profession, which is strongly oriented toward intervention and cure, to reconsider whether aging is a disease.

What Is Disease? Part of the difficulty with the question lies in unclearness of definition and criteria. H. T. Engelhardt[27] has suggested a number of criteria for establishing a state or process as a disease. Phenomena that are universal or common, or that are not dysfunctional, are not usually thought of as diseases. These two criteria are not sufficient for defining "disease," but technology, by extending and squaring the survival curve, could make aging abnormal and not universal.

Engelhardt, drawing on Talcott Parsons's[28] definition of the "sick role," suggests other criteria. Disease frequently involves pain, debility, and exemption from social and familial responsibilities. Disease states are brought about in, or imposed upon, individuals by natural biological or behavioral processes.

If the life-expectancy curve is extended or squared, aging as we currently understand it would still involve debility, exemption from responsibilities, and natural, isolatable causes. Indeed, the development of technologies to control the phenomenon of aging would make the aging process seem more like a disease.

What Is Aging?   One of the reasons for the confusion cited by Engelhardt, Caplan, and others[29] about aging vis-à-vis disease, is that the term *aging* denotes a complex of biological, psychological, and social phenomena. A number of theories—cross-linkage theory, free radical theory, genetic mutation analysis, and the autoimmunity hypothesis—locate the cause of aging at different levels of biological activity. The decision to label aging as a disease will hinge partly on the adequacy of these theories to pinpoint the source of aging since, as was noted, disease is usually identified with dysfunction or debilitation brought on by natural, determinable causes. Moreover, the available technologies lead to rather different conclusions concerning the status of aging. Curve-squaring does much to remove dysfunctional and universal aspects of aging, while curve-extension may do little to lessen their impact. Preventing or delaying aging seems far more important in labelling aging a disease than is curve-squaring.

Problems with the Notion of Disease.   The trend in medicine, as technological capacities increase, seems to be toward the classification of aging as a disease. This trend will continue especially if successful curve-squaring technologies increase awareness of the capability of manipulating the aging process.

However, some life-extending technologies, especially life-span extending ones, may present deterrents to that trend. First, life-span extension without curve-squaring will delay the debilitations of aging, not eliminate them. It might be argued that it is the technological ability to intervene in a debilitative process that allows it to be seen as a disease. If all people were still to become old and senile at some point, the sense of normality currently associated with aging might continue to exempt aging from the disease classification.

Second, if aging can be linked to environmental causes or to voluntary behaviors (for example, smoking, overeating), there may be resistance to viewing aging as a disease. The voluntary destruction of one's body may be viewed as criminal but it is not normally considered a disease. Society may be reluctant to allot time and money for medical research and application for those who forego life-extending opportunities. Thus those who age involuntarily might be thought of as diseased and those who age willingly as foolish, fanatical, or irrational, but not diseased.

Finally, life-extending technologies may revolutionize our understanding so that aging is counted as a disease but with altered professional and social consequences.

Some groups argue for the exemption of various behavioral and emotional states from the category of disease (criminality, homosexuality, violent aggression) while others press for the inclusion of those states and others (alcoholism, masturbation, gambling, neuroses, and psychoses). Inclusion or exclusion hinges on the benefits and services or stigmata and suffering that follow from the labelling. Eventually the decision to call aging a disease will depend not so much on biological or social criteria as on the pragmatic effects of such labelling in terms of privileges, rights, benefits, and status.

CELLULAR VS. HOLISTIC VIEWS OF MAN

Interest in life-extending technology has spawned diverse technological research strategies, such as disease amelioration, organ replacement, tissue regeneration, cellular and genetic engineering, and environmental and metabolic intervention. They flow from various conceptions of man as a biological entity. Debates among scientists are frequently stimulated not by the results of scientific investigation but by differing conceptions of the nature of humanness.

Cellular Reductionism. This view claims that all the properties of human nature—mental, physical, social and cultural—reduce to molecular or cellular biological processes. Much of the work in genetic, immunological, and cellular technologies vis-à-vis life extension indicates a belief in this reductionism, a belief shared by biologists[30] such as McFarland Burnet, Leonard Hayflick, Linus Pauling, and John Eccles, and philosophers[31] like Richard Rorty, Kenneth Schaffner, Wilfred Sellars, and Paul Feyerabend. Reductionism is most compatible with biochemical interventions to overcome specific diseases and biochemical, genetic, and other intracellular theories of aging.

Hierarchism.   This conception of organic life holds that while it is possible to reduce many of the observed phenomena to micromolecular laws, it is strategically more reasonable to recognize the body's complex levels of organic interaction and treat each separately. Thomas Nagel, Bernhard Rensch, Bernard Campbell, Clifford Grobstein, Morton Beckner, Howard Pattee, and many disease-oriented or organ-replacement advocates[32] are committed to this notion of distinct levels of organization and complexity. While they accept the possibility of reducing life properties at various levels of human organization to laws describing atomic or molecular events, they see no reason to do so before such reductions have been accomplished. Efforts at tissue regeneration and development of artificial prostheses are particularly attractive to them.

Holism.   Many physicians, scientists, and philosophers argue that molecular and cellular biological properties do not tell the whole story of human life. They argue for variables and factors not amenable to such reduction. Social, cultural, and value-related phenomena cannot be explained by scientific understanding at the micromolecular level. Advocates of this view such as Francisco Ayala, William H. Thorpe, Bernhard Rensch, Karl Popper, Eric Cassell, and many from the areas of psychiatry and psychology such as Thomas Szasz and Richard Laing, doubt the ultimate value of much of the work being done at the genetic, cellular, and tissue levels.[33] They implicitly emphasize the need for broad holistic approaches to biological phenomena and subtly urge an emphasis on environmental and personal factors in the assessment of specific research approaches and strategies. This leads logically to support of specific disease and life-span-increasing technologies oriented to broad environmental, sociocultural, and life-style changes. Although it is not necessarily implied by the view, holistic advocates in many cases opt for curve-squaring rather than life-span extending as the *desideratum* of research, since they emphasize quality of life rather than quantity.

Emergentism.   Some biologists, notably Michael Polanyi, Peter Medawar, Ernst Mayr, and Theodosius Dobzhansky, have urged a completely nonreductionistic conception of human life.[34] They argue that the complexity and organization of life is not amenable to molecular or even organic explanation. Attempts to extend or prolong life by biochemical or genetic intervention are looked at dubiously, since they ignore the fact that human existence is an emergent phenomena dependent on, but not reducible to, organic biological events. Human beings are more than the sum of their biological parts. Resistance to life-span-extending technology of any sort can often be traced to a philosophical or theological version of emergentism. Life must be respected as a given basic, not as a simple organic process.

Advances in life-span-extending technology will continue to challenge many of these philosophical views of human existence. As research at the cellular and molecular levels continues, it becomes more difficult for holists and emergentists to specify aspects of life not amenable to reduction. Many experiments in tissue culture and on animals seem to bear out the reductionist or hierarchist conceptions. At the same time, many of the most promising interventions are complex social and life-style changes.

An interesting ethical consequence of these diverse conceptions is that if reductionistic research proves fruitful, and life extension is attainable by cellular, organic, or molecular interventions, the reductionist and hierarchist viewpoints will converge toward a radical biologism of our conceptions of responsibility, guilt, and merit. Reductionism is closely akin to human determinism; life-extending technology could result in large numbers of criminals and deviants being considered medical cases and removed from the sphere of the law. If our reductionist-inspired understanding of basic biological activity increases, conceptions of punishment and free will, which are tied to holistic and emergentist outlooks, might decline in influence and be replaced by deterministic attitudes and measures. The 190-year-old who commits a crime is more likely to be sent to a biological engineer than to a judge, if present philosophical outlooks are maintained.

LIFE EXTENSION AND CULTURAL VALUES

Choices of alternative life-extending technologies will have a pervasive and sometimes dramatic impact on the family and on attitudes toward work, leisure, the elderly, and on value patterns themselves. As with other value choices, there is no clear methodology for resolving conflicts in this area. Our objective here is to point out some of the possible implications of life-extending technologies for cultural institutions and patterns.

The Family.   Changes in life expectancy resulting from artificial prostheses and cures for specific diseases will probably have little impact on the family. If morbidity is decreased, older family members may play a different role, their dependency may decrease, and consumption of resources for nursing home and custodial care may decline. Meanwhile, the percentage of elderly in the population will increase as the life-expectancy curve is squared, and the extended family may again become a common phenomenon.

A significant change in life *span*, however, will have a major impact on the family; more generations will be alive simultaneously (assuming no significant delay in the age of childbearing) and inheritance will come at a different point in life. If life span is extended by 50 to 100 percent, it may be practically impossible to maintain contact with all one's living progenitors and descendants; this would hasten the already advancing deterioration of the extended family. Certain religious and cultural groups may find this offensive, if they emphasize the family and have reservations about human intervention into the biological processes. The resistance of such groups to life extension may increase.

Work.   Perceptions of the nature of work will change with any major increase in life expectancy. If the worker-dependency ratio remains as it is now, there will be an impact on the habits and concepts of work. In any society, especially our own, work is more than a way of supporting oneself and one's dependents—it is a major part of life, a way of defining one's existence and a source of personal esteem and identity. In a culture steeped in the Protestant ethic, work gives meaning and purpose to life.

Curve-squaring will increase the likelihood of living past the productive years into retirement. Theoretically, this could enhance the importance of planning for that period and increase the value of the retirement years. It could increase the attention to, and possibly the value of, leisure time and even lead to new forms of valued activity. If the work ethic remains dominant, we might develop ways of legitimizing retirement activity by making it useful or productive. Whether or not the retirement years will become increasingly significant is highly speculative, in part because adults already expect to reach retirement and indicate this by supporting social security, holding pensions, and investing in retirement property.

Life-span extension may have a greater impact on the cultural value of work. Assuming a constant worker-dependent ratio, both work time and dependency time for any individual will increase. If the future holds increased time for each person both inside and outside the labor force, this may mean longer periods of career preparation. The value of schooling may increase—a pattern at odds with the current short-term concern about overly trained employees. Extended careers will mean the ability to develop skills over a long time, and unskilled labor will seem even less attractive than it does today.

Lengthier retirement with a likelihood of longer survival may radically change the retirement life-style; there may be a greater willingness to undertake long-term projects, learn new skills, even begin second careers. The usual preparation for labor and for retirement from it may change. The pattern of a brief period of "dropping out," which is emerging in contemporary culture, may increase. Interdisciplinary training in law, medicine, and humanistic disciplines would become more feasible. Women might go through reproductive years in the mother role and still pursue lengthy careers. On the other hand, if length of experience remains a prestigious characteristic within a profession, longer periods of commitment will be required. It is difficult to predict the precise impact of increased life span on the value of work, but it is safe to say that the impact will be great.

Value Patterns and Value Stability. Continuing technological innovations have an impact not only on health, happiness, and life-styles, but also on the most basic assumptions of a culture. Examples of this impact include the phenomenal change in judgments about birth control and abortion following the introduction of newer, more effective, and safer technologies. Our basic values may be affected equally by life-extending technologies. The concept of the heart as the seat of the soul, the center of passion, and the source of life has already changed with the development of open heart surgery, heart transplantation, and artificial heart research. Other technologies may have a similar effect.

Artificial prostheses may significantly change concepts of personal integrity and wholeness. The body may be seen not as an integrated and unique whole, but as a collection of replaceable parts. Orthodox Judaism places special value on the integrity of the body, requiring that unless other lives may be saved, the body should be buried as a whole. For this reason, organs removed during autopsy are restored to the corpse for burial.[35] If organs are removed and replaced over many years, maintaining this sense of integrity will be difficult.

Cultural values regarding manipulation of the body may change with the success or failure of life-extending technologies. Many people asked informally about the use of an antiaging pill are first intrigued and then repulsed, reporting that they would not take it if it were available. If freedom of choice were retained they would have the right to refuse such a pill. However, social scientists asking questions about future behavior are properly skeptical; they know that responses in the early phase of a technological development may not accurately predict attitudes once the newness wears off.

The perplexing problem is what weight, if any, should be given to the possibility that life-extending technologies will change our basic values. What is the value of value stability?

Two answers have been given. One is that we should avoid behavior whatever jeopardizes our basic and cherished values. The other is that there may be nothing wrong with either a new technology or new values. Our ancestors once thought slavery moral and birth control immoral—we do not regret the shift in those values. If we anticipate that new behavior will eventually be compatible with new values, should its incompatibility with our established values be a deterrent? Those protective of our values feel we must go slowly with new technologies to allow feedback from our values; change-oriented types consider such caution obstructionist.

RIGHTS, RESPONSIBILITIES, AND VALUES

JUSTICE AND LIFE EXTENSION

Along with questions of life evaluation, questions concerning the just distribution of life-extending technologies are probably the most pervasive and the most difficult. What rules of equity ought to apply? Can marketplace mechanisms be relied upon to distribute expensive technologies? Should technologies be incorporated into a national health insurance scheme and, if so, which ones should? What are America's obligations to other countries, particularly developing ones with an interest in life-extending technologies, as well as in more basic needs? What will be the differential effects on various individuals and groups such as the elderly versus the young, the present generation versus future ones, the wealthy versus the poor? Are triage considerations warranted?

The Hastings Center work on the question of justice covered two major areas. First, we considered basic theories of justice as they are being debated in contemporary Western thought. We asked: What are the major theories of justice and what are their implications for alternative life-extending technologies? Second, we asked: What major ways of placing value on human life grow out of these competing theories? Here we examined ways actually used in setting governmental policies as well as those that have been proposed.

The debate over theories of justice is one of the most interesting and controversial in contemporary political thought. Some argue that specific diseases should be conquered because of the desperate need of suffering people in our society. Others defend the right to buy experimental life-extending drugs on the open market. Still others hold that individuals and groups who have been the victims of past social wrongs, especially if these caused irreparably damaged health, have a special claim. From a different socioeconomic perspective comes the claim that the most useful or socially productive, those who have families or businesses or governments depending on them, merit special consideration. The problem for policy planners is to decide which, if any, of these competing claims ought to be given more weight.

DISTRIBUTING LIFE-EXTENDING TECHNOLOGIES

There are at least ten kinds of claims relevant to the distribution of life-extending technologies. We shall outline them, give examples of each, and then show how each of four major theories of justice synthesizes these ten claims into a coherent theory.

The first two claims are rooted in a theory of the equality of all human beings. The first approach holds that some goods are most fairly distributed when every person, regardless of need, merit, or usefulness, gets the same amount. The major dimensions of a future health policy might be decided by votes distributed this way. Every person might get a flat dollar amount of health care, say $50,000 per lifetime,[36] at government expense, to use as he sees fit for major lifesaving interventions, preventive medicine, or cosmetic surgery. This view has been defended as an efficient way of letting each individual realize his own values in seeking health care. A similar scheme could be devised for specific life-extending technologies. One could save his or her resources for later disease interventions and artificial prostheses, invest heavily in preventive medicine, or choose life-span-extending therapies. The problems with this, however, are obvious. Not everyone has the same needs, and some people would use their share in trivial ways. Furthermore, it is not clear that society could tolerate abandoning those who used up their share early and had a clear need later in life.

A second approach to distribution that treats everyone equally is based on some objectively measurable variable. Food might be fairly distributed, for example, on the basis of a person's weight; obese individuals might not have a full claim if the obesity was thought to be the result of voluntary behavior. Votes among shareholders in drug companies making life-extending drugs might be allotted by number of shares. Doses of life-extending drugs that are body weight-dependent could be distributed on that basis also.

Eight additional bases of distribution are worth considering. We can ask whether individual characteristics are relevant reference points or whether societal usefulness, previous harms, or commitments are more relevant. We can consider whether assets or benefits count, or whether deprivations or needs count more. Finally, we can consider whether objective factors count more than subjective factors.

Need seems an obvious basis for deciding who should have an opportunity for life extension and what that opportunity should be. Victims of diseases seem to have a special claim. Decisions about who is the most needy will depend on the kinds of life considered most valuable and the kinds of death most appropriate. Using need as a basis will give special weight to curve-squaring technologies such as treatment of specific diseases and use of artificial prostheses. Among the curve-squaring technologies, treatments would probably be chosen that best satisfy the criteria of an appropriate death— those combating diseases that produce unbearable pain or interrupt major personal life plans and responsibilities.

Ability might also be a basis for deciding which life-extending technologies to develop and who should get them. Should the lives of geniuses be prolonged? If so, since there is no way of predicting which diseases would strike them as a group, society might choose to distribute life-span-increasing technologies selectively to those with special abilities. Artificial prostheses might be given more easily to those with superior mental abilities, if these abilities seem to continue into later life.

Effort and desire constitute the chief subjective dimensions of the individual perspective on distribution. Effort is not the same as ability. Many try hard but lack talent. We reward effort with passing grades in school and with posthumous medals to heroes. It is hard to see the direct impact of rewarding effort when choosing among life-extending technologies, although it might be relevant in deciding who should benefit from them. Should those who have ignored proper exercise and diet have the same claim to an artificial heart as those who have shown valiant effort but suffer from heart disease? Life-span-increasing drugs could be offered first to those who have made an effort, but such judgments would be overwhelmingly difficult. Further, it is not yet clear that effort alone should be rewarded.

Desire is a strange basis on which to distribute most goods. We might give life-span-increasing drugs or artificial prostheses only to those who desire them, but a treatment that is simply "wanted" and is not a necessity of life is unlikely to have high priority in a national health program. The most plausible role for desire in this issue would be like the role it plays in the allocation of competing goods. If two apples and two oranges are to be divided between two people, it is not necessary for each to get one of each fruit if one likes only apples and the other only oranges. Analogously, there is no need for people to receive exactly the same life-extending technology if their desires differ.

It is also possible to base the development and distribution on a more societal perspective. Social utility is probably more relevant to distribution than to development, since it is not clear whether any of the technologies are uniquely beneficial in extending the lives of "useful" people. Whatever the technology, if usefulness is the basis of distribution, those judged useful should have a special claim on it. We should develop and distribute technologies to keep those people useful. The objective of both age-span extension and curve-squaring would be to make the most of the period of usefulness.

There are technical and ethical problems, however, with the notion of usefulness as a criterion of just distribution. A national debate about who the useful people are would be difficult and perhaps counterproductive, generating suspicion, power struggles, and so on. Nevertheless, it seems technically possible to decide which people are more useful to society than others. The more difficult question is ethical: Should usefulness per se be the criterion in making technology choices or do citizens have a claim to these choices independent of the accident of their usefulness? These questions will be explored later.

The subjective correlate of usefulness is willingness to serve, but it is not clear that willingness per se should be rewarded more than usefulness (or its counterpart, ability). In one sense, willingness to serve is useful in that it is an example of dedication. We might, as a society, decide that willingness to serve is so meritorious that it deserves reward over and above usefulness. Certainly it seems more plausible to reward willingness to serve society than to reward individual effort independent of any social commitment. If willingness to serve is relevant at all to technologies, it will be primarily regarding their allocation and not their development.

One of the more significant contemporary claims to justice is based on previous wrong done by society. Should blacks, women, and other previously oppressed groups receive special priority? The question is complicated because groups who have suffered previous social wrongs may also have claims based on need. If the rural poor have been excluded from the medical care delivery system, they may have greater health needs. The question is, should they get priority based on need or higher priority as compensation for previous injustice?

The policy payoffs of a claim for compensatory justice will be great in the life-extending-technology policy debate. If groups who have a particular claim on this basis can be identified, their life-extending-technology interests will get special attention. Diseases naturally cluster according to ethnic and sex groups, so it would be technically easy to give them priority. Should disorders of blacks (sickle-cell anemia and hypertension) get priority within the specific disease programs? Should men be given a higher priority for getting artificial hearts if they are considered a medically disadvantaged group because of their poorer survival rate? Should the medical interests of previously colonized nations (tropical diseases, diet, and public health, but probably not life-span-increasing technologies) take precedence over interests of the developed nations? Although life-span increase may be a special interest of the middle and upper classes of relatively wealthy nations, if compensatory justice is a relevant consideration, it may receive particularly low priority.

The subjective side of previous social harm—feelings of having been socially wronged—seems much less legitimate as a basis for public policy formation. Individuals and groups that protest the loudest about previous wrongs are likely, as a matter of political reality, to get special attention. It seems questionable, however, from a moral point of view, whether only ability to make noise should justify policy preference.

Each of these ten kinds of claims has defenders and probably all have some relevancy in the policy-making process. It would be helpful at this point to summarize the major current theories of justice or fairness in social life, to simplify the argument.

FOUR THEORIES OF JUSTICE

The Utilitarian Theory.   Economists, cost-benefit analysts, and some philosophers, members of the medical profession, and others hold that society should strive to choose the courses of action that will produce the greatest net benefits. Exactly what the benefits are depends on our answers to value questions raised earlier. The common thread among utilitarian groups is that, however the good is defined, the objective is to produce the most of it. A theory growing out of the classic utilitarianism of Jeremy Bentham, John Stuart Mill, and the liberal economists,[38] its method is to calculate the goods and harms to each individual as a result of alternative policy options and then sum them up across all individuals involved. The result is an aggregate of benefits and harms. The utilitarian objective is to produce the greatest possible net good when all individuals are considered.

In the case of life-extending technologies, we might take years of life as the good to be achieved. We would examine alternative life-extending technologies and choose, on an empirical basis, those that would produce the most years for the dollar. Childhood diseases might get the highest priority since a cure would add many years per child. If this were too expensive, however, we might consider getting more years of life by intervening in middle age or by attempting to extend the life span.

Adding years of life might not be the objective chosen. Some people would strive to maximize the aggregate relief of suffering, or minimize the number of life plans interrupted or the number of familial obligations unfulfilled because of death or morbidity. Still others would resort to more classical economic formulas, urging expenditure of resources on technologies that would add the most to the GNP or save the most in human capital.[39] Finally, some would try to realize the greatest aggregate good by also measuring social indicators such as overall health, diet, housing, happiness, and other values.[40] The aggregating tendency of the utilitarian formulas is a source of controversy, because adding fifty years to one life would be the same as adding ten years to five lives. If adding to the GNP were the objective, adding $100,000 for one individual would be the same as adding $1,000 for one hundred individuals. There is substantial ethical doubt about the legitimacy of aggregating goods and harms for purposes of public policy consideration. One major school of thought claims that individuals do count, that it does make a difference who gets the extra years of life, reductions in morbidity, or dollars added to the economy. Many argue that a legitimate goal of social policy is to increase efficiently net good over harm, but that that should not be confused with promotion of justice or fairness.

The Rawlsian Maximin Theory. The philosopher John Rawls has led a revival of interest in another theory of justice, which has its origins in Judeo-Christian thought, the work of Kant, and the contract theorists that stand behind the political philosophy of America's Founding Fathers. Rawls's view is that justice or fairness rests not in the total aggregate amount of good but in its distribution. He develops two principles of justice as the basis of social practices. First, liberty should be maximized to the extent that it provides similar liberty for all. Second, social and economic inequalities are justified and are to be arranged so that they are: (1) to the greatest benefit of the least advantaged, and (2) attached to offices and positions open to all under conditions of fair opportunity.[41] The resulting system will strive to maximize the position of the least well-off—that is, the position of the person in the society with the minimum of goods will be maximized. (This is sometimes called the "maximin theory.")

The implications of this theory for life-extending technologies are radically different from those of the utilitarian theory. If years of life are considered the good, the social policy objective is not to maximize the average years of life per person, but to maximize the minimal number of years the least well-off person can expect. Life-span extending technologies and even specific disease treatment for the young adult and middle-aged would receive very low priority. If relief of morbidity were the objective, the planners would not strive to minimize the average morbidity in society, but to minimize the morbidity of the sickest individuals. If GNP per capita were the goal, the target would not be maximizing the average GNP but maximizing the minimum. In each case the interests of those who are not least well-off would receive virtually no attention.

Life-span-increasing technologies and specific disease treatments for the elderly, middle-aged, and young adult do, however, bear indirectly on the Rawlsian theory. Possibly the best way to increase the life-expectancy of infants with genetic diseases would be to make sure that the life span of brilliant genetic scientists was increased. Pain and suffering from childhood diseases might best be reduced by giving life-extending resources to older medical scientists with special skills in this area. If GNP is the target, it might be possible to increase benefit from the GNP to the least well-off by paying successful business leaders very highly. The Rawlsian formula, although more egalitarian than the utilitarian ones that focus on aggregate effects, is not as egalitarian as it may seem at first.

The Egalitarian Theory. Egalitarians believe that Rawls does not go far enough. In the Rawlsian theory, to maximize the position of the least well-off person, it may be necessary to reward very highly those with the talent to help the least well-off. That, say the egalitarians, may be efficient, but it is not necessarily fair to give special compensation to those whose talents or opportunities are already far superior. Both egalitarian and maximin views see that justice may require compromising efficiency and that, as a result, the aggregate good may not be the greatest amount possible. The egalitarians, however, might make some choices to increase equality—which they see as inherently right—even if it means lowering not only the aggregate amount of good but also the position of the least well-off. People, even the least well off, might rationally choose to lower their own position somewhat in order to have a world that treats people more equally.

Clearly, pure egalitarianism, like the pure type of any other position, is not tenable. Some people are genetically determined to be so poorly off physically, that they could be made equal to others only by lowering the standard of life of the others to a point where the human species would collapse. Yet this does not rule out the policy goal of treating equality among other policy objectives as a characteristic to be sought.

The egalitarian understanding would have great impact on choices among life-extending technologies. As with other theories of justice, the impact would depend on what one wants to distribute more equally. If vital and productive life is the goal, the egalitarian might hold that everyone has an equal right to some minimal number of vital and productive years. The argument that certain life-span-increasing therapies should be developed to help those skilled in providing minimal years for others, the argument that made life-span extension a legitimate but secondary priority in the maximin position, would not hold any weight for the egalitarian. If everyone has an equal right to a minimal number of years, we should not only give absolute priority to life-expectancy extension over life-span extension, but we should give priority among life-expectancy-extending technologies to those most relevant to causes of death of the very young. Among technologies to extend the life of those who would otherwise die young, some, conceivably, would also be useful for the elderly. The technology for producing an artificial heart to replace an infant's congenitally defective one would probably also make feasible an artificial heart for the elderly, but it is possible that priority in distribution would go to the youngest.

Values other than life per se may mean developing and distributing technologies on a different basis. If, for instance, the goal is to make deaths as natural or appropriate as possible according to the subjective criteria previously outlined (when life projects are complete, obligations are fulfilled, and there is not unbearable pain), then life-expectancy technologies should be developed to give everyone an equal chance for a natural or appropriate death. Still, life-span-increasing technologies would receive low or no commitment under this general view.

The Entitlement Theory.   A fourth view about just social practices, in some ways the opposite of the egalitarian theory, has recently been articulated by Robert Nozick in a critique of Rawls from the right-wing libertarian position.[42] It holds that people are entitled to what they possess if they acquire it through a prior just distribution. They are entitled to own something that belonged to nobody or that was freely given by someone who acquired it justly. There is no moral reason why redistribution of goods justly acquired ought to take place except out of a sense of charity on the part of those who want to give their goods away. Thus, there is no particular pattern of just distribution in society.

The theory is not as anarchist as it at first sounds. Those who possess things that were not originally justly acquired are not entitled to them. The state functions to protect citizens from assault, robbery, and breaking of contracts. The implications for the role of the state in developing and distributing life-extending technologies are very different from those of the previous positions. The state should not directly develop or distribute, but should be an enforcement agency, making sure that privately arranged exchanges of resources (for example, money for technical skills and devices) are executed in an orderly way. It is irrelevant what the technology is or what it does. Those who want to buy life-span extenders could; those who choose to use their resources for specific diseases, artificial prostheses, or tissue regeneration could. Social interventions requiring societal cooperation in order to be effective, such as environmental controls, would depend on citizens agreeing to avoid mutually disadvantageous practices. When it is recognized that environmental pollution is done by a minority at the expense of the majority, it can be seen how difficult the entitlement theory may be to execute. Presumably it would require majority compensation of the minority so that it would be in their interest not to pollute, or it would mean that the minority were unjustly appropriating other people's resources by polluting their air, land, and water.

These four theories of distributive justice can be applied to different populations. Only the entitlement theory seems to justify limiting policy consideration to distribution within the United States. Utilitarian, maximin, and egalitarian theories potentially apply internationally, at least if the common human community is seen to extend beyond national borders. Even the entitlement theory has international implications when one considers questions of unjust appropriation through colonization and slavery.

The theories also seem to apply differently to contemporary and future generations. Future generations may be interested in different technologies from those of interest to the present generation. According to one view, the present generation and possibly its children and grandchildren are the only ones having an interest in distributive policy,[43] in part because it is hard to predict the basic values or factual situations of distant future generations. The obligation to future generations, however (suitably taking account of our uncertainties), is widely recognized in utilitarian, Rawlsian, and egalitarian positions.[44] Only the entitlement theory eliminates or radically reduces the claims of the future.

VALUING LIVES

The question of how various lives should be valued for purposes of choosing among life-extending technologies is closely related to the theories of justice.[45] A debate over technical procedures for placing value on lives has emerged in the literature of the policy sciences. In spite of the fact that the issues are closely related, the debate has generally taken place independently of the debate among philosophers on the theories of justice. Cost-benefit analysis and technology assessment techniques have, in some cases, been used to develop formulas for valuing different lives saved or extended, for purposes of choosing among medical interventions.[46]

It should be clear from the discussion of justice previously presented that lives may be valued because of some intrinsic worth or quality, or because of the relationship those lives have to society. The debate among economists, which has focused on techniques that are fundamentally utilitarian in nature and that have as their implicit goal maximizing some aggregate good, primarily concerns measuring that good. The following discussion considers some main positions in this controversy.

Aggregating Measures of Valuing Lives. Two major and competing aggregating techniques express value in economic terms: the human capital approach and the willingness-to-pay approach.[47] A third approach uses social indicators to measure and aggregate value.

The human capital approach asks the question: What are the benefits and costs in dollar terms of saving life from a particular disease or other cause of death?[48]

The impact on the GNP (corrected for certain nonmonetized labor such as household work) is calculated for competing possible interventions, yielding a set of comparative statistics expressed in dollar terms on their costs and savings. The numbers indicate benefits to society, not necessarily the value placed on their lives by the individuals whose lives are at stake. There are some clear moral problems with the techniques: Retired people (not engaged in household labor) are technically worthless, men are more valuable than women, whites more valuable than blacks, and so on.

The impact of this approach would be to aim policy toward technologies that have the most positive effect on the GNP. We would not make simple choices between life-expectancy extension and life-span extension, nor between tissue regeneration and artificial prostheses; rather we would search out technologies that kept the most people productive the longest. Since no such policy objective is clear in the first place (we may prefer to keep our worker/dependents ratio constant), there are serious problems with the technique.

The other aggregating economic measure is the willingness-to-pay approach developed by Thomas Schelling.[49] It relies on sophisticated techniques for finding out how much people would be willing to pay for reducing the risks of certain kinds of deaths. From those responses the value of different interventions can be calculated. Although this method begins with a more subjective measure of personal worth, it runs into many of the same ethical problems. Willingness to pay presumably depends heavily on present distribution of resources—on the status quo rather than on a just or fair ordering of society. It resembles the entitlement theory in this regard and, like that theory, could help to decide alternative life-extending technologies through modified marketplace mechanisms. The problem is whether the present marketplace mechanism, dependent on the current distribution of resources, is ethically adequate, or whether rights and responsibilities are independent of the status quo distribution.

More sophisticated measures have been developed to overcome the simplicity of the strictly economic measures of value implicit in these two approaches. These social indicators measure the general quality of housing, diet, recreation, work satisfaction, health, and the like.[50] As used in cost-benefit analysis and related policy planning techniques, however, they still tend to measure aggregate goods, and are subject to all the criticism of utilitarian theories. Increasing the value of one person's housing from $500,000 to $1 million, for example, has the same impact on the average value of housing as increasing fifty families' housing value by $10,000 each. Even with corrections for decreasing marginal utility, it is not at all clear, at least according to Rawlsian, egalitarian, and entitlement understandings of justice, that the goal of a social policy should be to maximize anything in the aggregate.

Expanding social measures to include goods other than life-expectancy increase is likely to shift policy choices in a way that will decrease the overall commitment to the technologies. Some resources will be diverted to medical areas to relieve suffering or to other areas outside the health sphere. The diviersity of choices among life-extending technologies, based on social-indicators approaches, will be as broad as the diversity among ways average citizens value different kinds of deaths. If life per se is valued, technologies that give the maximum number of additional years will be emphasized, whether life-expectancy or life-span extending. To the extent that the more personal interpretation of a good or natural death is adopted, technologies will be chosen that permit completion of life plans and obligations, and a death free from unbearable suffering. Those who see value in extending the life-span or holding to immortal life as an ideal may be more open to life-span-extending technologies, but even they will sacrifice this development for other priorities.

Nonaggregating Measures of Valuing Lives. The serious problems with any utilitarian measure that aggregates consequences have led to an exploration of a number of other theories for placing value on human life. These include the all-lives-are-equal position, the prime-of-life position, the younger-is-better position, and the older-is-better position.

The strand of American tradition emphasizing that all men are created equal rejects in principle the differential valuation of individual lifes. The view is not that all people have equal skills or make equal contributions to society, but that they are owed equal respect; they are equally members of the human community—the Kingdom of Ends, to use the Kantian phrase. The implication of the all-lives-are-equal position is that resources should be spread so that each person, regardless of age or station in life, has an equal claim to a technology that would extend his or her life. (The variant that would give each person an equal claim to a certain minimal number of years is considered below.) It is not clear whether this would mean that each person should have an equal chance to have his life extended or an equal amount of health resources expended on him in the attempt. The former seems the dominant interpretation among those writing from the egalitarian perspective.[51]

A second nonaggregating approach to the value of life is the view that life is most valuable in its prime. An individual begins life with value, which increases as experience and talent accumulate. This increase continues to a point (the prime) and then declines. The practical effect of this position is a valuing of life similar to the human capital and willingness-to-pay valuations, but the foundation is different, treating age as a more independent variable. The implication would be to give high priority to technologies that extend the prime of life, mainly treatments for specific diseases and other curve-squaring technologies, but possibly also life-span technologies that extend life's prime. Treatments of diseases or general aging processes for those past their prime would get the lowest priority. Treatments for infants and children whose prime of life could be created by preventing early death would get relatively high priority, but the interventions would be considered inefficient to the extent that they bought preprime as well as prime years.

Others hold a nonaggregating position that values younger life most highly, either because youth per se is valuable or because future life is valuable. In either case, priority would go to technologies that extend the life of the youngest. In the latter case, it would go only to young people on the assumption that more future life can come from medical interventions in the youngest lives.

In addition to seeing young life as more valuable, it is possible to conclude that young life deserves priority on grounds of justice. In other words, everyone is entitled to a certain minimal number of years because all people should be treated as equals. The egalitarian and Rawlsian notions of justice may require a special application of resources to give people this equal opportunity of living to the point the rest of the citizenry can expect to reach.

Whether the basis for the young's priority is the higher value of younger life or the greater claim of the young on justice, it is necessary to decide whether that priority is absolute or relative. The first view probably would include the qualifier that young life is only relatively valuable. Were it graphed, the value of life with this approach would be a gradually descending curve, resulting in relative priority to the young. The position that emphasizes simple justice might give absolute priority to the young. The egalitarian extreme would concentrate all resources on extending the life-expectancy of the young as would the Rawlsian position, if it were concluded that dying young made one least well-off, but adherents would qualify by developing and distributing life-extending technologies to older people who could help improve the lot of those who would otherwise die young.

The fourth possible nonaggregating answer to the question of life valuation is that older is better. As with the other answers, this one has both personal and social variants. The personal variant might be the position that personal memories have the real value, and the older person has more memories to cherish. The social perspective might be that it is wisdom from experience and/or training that has value. Assuming wisdom accumulates with age, the older population would be the most socially useful and therefore the most valued.

All of these general positions give uniquely high priority to lifespan extending in contrast with curve-squaring. From this point of view, it is better to extend the life-span of some people than to increase more equally the life-expectancy of every person.

FREEDOM AND LIFE-EXTENDING TECHNOLOGIES

The debate about alternative life-extending technologies turns in part upon what social policies will be required to produce behavior conducive to extending life. If it were known that life span could be increased significantly by educating pediatricians to instruct parents on the value of a particular diet (for example, to produce the McCay effect), we might opt for investing in such physician education at government expense. If, however, it were discovered empirically that this did not effect the desired change in children's diets, we might decide to achieve the life extension by more directly coercive control of children's nutrition. Such a policy would not be attractive to those who consider parental freedom an important right and responsibility. This freedom might be considered a right and responsibility to be preserved even at the expense of a certain decrease in the life span of the offspring. That it is parental freedom rather than the freedom of the primary beneficiaries of the technology makes the case more complicated.

The same conflict between life-extending benefits and freedom of choice arises with most of the technologies under consideration. If it were known that an artificial kidney would double the predicted five-year survival of a 65-year-old man with chronic but not acute kidney failure, we would presumably still recognize his right to choose freely to forego treatment. Likewise, if increased life expectancy or life span required coercive controls on fertility, life-style choices, or pollution levels, many would consider the infringement morally and politically relevant to the policy choice. Therefore, one who considers freedom as important as efficiency in extending lives will not be able to debate in the abstract the relative value of the various technologies and interventions. He will have to know empirically how much free choice will be surrendered to produce the various effects.

One might conclude on grounds of value choices and understanding of justice that curve-squaring technologies should take precedence over life-span-extending ones but that, since individuals should have the freedom not to extend their lives to the normal span, voluntary life-span extension should take precedence over compulsory curve-squaring, or even over elaborate programs to induce behaviors that would reduce premature death.

Another implication is that premature deaths thought to be the result of voluntary choices would receive particularly low priority or no priority at all. Premature deaths from mountain climbing, professional automobile racing, smoking, voluntary obesity, or failure to exercise would not have high priority, assuming that they result from voluntary choice and that individuals have the right to jeopardize their lives.

Different Meanings of Freedom. The literature on interpretations of freedom recognizes many meanings of the term. One's definition may heavily influence policy choices regarding life-extending technologies. The most adequate analysis is a three-term relation based on a person's being free from something to do something. That is, it must always be clear as to who is free, what he is free from, and what he is free to do.

Sometimes policy choices are made between different freedoms for the same individual and other times between different freedoms for different people. One must know what interferences one is accepting for particular goods and interests. This value-neutral concept of freedom facilitates expression of the trade-offs. Since one cannot have the freedom to do everything, he may have to give up some freedoms to achieve others. State administration of a life-span-extending drug would involve a choice between freedom from state control and freedom to function normally during old age. In the case of controlling factory air pollution, the choices are between the freedom of factory owners from state regulation, pollution controls, and attendant costs, and the freedom of other citizens from polluted air and consequent disease.

Such policy choices require value judgments about limits on freedom. Here at least two considerations are important. First, limits vary in degree from negative incentives such as taxes, to physical constraints such as being bound and gagged. While taxes limit freedom by making options more expensive, they allow a choice of action if a person desires it enough to pay the extra cost or give up some other activities. Other constraints do not allow any choice at all. Moreover, some people regard even rewards offered in certain circumstances as coercive—offering low-income individuals free meals fortified with a life-span-extending compound might be so interpreted. Severe social disapproval or even a social suggestion made over and over (via TV, films, and so on) is more and more regarded as coercive. The question remains whether positive incentives and these broad sorts of social pressure are coercive or limit freedom, and if so, whether they are preferred to other, better recognized forms of social restraint.

Second, Americans are much more averse to limits directly and intentionally imposed by others than to those that come from within themselves, such as disease. They are inclined to view state control, more than disease, as an unjustifiable limitation on their freedom. Indeed, many people do not regard disease, poor health, or even low income as limits at all, but as simple natural endowments. Once it becomes clear that a condition can be changed by intentional intervention, especially if its cause was a human action, such attitudes can change.

In American political thought, there are disagreements about the justifications for state-imposed limits to freedom. Among the generally accepted ones, however, are: (1) to prevent persons injuring other individuals, as by assault and battery; (2) to prevent harm to public institutions, as in destruction of public property; (3) to prevent injustice, as in racial or sexual discrimination; and (4) to preserve and promote the public welfare, as in proper disposal of garbage and prevention of contagious diseases. More controversial reasons are (5) to prevent persons harming themselves, as in suicide, riding motorcycles without helmets, or using drugs and (6) to prevent immoral conduct, as in gambling and prostitution. Reasons (3), (4), and (5) are particularly relevant to health policy choices. For example, official dispersal of new technologies may make life-extending possibilities, formerly available only to the wealthy, available to everyone, thus promoting equality. A substantial decrease in debilitating disease would undoubtedly increase productivity, decrease public expenditure for health care, and improve individuals' freedom to live their own lives.

Policy Problems Involving Freedom. One's interpretation of freedom will have a decisive impact on his life-extending technology choices. The following four probelsm deserve special attention.

The first involves freedom and efficient life-extension. It is likely that we as a society could obtain the greatest possible increase in life expectancy and life span through compulsory control of behavior rather than voluntary educational compaigns. Some life-extending technologies might be resisted for reasons, rational or irrational, that are rooted in life-style preferences, religious beliefs, or minority beliefs. People valuing freedom of choice would resist compulsory controls that conflicted with such preferences and beliefs. Furthermore, some technologies may lend themselves uniquely to either voluntary or compulsory use. Artificial organ technologies, tissue regeneration techniques, and specific disease interventions are likely to be administered to individuals and thus open to voluntary rejection. Environmental controls and some life-span-increasing technologies are likely to be more societal phenomena. Environmental approaches may require compulsory control of an air polluting industry, not for the benefit of the owners or employees, but for the benefit of others in the neighborhood.

If freedom has any ethical weight at all, policymakers cannot simply choose the technologies that will most efficiently increase life expectance. Indeed, it is not at all clear that the state has the right to require administration of even proven life-span-extending drugs.

If we consider state requirements for taking life-extending drugs, we must also consider the justifications for legislation depriving people of the freedom to refuse them, possibly through incentive systems. One might tax people more if they do not take a life-extending drug, or charge them higher rates for health insurance. Legal restrictions on smoking would prevent exposure to a high risk of cancer. But one should consider whether persons are capable of rational decisions in these matters, and whether rejection of life-extending drugs or other measures may be presumptive evidence that one has acted irrationally.

Certain freedoms, moreover, are given constitutional protection as fundamental rights that cannot be limited with a compelling state interest. Among these are the right to privacy, bodily integrity, marriage, and children.[52] Any policy that infringed on such rights would face not only significant legal challenges but also political opposition. They are fundamental freedoms that should be respected, although they may be limited for compelling reasons; whether the benefits of life extension constitute compelling reasons is not clear.

Neither is it clear whether one has the legal right and freedom to refuse life-extending treatments, either those that postpone death or those that restore one to a productive life, or whether a legal limit on this freedom would be sanctioned by society. Hence, in the future, more and more choices may be between life-extension and death. When, if ever, freedom will become secondary to other values and what role paternalism will play in social policies on these issues are questions whose answers have yet to be determined.

Blessings are usually mixed. Life-extension efforts, like any new therapy, may bring concomitant ill effects, such as the possibility of disease, early death, or deformity as a result of the treatment. Consequently, while freeing some people from disease for an extended healthy life, they would decrease the freedom of others from disease. This possibility, however, should be put in historical perspective. The risks are no different from those that accompanied past attempts to square life-expectancy curves. (For example, pneumonia vaccine that was found to be contaminated with simian viruses was introduced into the United States Army during World War II.)

The second problem involves who should pay for freely chosen health risks. If individuals do have the right to choose not to use the most efficient techniques for extending life expectancy, they may at some later point in life need medical treatment that would not otherwise have been necessary. An individual who chooses to smoke, avoid exercise, or eat fatty substances, or who refuses to take some hypothetical cholesterol-reducing drug, may later require, request, or demand an artificial heart. If freedom requires a society to permit such health-risky choices (assuming they are actually risky), many would argue that the individual himself should bear the responsibility for the additional costs of health care. Furthermore, if it were decided, as a matter of public policy, to give priority to curve-squaring over life-span-increasing technologies, this priority might not hold if specific disease intervention were necessary later in life because of voluntary risks to health. Such needs might be met out of humanitarian concern in a health crisis, but in general they might receive lower priority. This means that research and development of a specific disease technology or an artificial organ might receive low priority if seen as almost exclusively necessary for those who freely put themselves at risk. Moreover, such care might be delivered, but with the provision that it be paid for directly or indirectly by those requiring it; examples of this include insurance carried by a professional automobile driver, or a tax on cigarettes.[53]

The third involves parental freedom. One of the most difficult problems posed by the notion of freedom is that of parental liberties. Many life-extending technologies may have to be administered in childhood, when the individual is not legally capable of making his or her own decisions. While we may recognize the general right of competent adults to engage in life-risking behavior, it is not clear that parents should have the freedom to select such a risk for their children. On the other hand, the family is a fundamental unit in our society and has substantial latitude in choosing life-style preferences. Parents have the right to choose their children's education, but not to refuse education; they have the right to refuse certain medical treatments, but not those that would safely and simply restore a child to normal health (such as a blood transfusion). If control of diet or the taking of drugs early in life turns out to be important in increasing life-expectancy, policy planners will confront the enormously complex problem of whether parents have the freedom to withhold these options from their children. They may also consider avoiding this problem by concentrating on technologies for the adult, who is capable of controlling his own care.

The fourth problem is a traditional disagreement over whether freedom means the right to pursue a course independent of external, active constraint, or whether it implies an obligation on the part of someone else to provide the resources required to pursue that course. Does the freedom to choose an artificial heart or to take a drug with potential life-span-extending properties mean simply that no one will actively prevent use of these technologies, or that someone or some agency (such as the federal government) has an obligation to supply them if the individual cannot otherwise afford them? Freedom to take drugs with a potential life-span-extending effect might imply only that no one will prevent an individual from taking them. If the FDA did not place constraints on physicians' prescriptions for L-Dopa or dimethylaminoethanol, which may have life-span-extending properties, physicians would be free in this sense. If the FDA did not require a prescription to obtain them, consumers would be similarly free. If, however, they were free in the second sense, the state or someone might have an additional obligation to make the drugs available at an affordable price.

There is a growing discussion on the right to health care.[54] Although this debate is far from settled, it appears, in light of the increasing discussion of national health insurance, that policy planners should consider that individual citizens may claim a right to life-extending technologies under national health insurance.

KNOWLEDGE, UNCERTAINTY, AND LIFE EXTENSION

As we have seen, the use and consequences of life-extending technologies that would result in either the squaring or the extension of the population survival curve raise serious ethical dilemmas. In contemporary Western society, decisions, plans, life-styles, expectations, and valuations rest on a probabilistic knowledge of the quality and quantity of life that these technologies are likely to change drastically.

Knowledge and Life Span.   Many individuals' ethical and valuational decisions rest on current perceptions of the likelihood of their life span and the number of years of vigorous activity they can expect. Choices concerning careers, marriage, education, personal habits, jobs, expenditures, savings, and life styles center around particular perceptions of the statistically average life span for men and women. Undoubtedly, accidents, disease, war, and chance take their toll, but personal planning is done in light of reasonable expectations of living to sixty, seventy, or eighty years of age.

In terms of uncertainty in personal planning, the impact of life extension would be enormous. The effectiveness of much of the technology, particularly environmental alterations or genetic and cellular engineering, and the possible risks, would not be known with certainty for many years. Uncertainty would exist not only for individual participants in the new technology but also for government and private organizations involved in public policy formation and long-term planning. Food, housing, industry, recreational facilities, and natural resources would have to allotted on the basis of fundamental uncertainties as to the size and composition of future populations.

Life-span-increase technologies introduced without any concomitant curve-squaring will greatly increase uncertainty, particularly in the early decades of use when the long-term impacts are unknown. Thus, they will appeal to those who can tolerate uncertainty and those who want to increase their chances of long-term survival, even with the increased risk of premature death from any unexpected side effects. They will be unattractive to those with a lower tolerance for uncertainty; one who prefers a predictable future to a longer one will opt against life-span-increasing technologies.

Curve-squaring technologies may have opposite implications. In an ideal world of a perfectly squared life curve, everyone would know precisely the moment of his death. In the less than perfect world, that would never be the case, but the more curve-squaring technologies developed and perfected, the more certain would be the time and manner of one's death. There are significant differences among people over the desirability of this increased knowledge. Some find it repulsive, perhaps another example of Promethean usurpation by man of knowledge appropriate only for the gods. Others committed to the value of knowing and planning would find the possibility attractive, legitimate, or useful.

Uncertainty and Truth.   In the face of widespread uncertainty about the makeup of future populations in a society where life-extending technology is available on a broad scale, the potential for deceit and abuse would also be tremendous. Capital investment, advertising, insurance, inventories, and depreciation are all variables that demand accurate information if the economies of most large industrial states are to function in a fair, just, and equitable manner. Life-extending technologies would place a great premium on truth-telling in agencies or corporations involved in long-term projects and investments. The public would want to know if life insurance premiums were being assessed on the basis of curve-squaring, life extending, or status quo estimates of future population compositions.

It is conceivable that full and open disclosure of the development of certain life-extending technologies might conflict with other societal goals and even with the production of the greatest possible extension of life expectancy. Open disclosure of government-funded research projects could decrease their attractiveness for investigators accustomed to research being confidential. Possibly the initial users of developing technologies would be researchers with a greater likelihood of living longer and improving technologies that could eventually be more equitably distributed. Public disclosure of such a policy might lead to opposition and eventual failure.

The duty to be truthful and open in disclosing to the public what a government is doing may, on occasion, conflict with other goals; the appropriate response depends on how one views the duty to tell the truth. If such a duty exists, independent of the consequences of being truthful, there is reason to adopt a policy of openness even if some price will be paid in terms of life-expectancy extension. Overwhelmingly negative consequences might be seen as justification of secrecy, but at least there is an initial prima facie reason to consider disclosure. If, on the other hand, telling the truth is only a rule of thumb that generally produces good consequences, then every case would have to be evaluated on its own merits, and withholding of information about new technologies would be much easier to justify.

SUICIDE, EUTHANASIA, AND LIFE-EXTENDING TECHNOLOGIES

The current laws regarding suicide, euthanasia, allowing one to die, and refusal of treatment have evolved over the years from common law, and depend on a number of key distinctions that are related to empirical facts about what can and cannot be done by medicine to extend life.[55] The development of new technologies with the potential for extending life expectancy and life span is likely to have impact on our traditional patterns of analysis of what is ethical and legal.

The Present State of the Law.   Currently no state makes suicide or attempted suicide a crime, although many states consider aiding a suicide criminal, normally under the general law of homicide. Texas has a special statutory crime of aiding suicide, reducing the offense from the level of homicide. The view that aiding a suicide is murder is accepted by all but a few European and South American countries, which allow a plea of noble motivation either in mitigation of, or as an excuse for, a murder charge.

It must be remembered that suicide, even if not illegal, is frowned upon by both society and the state. In many states, suicidal tendencies are grounds for civil commitment. Most suicides are perceived as a "cry for help" on the part of an anguished soul, and the burden is on the potential suicide to convince us of the contrary.

The legal position regarding what has variously been called "euthanasia," "mercy killing," "the right to die," or "the right to refuse medical treatment" is more complex. Again, there are no laws specifically making euthanasia a crime, but the law, in American jurisdictions, still classifies active killing for mercy as murder.

Refusing medical treatment, whether one is terminally ill or not, is legally acceptable provided one is mentally competent and the treatment is offered for one's own good (public health treatments and those proposed for the benefit of one's offspring are thereby excluded). For mentally incompetent patients the legal situation is less clear, but a moral and possibly a legal consensus is emerging that in some circumstances guardians may refuse treatment for incompetent wards. Acceptability of that refusal might hinge on whether the treatment is useless for the patient given his or her condition, or whether the treatment, even though useful, is gravely burdensome. The Quinlan case has increased the momentum for this kind of policy.

The Impact of New Life-Extending Technologies.   Some life-extending technologies will have significant impact on current thinking about rights and responsibilities with respect to suicide, euthanasia, and the right to refuse treatment. At present the policy consensus depends on the empirical fact that for virtually all cases, simple withdrawal of treatment combined with adequate pain-relieving medication is sufficient to overcome the burden and indignity of prolonging the lives of hopelessly ill patients. (Deaths resulting indirectly from the side effects of pain-relieving medication are widely held to be tolerable, legally and ethically.)

Legal institutions will respond to cultural change. Any effects of new life-saving technologies on laws regarding euthanasia or suicide will be mediated through cultural and religious beliefs. Technology can only increase cultural strain and point up seeming legal anachronisms. As an example, consider nineteenth- and twentieth-century changes in autopsy laws that were brought about largely by the opportunities developed by new medical technologies. That such legal innovations regarding utilization of the dead body and its parts are a cause célèbre among religious groups in Israel, who reject secular attitudes toward the physical body, demonstrates that culture and not technology is the ultimate organizer of legal relations.

The present law and much present ethical thought depends heavily on the distinction between actions taken to hasten a death ("commissions") and mere omissions or refusals of treatment. This distinction, already difficult to maintain in some cases, may be disappearing. Stopping a respirator, for instance, is considered an omission by most philosophers and theologians who find the distinction important, but is treated as an act of commission by most physicians and other health care professionals. The development of new technologies may place greater strain on this distinction.

If persons use antiaging drugs from birth, are provided with long-life cardiac pacemakers, or adopt life-span extending diets, they may not be able simply to omit an "extraordinary" means. If one begins at birth a course of pill-taking to retard aging, or has a cardiac pacemaker, which is good for many years, implanted at age 80 it is difficult to argue that halting the drug regimen or removing the artificial prosthesis will merely restore a previous natural state. If society adopts patterns of widespread use of medicine to delay aging, all of us will be kept alive by varieties of artificial techniques. There will be no "state of nature" as regards health practice. It will thus be more difficult to argue that refusals to treat are only acts of omission. Some now hold that stopping a respirator is more akin to an omission than an action, but it might be much more difficult to consider removing an artificial heart a mere omission.

A great deal of confusion exists in our society at both legal and ethical levels about care that is required and care that is expendable. We can anticipate the rapid proliferation of new, highly diverse, potentially life-extending technologies, many of which will not be in common use and the selection of which will depend upon highly personal value choices. All members of the society will be even more uncertain about what constitutes expendable care, leading to disputes among physicians, and frustration and litigation on the part of patients and their families.

The concept of extraordinary care, as previously noted, is a cultural and not a technical phenomenon.[56] Technological advance may make certain medical innovations (such as dialysis machines) cheaper and therefore more likely to be culturally acceptable. Also, the extent to which a particular therapy occurs often changes the ways in which society perceives it (for example, the general acceptance of insulin and kidney dialysis). For a therapy to be expendable, it need not be esoteric. At the same time, an intervention need not be common for a physician to be held responsible for using it. Many factors must be considered before a recent medical innovation is deemed to be required at both the legal and ethical levels. The proliferation of new technologies seen as essential by some but expendable or even malicious by others can only heighten our confusion in determining which life-extending technologies ought to be developed and used.

An increase in the proportion of the aged in the population will pose the issue of suicide and euthanasia more often for individual citizens, members of their families, and professionals with whom they interact. We know little about what life would be like for the older members of a population in the context of life-extending technologies; their impact on our cultural values is difficult to anticipate. We may well lose our collective youth orientation as our proportion of elderly grows. The possibility exists, however, that allocation problems will result in social pressure for life termination upon the failing of ones *élan vital* whenever it occurs. On the other hand, assured of extensive longevity, one may be less likely to "rage against the dying of the light" and more likely to accept death when it comes.

Different projections of the impact of life extension lead to radically different judgments of the social value of suicide or euthanasia. If life per se is the objective of life-extending technologies, there may be an increase in the number of suicides and treatment refusals. If life is preserved in an immobilized and semicompetent condition, suicide will not be an alternative, because the patient will be unable to effectuate his or her desires; here treatment refusal and treatment-omitting decisions on the part of others will be most plausible. If a technology significantly extends the life span without affecting or increasing the time spent in senility, pressures to commit suicide or refuse medical treatment may grow, at least if allocation is a social concern. Pressures to let incompetent patients die may increase similarly.

If the policy objective is to extend life of high quality with individuals physically and mentally mobile, pressures to commit suicide, refuse treatment, or make treatment-stopping decisions for incompetents may diminish. Decisions to end life will have to be active and made by the individuals themselves while competent. This would eliminate some of the diffiuclt policy questions pertaining to assisting in stopping treatments when the patient is unable to do so, and deciding for the incompetent patient.

Curve-squaring technologies in general will minimize the number of decisions of this sort. If the curve of life expectancy were perfectly square, everyone would live to a sharply predictable life span. If curve-squaring technologies also reduced morbidity, active killing for mercy or treatment refusal would be unnecessary. Life-span-increasing technologies that did nothing to square the life-expectancy curve and reduce morbidity might actually increase the amount of mercy killing, suicide, and treatment refusal because of the prolonged time spent in an unbearable condition. If we adopt technologies that only extend life span, we might see a change in cultural evaluation of suicide, euthanasia, and treatment refusal.

Such a drastic change in our legal institutions would require a cultural shift of great magnitude: perhaps one in which we valued not the dignity of the individual but his social worth or his right to personal autonomy. Diana Crane suggests that this shift has already occurred, at least regarding a willingness to consider the social value of a life in determining whether to save it.[57] The Quinlan decision also suggests this shift. Present-day Anglo-American law, for better or worse, is still dominated by the Judeo-Christian concept of the sanctity of life, and opposes judgments based on social worth alone. New technologies may force us to revise this foundation of present legal relations if biological life becomes almost indefinitely extendable.

It is worth noting that two cultural trends on the horizon—the shift to self-determination over a wider range of issues and the recognition of social duties flowing from possible scarcity of resources—may reinforce the acceptability of suicide and euthanasia.

This raises once again the question of whether we ought to adopt a technological innovation that will predictably change existing basic values. We should at least be aware that major life-extending technological innovations may produce fundamental changes in social values and life-styles that cannot be ignored when policy choices are being made.

The ethical and other value implications of choices among life-extending technologies raise extremely complex and fundamental questions. It is possible that once all the technical facts are understood one technology or group of technologies will be seen as clearly preferable regardless of these value questions, but it seems extremely unlikely. If different policies can be justified as serving various contradictory sets of ethical and other values, as seems likely, then careful exploration of the issues raised in this analysis will be essential.

Without a clear understanding of the radically different positions regarding the concept of natural death, and the relationship between death and suffering and that between medical needs and other human needs, errors in public policymaking are likely. Without exploration of the effect on concepts of illness, disease and aging, and understanding of the long-term impact on our basic cultural values, we may choose to develop and deliver health care technologies that we as a society will live to regret. Without consideration of the ethical principles of justice, freedom, and truth-telling and of the ethical obligations pertaining to suicide and euthanasia, we may make a similar error. We may also fail to develop those life-extending technologies that ought to be developed.

NOTES

1. Harvard Medical School, Ad Hoc Committee of the Harvard Medical School to Examine the Definition of Brain Death, "A Definition of Irreversible Coma," *Journal of the American Medical Association* 205 (August 5, 1968): 337–340; Institute of Society, Ethics and the Life Sciences, Task Force on Death and Dying, "Refinements in Criteria for the Determination of Death," *Journal of the*

American Medical Association 221 (July 3, 1972): 48–53; P. Ramsey, "On Updating Procedures for Stating That a Man Has Died," in his *The Patient as Person* (New Haven, Conn: Yale University Press, 1970), pp. 59–112; D. M. High, "Death: Its Conceptual Elusiveness," *Soundings* 55 (Winter 1972): 438–458; R. M. Veatch, "The Whole-Brain-Oriented Concept of Death: An Outmoded Philosophical Formulation," *Journal of Thanatology* 3, no. 1 (1975): 13–30; and A. M. Capron and L. R. Kass, "A Statutory Definition of the Standards for Determining Human Death: An Appraisal and a Proposal," *University of Pennsylvania Law Review* 121 (November 1972): 87–118.

2. For a fuller analysis of the uses of the term *natural* with regard to death, see Robert M. Veatch's chapter "Natural Death and Public Policy," in his *Death, Dying and the Biological Revolution* (New Haven, Conn.: Yale University Press, 1976), pp. 286–289.

3. T. Parsons and V. M. Lidz, "Death in American Society," in *Essays in Self Destruction,* ed. E. S. Schneidman, (New York: Science House, 1967), pp. 133–170.

4. T. Parsons, R. C. Fox, and V. M. Lidz, "The 'Gift of Life' and Its Reciprocation," *Social Research* 39 (1972): 367–415.

5. P. Ramsey, "Shall We Reproduce?" *Journal of the American Medical Association* 220 (June 5, 1972): 1346–1350 and (June 12, 1972): 1480–1485; and L. R. Kass, "Making Babies: The New Biology and the 'Old' Morality," *Public Interest* 26 (Winter 1972): 18–56.

6. See D. Callahan's chapter, "Natural Death and Public Policy," in this volume.

7. J. Fletcher, "Ethical Aspects of Genetic Controls," *New England Journal of Medicine* 285 (September 30, 1971): 776–783; and J. Fletcher, *The Ethics of Genetic Control: Ending Reproductive Roulette* (New York: Doubleday, 1974).

8. R. Sinsheimer, "Troubled Dawn for Genetic Engineering," *New Scientist* 68 (October 16, 1975): 148–151.

9. J. Lederberg, "DNA Splicing: Will Fear Rob Us of Its Benefits?" *Prism* (November 1975): 33–37.

10. W. S. Ross, "The Best Medical Care for the Hopeless Patient," *Medical Opinion* (February 1972): 51–55.

11. P. Ramsey, "The Indignity of 'Death with Dignity,' " [*Death Inside Out,* ed. P. Steinfels and R. Veatch (New York: Harper & Row, 1975), pp. 81–96.] Cf. his "On (Only) Caring for the Dying," in Ramsey, *The Patient as Person,* pp. 113–164.

12. For a fuller exploration of these issues, see Robert M. Veatch's, "Natural Death and Public Policy," in this volume. The study leads to the conclusion that the acceptability of death and the right to refuse treatment are compatible with a commitment to constant struggle to conquer death.

13. For a fuller discussion see the chapter by L. McCullough entitled "Pain, Suffering, and Life-Extending Technologies" in this volume.

14. As cited in I. Illich, "The Political Uses of Natural Death," in *Death Inside Out,* pp. 25–42.

15. See I. Jakobovits, *Jewish Medical Ethics: A Comparative and Historical Study of the Jewish Religious Attitude to Medicine and Its Practice* (New York: Block, 1959); and F. Rosner, *Modern Medicine and Jewish Law* (New York: Yeshiva University Press, 1972).

16. See B. Haring, *Medical Ethics* (Notre Dame, Ind.: Fides, 1973); and C. J. McFadden, *Medical Ethics,* 6th ed. (Philadelphia: F. A. Davis, 1967).
17. Pope Pius XII, *The Pope Speaks* 4 (1957): 393–395.
18. Council on Wage and Price Stability, Executive Office of the President, *The Problem of Rising Health Costs* (Washington, D.C.: U.S. Government Printing Office, 1976).
19. V. R. Fuchs, *Who Shall Live? Health, Economics, and Social Choice* (New York: Basic Books, 1974). See especially Chapter 2, pp. 54–55. See also R. Dubos, who observed in *The Mirage of Health* (New York: Harper & Row; 1959) that "To ward off disease or recover health, men as a rule find it easier to depend on the healers than to attempt the more difficult task of living wisely," p. 110.
20. A. L. Caplan, "The 'Unnaturalness' of Aging and Its Implications for Medical Practice," *Man and Medicine,* forthcoming, 1979.
21. C. Boorse, "On the Distinction between Disease and Illness," *Philosophy and Public Affairs* 4, no. 4 (1975): 49–68; T. S. Szasz, *The Myth of Mental Illness* (New York: Harper & Row, 1961); A. Flew, *Crime or Disease?* (New York: Barnes & Noble, 1973).
22. D. Mechanic, "Health and Illness in Technological Societies," *Hastings Center Studies* 1, no. 3 (1973): 7–18.
23. P. Sedgwick, "Illness—Mental and Otherwise," *Hastings Center Studies* 1, no. 3 (1973): 19–40.
24. H. Fabrega, Jr., "Concepts of Disease: Logical Features and Social Implications," *Perspectives in Biology and Medicine* 15 (Summer 1972): 583–616.
25. I. Illich, *Medical Nemesis* (New York: Bantam, 1976).
26. H. J. Geiger, "Review of Medical Nemesis," *New York Times Book Review,* December 18, 1975.
27. For a full discussion, see H. T. Engelhardt's chapter "Is Aging a Disease?" in this volume.
28. T. Parsons, *The Social System* (Glencoe, Ill.: The Free Press, 1951), pp. 428–479.
29. A. L. Caplan, "The 'Unnaturalness' of Aging and Its Implications for Medical Practice," forthcoming. See also D. B. Hausman, "What is Natural?" *Perspectives in Biology and Medicine* 19 (Autumn 1975): 92–101; and R. M. Veatch, "The Medical Model: Its Nature and Problems," *Hastings Center Studies* 1 no. 3 (1973): 59–76.
30. Cf. F. Ayala and T. Dobzhansky, eds., *Studies in the Philosophy of Biology: Reduction and Related Problems* (Berkeley, Cal.: University of California Press, 1975).
31. K. F. Schaffner, "Approaches to Reduction," *Philosophy of Science* 34 (1967): 137–147.
32. Cf. R. Munson, ed., *Man and Nature* (New York: Dell, 1971).
33. A. Koestler and J. R. Smythies, eds., *Beyond Reductionism* (London: Hutchinson, 1969).
34. M. Grene and E. Mendelsohn, eds., *Topics in the Philosophy of Biology* (Boston: D. Reidel, 1976).
35. I. Jakobovits, *Jewish Medical Ethics: A Comparative and Historical Study of the Jewish Religious Attitude to Medicine and Its Practice.* (Rabbi Jakobovits cites this stricture as forming part of an agreement between Chief Rabbi Isaac

Herzog acting on behalf of the Chief Rabbinate of the Holy Land, and the Hadassa University Hospital of Jerusalem, concerning the sanctioning of postmortem examinations.)

36. See the national health insurance proposal sponsored chiefly by Representative Railsback (HR 2618), family health insurance plan provisions, taken from R. M. Veatch, "What Is a 'Just' Health Care Delivery?" in R. M. Veatch and R. Branson, eds., *Ethics and Health Policy* (Cambridge, Mass.: Ballinger Press, 1976), p. 144.

37. Taken from R. Veatch, "What Is a 'Just' Health Care Delivery?" p. 131.

38. See J. Bentham, *An Introduction to the Principles of Morals and Legislation,* ed. J. Lafleur (New York: Hafner Press, 1948); J. S. Mill, *Utilitarianism and Other Writings* (Cleveland: Meridian, 1962); G. E. Moore, *Principia Ethica* (Cambridge: Cambridge University Press, 1903); and H. Sidgwick, *The Methods of Ethics* (London: Macmillan, 1907).

39. See D. P. Rice, *Estimating the Cost of Illness* (Washington, D.C.: U.S. Public Health Service, 1966), for the most thorough development of this position. Rice's work contains the economic data on which to make such determinations. More recent data are in B. S. Cooper and D. P. Rice, "The Economic Cost of Illness Revisited," *Social Security Bulletin* (February 1976): 21–36.

40. See R. A. Bauer, ed., *Social Indicators* (Cambridge, Mass.: M.I.T. Press, 1966); Stanford Research Institute, *Minimum Standards for Quality of Life,* PB–244–808, prepared for the Washington Environmental Research Center (Springfield, Vir.: National Technical Information Service, 1975); and Statistical Policy Division, Office of Management and Budget, U.S. Department of Commerce, *Social Indicators 1973: Selected Statistics on Social Conditions and Trends in the United States* (Washington, D.C.: U.S. Government Printing Office, 1973).

41. J. Rawls, *A Theory of Justice* (Cambridge: Harvard University Press, 1971).

42. R. Nozick, *Anarchy, State and Utopia* (New York: Basic Books, 1974).

43. M. Golding, "Obligations to Future Generations," *The Monist* 56 (January 1972): 85–99.

44. D. Callahan, "What Obligations Do We Have to Future Generations?" *American Ecclesiastical Review* 164 (April 1971): 265–280.

45. For a more detailed background analysis of the debate on valuing lives, see R. M. Veatch's chapter, "Justice and Valuing Lives," in this volume.

46. See R. M. Bailey, "Economic and Social Costs of Death," in *The Dying Patient,* ed. O. G. Brim, Jr., et al. (New York: Russell Sage Foundation, 1970), pp. 275–302; E. B. Drew, "HEW Grapples with PPBS," *The Public Interest* (Summer 1967): 9–29; V. Held, "PPBS Comes to Washington," *The Public Interest* (Summer 1967): 102–115; W. Hoffer, "What Price Is Right for Human Life?" *Prism* (August 1974): 13ff.; H. E. Klarman, "Application of Cost-Benefit Analysis to Health Systems Technology," ed., M. F. Collen, in *Technology and Health Care Systems in the 1980s* (Washington, D.C.: United States Government Printing Office, 1973), pp. 225–250; D. R. Rice and B. S. Cooper, "The Economic Value of Human Life," *American Journal of Public Health* 57 (November 1967): 1954–1966; V. Taylor, "How Much Is Good Health Worth?" *Policy Sciences* 1 (1970): 49–72; and R. Zeckhauser, "Procedures for Valuing Lives," *Public Policy* 23 (Fall 1975): 419–464.

47. For a critical comparison see J. P. Acton, "Measuring the Monetary Value of Lifesaving Programs," *Law and Contemporary Problems* 40 (Autumn 1976): 46–72.
48. See D. P. Rice, *Estimating the Cost of Illness;* and B. S. Cooper and D. P. Rice, "The Economic Cost of Illness Revisited," *Social Security Bulletin* (February 1976): 21–36.
49. T. C. Schelling, "The Life You Save May Be Your Own," in *Problems in Public Expenditure Analysis*, ed. S. B. Chase, Jr. (Washington D.C.: The Brookings Institute, 1968), pp. 127–162.
50. See R. A. Bauer, ed., *Social Indicators;* Stanford Research Institute, *Minimum Standards for Quality of Life;* Statistical Policy Division, Office of Management and Budget, U.S. Department of Commerce, *Social Indicators 1973: Selected Statistics on Social Conditions and Trends in the United States.*
51. See G. Outka, "Social Justice and Equal Access to Health Care," *Journal of Religious Ethics* 2 (Spring 1974): 11–32; J. F. Childress, "Who Shall Live When Not All Can Live?" and F. B. Westervelt, "Reply," *Soundings* 53 (Winter 1970): 339–362; N. Rescher, "The Allocation of Exotic Medical Life-Saving Therapy," *Ethics* 79 (April 1969): 173–186; and R. M. Veatch, "What is a 'Just' Health Care Delivery?" pp. 127–153.
52. For a full discussion, see the chapter originally prepared for the Research Group by M. Breger entitled "Privacy, Suicide, Euthanasia, and Life-Extending Technologies" in this volume.
53. For a debate over this policy issue see R. M. Veatch and P. Steinfels, "Case Studies in Bioethics: Who Should Pay for Smokers' Health Care?" *Hastings Center Report* 4 (November 1974): 8–10.
54. See C. Fried, "Equality and Rights in Medical Care," *Hastings Center Report* 6 (February 1976): 29–34; L. Kass, "Regarding the End of Medicine and the Pursuit of Health," *The Public Interest* 40 (Summer 1975): 11–42; D. Mechanic, "Rationing Health Care: Public Policy and the Medical Marketplace," *Hastings Center Report* 6 (February 1976): 34–37; R. Morison, "Rights and Responsibilities: Redressing the Uneasy Balance," *Hastings Center Report* 4 (April 1974): 1–4; C. Fried, "Rights and Health Care—Beyond Equity and Efficiency," *New England Journal of Medicine* 293 (July 31, 1975): 241–245; R. Sade, "Medical Care as a Right: A Refutation," *New England Journal of Medicine* 285 (December 2, 1971): 1288–1292.
55. For a full discussion see M. Breger, "Privacy, Suicide, Euthanasia, and Life-Extending Technologies" in this volume.
56. This is clear even from Pope Pius XII's evocation of the concept, when he writes regarding a physician's duty to care for an ill patient: "Normally one is held to use only ordinary means—according to circumstances of persons, places, times and culture," when treating a patient. See Pope Pius XII, *The Pope Speaks* 4 (1957): 393–395.
57. D. Crane, *The Sanctity of Social Life: Physicians' Treatment of Critically Ill Patients* (New York: Russell Sage Foundation, 1975).

3

Guidelines for Research, Development, and Delivery of Life-Extending Technologies

THE HASTINGS CENTER RESEARCH GROUP

The Death and Dying Research Group of the Institute of Society, Ethics and the Life Sciences has explored the social and ethical questions of choosing among alternative life-extending technologies. Our objective has been to examine the ethical and other value foundations and policy options of such choices by governmental agencies, foundations funding health care research and development, and local institutions having to make priority decisions. The Research Group has examined whether some deaths are more natural or appropriate than others, what principles ought to govern the distribution of resources for research and development, and what other values are at stake in such choices.

This has not been an effort to direct the choices of individual patients and their families. Some individuals may find appropriate a technology not generally seen as appropriate by other members of society; others may choose to forego certain technologies generally seen as worthwhile. Our efforts have focused on the formation of a health policy—upon the criteria for decisions regarding the support of the research and development of life-extending technologies. We use the general term *life-extending technologies* to include two kinds of interventions: those that increase life expectancy by permitting more people to live a full, normal life span and those that extend that normal life span itself.

What follows is a set of principles we have found to be appropriate. They reflect the considered judgments of the Research Group members. Not every member necessarily accepts every statement in detail, but we share the general conclusions expressed here. Often claims about what ought to be done conflict with one another. We recognize this. It would be convenient if there were a single formula for reconciling such conflicts. We are convinced, however, that any such formula would inevitably be overly simplistic. It would lead to policy judgments in some circumstances that would be very implausible. These guidelines, however, present a list of criteria we find relevant in making choices among life-extending technologies.

1. The value of life is the positive warrant for the research, development, and delivery of technologies that extend life expectancy, but they should be subject to the constraints and discriminations developed in the guidelines that follow.
2. In general these discriminations and constraints reflect a variety of different and sometimes competing legitimate aspirations and goals. Any evaluations of life-extending technologies must take into account the competing claims from sectors other than health, and the impact of the alternative life-extending technologies on elements of welfare in those sectors.
3. Prevention of pain, suffering, and long periods of debilitation is as legitimate a public policy objective as the delaying of death. Therefore, evaluations of alternative life-extending technologies should include consideration of their impacts on pain, suffering, and debilitation, as well as life extension per se. Further, other things being equal, preventing deaths that are accompanied by pain, suffering, and debilitation deserves higher priority than preventing the same number of deaths at the same age that are not attended by suffering.
4. Funds for health research, development, and delivery should not be committed to life-extending technologies if such allocation would seriously impair efforts that help alle-

viate pain, suffering, and debilitation but have no impact on mortality. For example, treatment of arthritis reduces morbidity but does not reduce mortality.

5. Other things being equal, the forestalling of deaths that occur at a relatively young age deserves special priority. Technologies whose primary impact will be in allowing more people to live a relatively normal life span should receive priority over technologies whose primary impact will be in extending the normal life span.

6. At the present time there are many competing concepts of illness and disease in our society. Whether aging itself is regarded as a disease may depend on one's concept of disease, as well as on other conceptual and evaluative judgments about aging. These concepts will influence which life-extending technologies are emphasized. Successful development of life-extending technologies will in turn influence our concept of illness and disease. Serious attention should be given to technologies that are based on holistic and sociopsychological views of man as well as more biological views. Social structures and environmental technologies should be included in the development of means to pursue life extension.

7. It is unacceptable to decide among life-extending technologies solely on the basis of maximizing benefit/cost ratios, days of life added per dollar invested, or any other technique focusing only on total impact, whether the total costs and benefits are measured by projected lifetime earnings lost, willingness to pay, or any other way of calculating costs and benefits. One must also assess the distribution of the impact. This might argue, for example, for eliminating certain kinds of early deaths rather than a general increase in life expectancy.

8. Equity and fairness are important factors in choosing whether to develop and distribute life-extending technologies. When individuals who are least healthy and generally least well-off may benefit from research, development, and delivery of life-extending technologies, these efforts deserve priority even if they are not the most efficient use of resources measured in terms of average life expectancy or similar measures.

9. Some patterns of behavior increase risk of death. Educational programs should be undertaken to make clear the risks of such behavior. Efforts to delay deaths that are perceived as stemming from acts clearly beyond individual control deserve priority over risks of death perceived as resulting primarily from personal free choice to take such risks. At the same time, policy planners must be aware that many apparently voluntary risks are undertaken because individuals perceive no plausible option. Policies to extend life should include efforts to increase the opportunities of such individuals.

10. Freedom is a fundamental value. While some restrictions of freedom may be necessary, those technologies that are consistent with maintaining freedom should be given priority. Compulsory or highly coercive policies that promote lifestyle changes in order to extend life expectancy should be avoided. Compulsory changes in behavior, diet, smoking, exercise, and driving should be avoided when those behaviors affect only the individual who undertakes the risk.

11. Technologies should be avoided that would seriously increase the likelihood of continuing states of misery so that individuals would be provoked to suicide or to active mercy killing as the only plausible ways of ending an unbearable existence. When possible, the option of simply stopping treatment should be left open.

12. Technologies should be avoided that have a significant negative impact on social organizations such as the family, the school, the work place, the health care system, and voluntary communities.

4

Life Extension and Cultural Values: Family, Work, Leisure, Value Patterns, Old Age

RICHARD A. KALISH

The effects of life-span extension on social, psychological, and cultural values are immense. For those who enjoy life, there is more time for enjoyment; for those who are bored, depressed, or resentful, there is more time for anticipation of those states. More books can be read; more concerts attended; more languages learned; more brook trout caught; more broken legs suffered; more friends killed in accidents; more old, comfortable, and traditional values and ways of living threatened by new ones.

These comments suggest the effects of life-span extension on the individual, but what about the impact on societies and cultures? What happens to the family when it routinely spans five generations? What happens to education when knowledge changes more rapidly and each life encompasses several generations of knowledge? What happens to careers when nearly half a person's life expectancy occurs after today's retirement age? What happens to the meaning of death when its timing becomes more predictable? Or, perhaps, less predictable?

ON GENERALIZING

Social, psychological, and cultural values can be described across large societies, such as that of the Western world or that of the United States and Canada. Within these broad groups, however, are innumerable subcultures that partake of the dominant values but integrate them with their own value systems. These subcultures may be regional (southeastern United States, New England), ethnic/racial (Black American, Asian American, French Canadian), religious (Jewish, Roman Catholic, Pentecostal), vocational (physicians, police, coal miners), and so forth.

In contemplating the effects of life-extending technologies on cultural and social institutions and on psychological functioning, it is essential to keep in mind the role of the many subcultures. Great care must be taken to avoid the familiar pitfall of overgeneralizing from one subculture to another or of exaggerating the differences. Finally, within each subculture there are vast individual differences, although usually less radical than the departures from the culture as a whole.

This chapter focuses on modal psychological, social, and cultural values and resulting behavior; it does not offer frequent reminders of subcultural or individual differences. I discuss values in the context of mainstream United States and Canada, to a lesser extent of Western society, and to a still lesser extent of other communities around the world that resemble the United States and Canada in salient ways. However, it is essential that the discussion of modal values not obscure the real and important subcultural and individual differences that exist and that must be considered carefully in policy and programming decisions.

I have selected a handful of major social institutions to serve as a base for examining the effects on values of life-span extension. The topics have been grouped into three sections: (1) the self, personality, and the meaning of death; (2) the family; and (3) work, education, leisure, and retirement.

THE SELF, PERSONALITY, AND THE MEANING OF DEATH

One's own death, as well as the deaths of others, is not an abstract or vague concept, subject only to some form of mystical denial and of interest only to caring family members or health professionals. Regardless of denial, love, care, or even beliefs about immortality, death is a boundary of this life, and as such it receives and deserves recognition.

At the present, this boundary is perceived in our society as occurring some time between the mid-sixties and mid-seventies. It is almost as though a person born in America, particularly middle-class America, receives with his birth certificate a birthright to live to be at least sixty-five or seventy years. If he finds out that he will die sooner, he feels cheated; if he lives an additional decade or more, he often expresses the feeling that he has lived his life and can die at any time. Thus, we find that the elderly, when asked directly, indicate that they fear death less than either the young or the middle-aged,[1] not because they wish to die but because the losses they suffer in dying (for example, roles, futurity, vitality) do not appear as severe.

CURVE-SQUARING AND THE MEANING OF DEATH

With curve-squaring, the outer boundary of life remains much the same, but the probability of continuing to that boundary increases. To some extent it redefines what it means to be old. Life-span extension, on the other hand, moves the boundary a few, many, or even an infinite number of years into the future; it would most probably extend the period called "old age," but if the original shape of the life-span curve remains intact, with only the range and standard deviation becoming greater, the overall impact on what it means to be old would be less certain and less direct.

Two or three centuries ago, deaths occurred with considerable frequency all across the age spectrum although they were most common during infancy, early childhood, childbearing years for women, and old age. Today, any person who lives through the first two weeks of life—and almost all do—has an extremely good chance of living into his or her seventies. Although deaths from accidents, suicides, homicides, and war still occur with disproportionate frequency among younger people, these are normally not sufficiently numerous to have much impact on overall life expectancies.

We already associate death with old age, since that is the time during which most deaths occur. I believe that our "birthright" for longevity is about seventy years; about half the population lives beyond that age. When curve-squaring technologies cause life expectancy to be about ninety years, the "birthright" will slowly shift to that age. However, relatively few people will live much beyond the age of 90 and, if they do, their future life expectancy would be brief.

A 75-year-old woman today has a life expectancy of eleven years.[2] With curve-squaring, a comparably aged woman would be, perhaps, ninety-five years old, but with a probable life expectancy of two or three years, maybe less. Two issues need to be addressed: First, in what ways does this affect the way people in general value old people and their own aging process? Second, how does this affect the older person him- or herself?

There is speculation that older people are avoided because they are associated with death and dying. For the elderly, death is very salient because it is so much more imminent than it was in their younger days, and those who relate closely to them are often aware of this. Today death is largely the province of the elderly; if it became almost completely theirs, avoidance of the elderly might become more marked. This depends, of course, on how changing values regarding the meaning of death affect any individual. If death and dying become less anxiety-producing, avoidance of the elderly will diminish.

An alternative possibility is that the increased predictability of the time of death would reduce the anxieties of persons who interact with the elderly, because the potential for unpredicted loss or for slow and agonizing death would decrease. Neither anticipation of the death nor the duration of the dying process would be as anxiety-arousing.

Ernest Becker contends that anticipation of vulnerability, decay, and death forms a major—very likely *the* major—motivating force in social and individual behavior.[3] Alignment with the heroic or the transcendent can only reduce and not eliminate anxiety and tension concerning these pressures. Therefore, the obvious association of the elderly with vulnerability, decay, and death, assuming Becker to be correct, would increase their roles as taboo persons. The relative certainty of death at a particular age would lead either to strong repulsion toward people of or near that age or to oversolicitude, which might be almost as bad.

Conversely, curve-squaring would reduce the duration of any such feelings. Since the duration of the decaying process would constitute a relatively smaller portion of the life span, the individual would be taboo for a briefer period.

Whatever occurs, the value of the elderly is not likely to remain the same as today. One possibility is that society will place a higher value on them before their relatively brief period of terminal decline and a lower value on them after that. There may actually be substantial demarcation between those who are old and those who are old and dying, with the former more rewarded in many ways and the latter, less so. I would also speculate that the reduced value of the dying older person will be compensated for by increased financial support for care during this period.

Now to look at the effects on the older person himself. Two alternate and conflicting possibilities come to mind. First, the older person might find himself increasingly anxious as the time of his highly predictable death approaches. In effect, he would have the same perceptions that the nonelderly would develop of the elderly; that is, fear and dread would build, so that with increasing age, he would resent his own aging process more and feel more tension in his daily living.

Second, death for the old person would be so inevitable, predictable, and expected, that he or she would have rehearsed the death before the time came to die. It is possible that he would have worked through many of his anxieties. Also, he will not feel cheated, since he will have had roughly the same length of life as everyone else. Since the evidence is considerable that the elderly fear death less than younger persons it is logical that additional years of life would add to the probability of further fear reduction.

At the same time, there would be margin for error in life expectancy, since accidents, suicides, and homicides will still occur, as will the possibility of a "premature" death or an unexpectedly long life, even though these two occurrences will be less frequent and will lead to less variability than is seen today. It is difficult to speculate upon the outcome of the curves becoming totally rectangular, but at this juncture that seems infinitely far in the future.

Curve-squaring would have a number of other effects on the individual. First, it would increase predictability so that life insurance, health insurance, and retirement annuity programs would probably become less necessary, since the risk of death and serious illness would be modified and no longer require the "spreading the risk around" approach that insurance is based on.

Second, deaths of the elderly, in part because they are already moderately predictable, have less apparent impact on survivors than deaths at other ages. The death of an older person is perceived as less tragic than the death of someone younger.[4] As deaths become more predictable, survivors-to-be will have ample time to pass through anticipatory bereavement, so that the eventual death will be effectively mourned before its occurrence. At the same time, with curve-squaring, the death of a young person might have greater impact and destructive qualities for the survivors, because it would be unanticipated and unfamiliar. Indeed, such deaths would occur almost completely as a function of accidents, suicides, homicides, and war, along with some residual incurable illness, so that most nonelderly deaths would be sudden and unexpected.

Third, as people grow older, they tend to move from *active mastery* to *magical mastery* in order to function in their human and physical environments.[5] That is, they are less able to function in their environments through physical strength or production of goods and services, and come to rely more on religion, mysticism, and eventually memories, identification with stronger people, and denial. This change seems to occur regardless of cultural background. With death more predictable, there will be little need to speculate why one person was "taken" and another person was "left," since—with few exceptions—both will be left until both are taken. Divine power, to the extent that it remains pervasive in Western thought, will no longer be perceived as "taking people before their time"—but this does not mean that denial of one's own death will cease to occur. It is possible, then, that as people approach their anticipated deaths, they will make greater use of magical mastery to defend themselves against it, through religious rituals and ceremonies, intellectualization, denial, or attempts to develop close human relationships as a buffer against the isolation they fear.

Fourth, since people appear never to tire of expecting more and more of the biomedical sciences, I would assume that there would be greater pressure not only to complete the squaring of the curve, but also to extend outward the age at which the squaring occurs. That is, success at curve-squaring as well as success at life-span extension will only whet appetites for more of both.

LIFE-SPAN EXTENSION AND THE MEANING OF DEATH

If the curve of potential life expectancy retains its present shape but extends for 150 years rather than its present 100 or so, a different set of dynamics develops. First, the time of death would remain unpredictable, with the death rate mounting slowly over the years, albeit accelerating during the later years (ages 110 to 140 instead of the present 75 to 95). People would gear their expectation to an average life expectancy of 125, so that death at 100 years would elicit the same frustration and unhappiness that now arises over death at 45 or 50.

Life-span extension approximately doubling today's expectancies would undoubtedly have much greater impact on both societies and individuals than would curve-squaring. Consider some of the effects of having an electorate, 30 to 50 percent of whom have personal memories of life a century earlier. These individuals might well slow down social change because they would adhere to the values they had been socialized to many decades earlier. Social and cultural changes often develop when younger generations are socialized to newer values, then carry these values with them as they mature into middle-aged adults commanding positions of power and policy formation. If, however, life-span extension means that people maintain power positions not just for ten to twenty years, but for as many as forty to seventy years, new ideas will have been replaced by newer ones well before their advocates are in a position to put them into practice.

On the one hand, the large numbers of very long-lived persons retaining the vote and other forms of power would be a conservative force, slowing down the movement of social change. On the other hand, the life experiences of any given individual would include value demands so varied that they could become distressing. A 40-year-old friend of mine said that she would not wish to live 150 years because life that far in the future would be so dissonant with what she grew up with and was accustomed to that she would not approve the changes. She felt her children were in a much better position to adapt to the future because they did not share her memories and because their socialization was more in keeping with present and future life-styles and social values. She spoke particularly of the demands of the poor that world resources be more evenly shared; she was simultaneously aware of the present immoral inequality and reluctant to give up her large home, comfortable car, and access to energy resources. She projects considerable change thirty to forty years from now, when she may well be alive, but feels that the changes seventy or ninety years from now will require more adjustment than she is willing to make.

Whether my friend's concerns will actually become a problem is not known. Perhaps the changes will occur slowly enough for her to become accustomed to them, retaining some nostalgia and regrets, but little pain. Individual differences in this matter will obviously be immense; some changes will be fully compatible with the internalized values of a given person, while others will violate that person's standards. The sudden imposition of new standards, such as occurred in Russia after the Revolution, was extremely disturbing to many people (although very satisfying to others); however, changes that occur over 100 years rather than 100 days would have much less impact. This issue could be examined by interviewing 80-year-olds and 60-year-olds to determine the relative effects of experienced social change and anticipated future changes.

Another effect of doubling the life-span expectancy would be to change the definition of old age. With the hypothesized changes, it is unlikely that anyone 60 or 65 or 70 would be considered chronologically old although it is also likely that the definition of old age would encompass many more years than it does today.

Similarly, given a high probability of living to be 125, the anticipation of death by a 70-year-old would not differ too much from the anticipation of a 30-year-old today. This would be especially true if the death rate did not begin to accelerate meaningfully until 90 years of age or so. The population would become neither more nor less death-conscious, but the number of years during which death seemed far away would be greatly increased, as would the number of years a person perceived himself as elderly, perhaps even "dying."

With life-span extension, however, some individuals will accumulate deficits on the basis of being alive, and therefore susceptible, for a longer period of time.[6] Consider, for example, all the ways in which an individual might lose his vision. Some are related to the illnesses of old age, such as stroke and glaucoma, and would probably occur at a much later chronological age than at present. Other causes, however, occur randomly across the age spectrum, for example, accidents and infections. If a given proportion of people suffer serious visual decrements for one of these reasons by the time they are 60, we can readily hypothesize that at least twice that proportion will have lost their vision for these reasons by the age of 110.

It is possible, but more debatable, that psychological deficits may also accumulate.[7] Unless society changes in other ways, a 110-

year-old man or woman will have had more failures (and successes), more stresses (and rewards), more feelings of inadequacy (and of adequacy), and more crises (and more crises successfully survived). This assumes, of course, that people remain at their prime for a longer time. If they do not, the ratio of positive to negative will be a function of the ratio of prime years to decremental years.

A major fact that must be known before predictions can become meaningful is the rate at which age-related decrements occur with life-span extension. Assuming that life span is doubled, there are several possible decrement curves. The preferred one is that all decrements are postponed until the later segment of the life span; the least preferred is that decrements continue to occur at about the same age they now do, but that life be maintained in spite of the decrements. The most probable is that the decrements will begin at about twice the age they now occur, which means that the curve retains its shape, but that a given individual will have to put up with any decrement for roughly twice as long as at present. Therefore, a person who today loses her hearing at age 63 and dies at 71, would, in this brave new world, lose her hearing at age 126 and die at age 142, meaning sixteen additional years of hearing loss and its concomitant stresses.

Society may not, of course, take kindly to a drawn-out process of diminishing capacities and the need for care. I can see the possibility of increasing irritability and even anger directed against older people as a result of society's lengthy involvement, both financial and psychological, with their dying. Social values that in the past decade have seemed to enhance the value of the elderly may well change to an increasing deprecation of people who utilize society's resources without adequately reimbursing that society.

THE INFLUENCE OF SPECIFIC TECHNOLOGIES

The specific mechanism that promotes either curve-squaring or life-span extension seems much less important than such factors as how long life is extended, the accessibility of treatment and its possible side effects, the likelihood of an extended period of confusion and what we term "senility," and so forth.

If life is extended through the elimination of specific diseases, such as heart attacks, stroke, or cancer, we eliminate a potential source of considerable pain and discomfort, but what would replace these diseases as causes of the end of life? Disintegration of bones? Paralysis that causes death by choking? Deterioration of thought processes so that eventually the the organism processes input at a primitive level, perhaps at that of a three-month-old infant? In the past, as medical scientists eliminated causes of death, they ignored the obvious fact that something was still going to cause it. Without depreciating their contributions, we should begin now to develop some sense of what death will be like when present causes are substantially reduced and—at least as important—learn how people feel about these new forms of death.

The use of artificial prostheses presents a different set of concerns. Machine-dependent survival is no longer rare, but at present people who depend.on machines also depend on the technicians who keep the machines in good running order; we have only begun to probe how they feel about what we might term their "person-machine" relationships. What little is known suggests that, like all intense relationships, these are as likely to involve love-hate as the stormiest of happy marriages.[8]

The impact of tissue regeneration, another potential path to prolongation of life, depends on the nature of the treatment, the dependency on its provider, and the nature and timing of eventual death. Similarly, perceptions of environmental interventions are a function of their psychological, social, and financial cost. That people presently smoke, eat excessively, take in too much alcohol, and live in smog-saturated urban areas where they commute twice a day in forty minutes of tension suggests that environmental interventions will be accepted only if the toll they exact is minimal.

Of the four technologies described, two (specific disease interventions and environmental interventions) are most probably going to result in curve-squaring; the other two (artificial prostheses and tissue regeneration) permit the hope, at least, that additional prostheses and further regeneration can be provided that will extend the life span beyond what is presently considered the outer limit.

The acceptability of the various technologies differs as a function not only of their adequacy in terms of accomplishments, but also of the individual value systems of recipients. One gerontologist remarked that "we will soon all live 300 years, 50 years of virility and 250 years of senility." Even allowing for hyperbole, this kind of life might be acceptable to some (note Aldous Huxley's *After Many a Summer Dies the Swan*), but totally out of the question for others. Thus policy questions concerning which technologies to pursue must be integrated with some recognition of their results, e.g., number of additional healthy years, financial cost, side effects, dependency on treatment providers, frequency and duration of individual treatments, and the quality of the extended life that will be experienced.

As a brief aside, it has not often been noted that the diminishing birthrate coupled with an increased life span, whether extended or squared, will produce a constituency of the old and the very old, large proportions of whom will be living as a result of intervention. These individuals, by virtue of their numbers, will wield considerable power in the political process, especially in democracies but also in nations with other forms of government. The possibility is great that they will demand that their leaders respond to their needs even at the expense of others' needs (school children's, younger welfare recipients'). Thus, both the quality of their lives and hopes for additional years will undoubtedly become pervasive and volatile political issues.

THE FAMILY

The debate about the family rages in the popular media, at cocktail parties, and in the living rooms of liberals and conservatives alike. Is the family doomed? When life prolongation as we have been describing it becomes a reality, the debate topic is likely to shift slightly: Whither the family *now*? Once again, the answers are a function of whether the mediating influence is curve-squaring technologies or life-span extension technologies.

We approach this section of the chapter topically, rather than in terms of curve-squaring and life-span extension as in the previous section. The major topics to be considered are intergenerational relations; inheritance; marriage, and divorce, and remarriage; women; and homes and hospitals.

INTERGENERATIONAL RELATIONS

With curve-squaring technologies, four- and five-generation families will become the norm rather than the exception. Assuming that the parental age at which the first and last children are born does not alter meaningfully, virtually all children will have four living grandparents; and it will not be unusual for a young child to have eight, ten, or more living great-great-grandparents.

It is not difficult to see what this might mean. Even assuming zero population growth (ZPG), one living great-great-grandparent will have two children, two children-in-law, four grandchildren, four grandchildren-in-law, eight great-grandchildren, eight great-grandchildren-in-law, and sixteen great-great-grandchildren, whom we will presently assume are too young to be married. Thus, in a ZPG family, there will be forty-four direct descendents and descendent spouses. The young child who has not suffered any loss of progenitors for five generations will have thirty older persons to whom to relate. And these figures are fairly conservative—they do not take into account second marriages, cousins, other relatives, or more than two live births. (The centenarian whose descendents average three rather than two children will have 159 direct descendents!).

There are families that approximate these numbers today, but their reunions make the family section of their local newspapers. It is unlikely that close relationships among these numbers of people would occur frequently, especially as the family members of the great-great-grandparent looking down the age span, and of the great-great-grandchild looking up, have only modest overlap.

But it is not only the numbers that bring into question the possibility of a sense of family encompassing these related persons. My own observations and those of people with whom I have talked suggest that warm personal contact rarely goes beyond three generations: The great-grandmother really does not know her great-grandchild and, indeed, may not be especially eager to know him. Of course, if her health is good and if she remains vigorous, they may not drift apart. In any event, we cannot assume that four generations will relate closely.

However, life prolongation through life-span extension rather than curve-squaring raises a different set of possibilities. Now we have eight, ten, and even twelve generations in direct line of descent. There appears to be no way in which the 140-year-old elder will have contact with a 14-year-old descendent; as even allowing for more early deaths than through curve-squaring, there may well be several hundred such descendants. Indeed, to avoid incest—since age will obviously play a much different role in marriages—we will need to establish a kind of premarital verification of nonrelatedness, or at least reconsider the taboo aspect of incest.

Some people might contend that increased family size will enhance the value of the family within the society, but my own intuition is just the opposite. The extended family will become so cumbersome, not only in numbers but also in its inability to communicate or even know each other, that only the present nuclear family will survive as a unit. Different generations may interconnect in the sense that young people today seek their origins, but they will not do so in an intimate interpersonal sense, except—as today—in a very modest number of instances.

INHERITANCE

A special instance of intergenerational relations is that of inheritance. In times past, property went from parents to children—sometimes to all children, sometimes only to males (in a few societies, only to females), and sometimes primarily to the oldest son. More recently, property has begun to go from grandparents to grandchildren, for college funds, a trip to Europe, or just to keep memories burning.

With curve-squaring, the deaths of the elderly will occur at about the time that the next generation is moving into retirement (I assume some postponement of retirement age), and the legacies may be welcome to supplement the reduced income. I personally believe, however, that bequests that skip a generation will increase in proportion, so the middle-aged will receive the money, although their parents may receive art pieces and similar property. Since the psychological connectedness between generations 1 and 4 is too remote for warm feelings, it is unlikely that property will be left to great-grandchildren, except under unusual circumstances.

Already the potential legacy of the elderly provides little control over younger family members. Longer life would increase this tendency since children would be elderly themselves before receiving parental largesse. However, some economic differences will result, since the elderly use money differently from their middle-aged grandchildren. If the age of retirement is postponed, financial assets might be used as capital as much as possible, to generate additional income. When money is eventually willed to the middle-aged, it will probably be spent, but since more older people will live to be older still, there may be more money tied up in investments and less money circulating. This is highly speculative, however, both economically and psychologically.

Curve-squaring technological success will also bring other changes. Life insurance will probably become much less popular since by the time of death, younger dependents will have become established; and with increasing numbers of women in the labor force, insurance will seldom be needed for future spousal support. Costs of life insurance should drop, since fewer people will die, and those who so desire can maintain high coverage in term insurance. On the other hand, annuities or anything with a guaranteed payback will be more expensive because more people will collect over a longer period of time. Given this prediction, the life insurance industry may need to change its marketing strategies, and develop new forms of policies.

Life-span extension will create other concerns. Since it is likely that 110-year-old children will die before their 135-year-old parents with greater frequency than our present life charts indicate, life insurance will be more erratic. Indeed, people will probably drop it as soon as children are independent. Annuities, on the other hand, will be riskier for both the customer and the insurance company if the curve of decline remains unchanged. If the decline is postponed until the very end of the life span, risks are diminished, but the probability of a long payoff period may endanger the insurance company. This is especially true if prolongation technologies change life within a relatively brief period of time, so that insurance companies will have many previously arranged annuities that would pay back far longer than initially anticipated.

All in all, I suggest that both legacies and life insurance will diminish in importance to the recipients, while annuities may become less profitable to the companies. I have, however, seen no sign that the insurance industry is looking seriously at this issue. Conversely, I see no need for the family to look seriously at it; they can make changes at appropriate times, and it is difficult to know now whether annuities would be a good investment because of the possibility of a longer payoff period, or a poor investment because many companies will go bankrupt. Most probably, the government will have to cover insurance company losses, since the public outcry would be immense if these predictions came to pass.

Further, since the elderly tend to be valued, in part, in terms of their power over wealth, jobs, succession, and so forth, the changing circumstances of inheritance may or may not enhance that value. If the wealth distributed by the older person at the time of death is appreciable in relationship to the earnings of the survivors, the elderly may be more highly valued; if this wealth remains—as today—a nominal amount in most instances, the elderly will probably not be valued more than at present. Also, valuing the elderly is a function of the generation of the survivors: If the wealth is primarily distributed to the middle-aged grandchildren, the elderly children may lack respect for the aged, but the middle-aged will be highly supportive.

The overall impact of inheritance on the general valuing of the family unit is almost impossible to evaluate, but anything that increases income transfer from the older generation to a younger and leaves the nature and conditions of the transfer to the older person, is likely to tighten family unity and heighten the value placed on family.

MARRIAGE, DIVORCE, AND REMARRIAGE

The bases for marriage have shifted from familial to personal, from society-based to individual-based, and from sacred to secular. In increasing numbers people state that they marry or enter into comparable relationships for their own personal growth rather than to satisfy parents, to gain immortality through progeny, or to be accepted by age peers.[9] Assuming this trend continues, divorce rates are likely to remain high. If the purpose of marriage is growth and happiness, it logically follows that feelings of stultification and unhappiness will lead to unmarriage. And that is what happens.

With any form of life prolongation, divorce rates will probably increase further. First, the binding force of children, already diminishing as the birthrate diminishes, will continue to lose power. On a straight chance statistical basis, the simple fact that there will be more years of life after children are grown increases the divorce probabilities for any given couple. As more women take jobs and have the potential for financial independence, their willingness to leave an inadequate relationship will increase.

Second, a physically healthy person will probably be more willing to seek divorce than an unhealthy person; similarly, it may be more difficult emotionally to divorce an unhealthy person than a healthy person. Therefore, with ill health postponed by a decade or many decades, divorce becomes more possible.

Third, a 65-year-old woman has a future life expectancy of 17½ years today; a 65-year-old man can anticipate about four fewer years.[10] If they have made a moderate commitment to each other and are not truly unhappy in the relationship, inertia and the predictable nature of their present status are likely to keep them together. The same two people, however, anticipating thirty or more years of future life, might feel differently about an unfulfilling relationship.

Fourth, living longer also means living through more changes in fads, fashions, trends, and social values. However, there is no reason to expect both members of a couple to experience these changes in the same way. In the 1970s many women changed their perceptions of appropriate sex roles, while their husbands adhered to more the traditional ones; one result was a sharp rise in divorce rates. The more years a couple live through together, the greater the chances that changing values will pull them apart. With life-span extension allowing 140 years of anticipated life, there will be about one divorce per person per lifetime; curve-squaring technologies might have less impact—it would depend on the age at which the right-hand boundary of the rectangle began to take shape.

Fifth, whatever technology is applied will presumably also extend the period of sexual activity relative to the extension of life expectancy. "It will be commonplace for 60- and even 70-year-old men and women to be sexually attractive and attracted, and sexually capable. If the spouse with whom one has lived for 25 years is no longer seen as attractive, the motivation to leave will be accentuated by greater sexual appetites and a longer potential time period for pay-off."[11]

With a rise in divorces will come a comparable rise in remarriages, although these marriages will probably not adhere to the traditional age differences between spouses. Especially if the mechanism for life prolongation is a life-span extension, couples who differ widely in age will be marrying, as will couples in which the woman is older. Although both a 100-year-old man and a 60-year-old woman (or reverse the ages if you prefer) will still be in their prime, however, the forty years separating them means that their life experiences probably differed considerably due to the technology and social value systems that existed when each was 30, 40, or 50. Although attractions between persons of widely disparate age will become more common, the success of crossgenerational marriages is very difficult to predict.

The effect of all this on the institution of marriage is uncertain. I would say that marriage as a lifelong commitment will diminish as a societal value, but that marriage as a long-term commitment will remain the same or even enhanced. To continue to emphasize marriage as a lifelong commitment would appear to doom the institution altogether. Since we have not recently been successful in maintaining marriages of thirty and forty years, it seems counterproductive to try to sustain marriages of eighty and one hundred years within today's social context. At the same time, the transient marriage of four or five years would probably also lose value. Among divorced and widowed people today, a great deal is heard about the tedium of short-term relationships—the anticipation of forty years of four-year relationships would be highly distressing. Therefore, it seems possible that the thirty or forty-year marriage, which was the expectation in our society before the high-divorce-rate era, would become more valued. Perhaps a greater emphasis on the lifelong commitment would evolve, since the pain of breaking up a thirty-year relationship is great. This topic remains highly speculative.

WOMEN IN PARTICULAR

Life-span extension in particular and curve-squaring technologies in general may have an additional effect that is seldom mentioned. If life expectancy reaches 140 years, or even if almost everyone is assured of eighty-five or ninety healthy years, people may feel that they have enough time for both families and careers. (We discuss education and work in the next section.) Many women today, and some men as well, have opted against having children because the youngsters would interfere with their careers. Although any life-span-extending technology is likely to extend the years of fertility, the present combination of birth control methods and abortions would probably counteract any potential population increase.

Knowing that their work life might last 50 or even 110 years, however, some women may decide there is ample time for both a career and motherhood. These roles might occur one after the other, or they might be simultaneous or even alternating. If they occurred at a time when childbearing was highly valued, as during the 1950s, there could be an immense population explosion; if they occurred at a time when this was not so—like today—the population increase would be moderate or minimal.

A related concern is that today a woman who enters the labor force at a somewhat older age is at a disadvantage; the disadvantage may follow her throughout her career. With an extended life expectancy, the loss of a few early years in childbearing and childrearing may not cut heavily into careers. Although a late start may still permanently handicap a woman's achievement and status potential, a case could be made that the longer the time available for work, the greater the possibility of compensating through diligence or ability.

An alternative pattern would be to work until the early thirties, take fifteen or twenty years off to raise children, then return to work in the early fifties, and still have a future work life potential of seventy-five to ninety years. Obviously, the contemporary pattern of taking only enough time off to have the child and provide initial care is also likely to continue for some women.

So far the assumption seems to be that only women should consider taking hours or years off for childrearing, but it is entirely possible, even probable, that extended life will allow men to take several years off without concern about career sacrifices. Given the present egalitarian trend in man-woman relationships, the expectation of ample years for career and family might expedite the present incipient process of the man being the primary caretaker of the children. (All this presupposes that, although the decremental aspects of aging are slowed down, the social and physical maturity necessary to function as an adult will occur at the same rate as today.)

A number of factors have recently lowered the value of both childbearing and childrearing. These include population pressures, the changing role of women in relation to men, broadened work opportunities for women, their increased desire for careers, and the costs of housing and family living. Possibly when life-extension is added, the long time allocated to work will be less appealing, and both motherhood and fatherhood will be more highly valued, not just as status or family continuity, but as a legitimate respite from the tedium of pursuing work and careers.

One unknown is whether curve-squaring will raise the life expectancy of men to equal that of women, or whether women "naturally" live longer. If the former, then widowhood would be sharply reduced, except to the extent that women marry older men; widowhood might increase slightly, but for brief durations for the very old. On the other hand, life-span extension would most probably increase the duration of widowhood since, as societies become healthier and live longer, the life expectancies of women increase proportionately more than those of men. It is debatable whether women are blessed, cursed, or left neutral in their capacity to outlive men, but to the extent that widowhood is distressing, life-span extension would probably lead to more distressed widows for longer periods of time.

HOMES AND HOSPITALS

B. L. Neugarten has pointed out that "there has been a dramatic trend toward separate households for older persons,"[12] although she does not predict whether the trend will continue. Regardless of which form of life-prolonging technology develops, the elderly are increasingly likely to have elderly children still living. With curve-squaring these children will probably be in good health, while with life-extension, they will be in roughly the same state of health as 60-year-old children of 85-year-old parents today.

With life-span extension, the probable period of widowhood will be even longer than at present; there will be more years of living alone and having no one to care for or be cared for by. Although homes will probably remain in the family for longer periods of time, many elderly will be unable to maintain independent households, especially in homes they shared with the now-deceased spouse.

The location of these homes is a matter of concern. Middle-aged people today live primarily in the suburbs, often in tracts, where they settled when they were younger. If they sold their first home, they frequently bought another in the same or a more expensive community or tract. Today they are growing old in those suburbs, which often lack transportation, shopping, access to physicians, recreation areas, and other attributes appropriate for the elderly.[18] Since the life-extending technologies being discussed are likely to be developed while today's suburbanites live in their present communities, these individuals will be affected. Life prolongation will probably serve to keep the present owners in their homes, coping with mounting taxes and aging buildings.

Institutions for the elderly will also undergo change. With curve-squaring the implication is that health and presumably cognitive capacities will be maintained until close to the end of life (although this assumption is not necessarily valid). This situation would reduce protracted confusion and disorientation, the maintenance of stroke and cancer patients for indefinite periods, and the duration of frailty and rapid fatigue. In effect, the present nursing homes and board-and-care homes would be less necessary.

Life-span extension will have the opposite impact. Assuming the same curve of decrement, there would be more years of confusion and disorientation, longer periods during which terminal stroke and cancer patients would be kept alive, and more frail and readily fatigued elderly. Also, since the death of a spouse will likely produce a longer period of widowhood, even the psychological factors of isolation and loneliness might encourage longer institutionalization.

Some recent health care innovations will probably reduce these problems to some degree. The hospice movement, growing rapidly in Europe and just beginning to be known in the United States, provides effective in-patient care and vastly improved out-patient care for the terminally ill. Also, increasing pressures for home health aides, visiting nurses, and other home-related services may well improve community medicine, while reducing the need for hospital medicine.

These changes will enable ill people to remain in their homes longer than at present. The thrust of both hospice and home care is to encourage out-patient care and family involvement. Regardless of improved care, however, life-span extension will mean that more people will require institutionalization for longer time periods, with a concomitant rise in health care costs. Curve-squaring will reduce the length of such institutional care, although it might not reduce and could increase the number of recipients. Obviously, the former would lower the value of the older person and the latter would leave the value at approximately its present level.

BACK TO SQUARE ONE

We began by discussing the nature of the family and whether life-prolonging technologies would further disrupt the family system. My personal reaction is that it would both help and harm families, and on balance would have little or no destructive effect on the institution of the family. Technically speaking, family units would become larger, but psychologically family identification would probably be restricted to three generations. Although divorces would become much more common, so would remarriages. The individual family is more likely to undergo change in its constituent parts than it has recently, but a century ago families were broken by early death more frequently than they are by divorce today, and the institution survived. Families may come to be seen as more fluid than they are today.

It is not necessary to await the arrival of treatment Z, which extends life, in order to investigate the effects of multigenerational families. There are enough four-generation and five-generation families today to gain some initial insights; these avenues have not, to my knowledge, been pursued.

WORK

This and the following three topics (education, leisure, and retirement) are interrelated, but they also stand as separate issues. I will discuss them singly, always keeping in mind that their interconnectedness makes such divisions artificial. In presenting the following comments, I will begin with several premises: (1) that retirement age will become less arbitrary and more flexible, (2) that some form of guaranteed annual income will replace the present social security system (perhaps supplemented by flexible and portable annuities), and (3) that the age at which job discrimination becomes a factor will rise.

The issues that life prolongation presents to values and practices concerning work resemble those of many other facets of the social milieu. These include the potential for extending flexibility, the problems of obsolescence of knowledge, the long wait for job openings and promotions, second and third careers, and boredom and overfamiliarity.

A familiar complaint about the elderly is that they become conservative, cautious, and rigid. Although such claims are frequently exaggerated, there is a kernel of truth in the stereotype. To some extent, caution is created by life circumstances, which incline the older person to guard what he has accumulated rather than risk it. And to some extent, it is the result of having been socialized to job-related values and practices at an earlier time in the history of the organization and the organizational system, so that it is difficult to keep up with rapid changes.

With curve-squaring technologies, there is every reason to believe that the older worker's flexibility would be extended to the same degree as his work life. If 65 is still ten years away from probable retirement, the worker will likely be as flexible at 65 in this future as at 55 today. This presupposes that employing organizations will introduce continuing education programs to update their employees on changes in values, practices, and technologies, as well as in more general knowledge. Each educational program will have to deal with both information and socialization to new values and concepts, since either without the other reduces the older employee's value to the organization.

Obsolescence is one of the major concerns in extending the duration of work life. Knowledge is increasing so rapidly in many fields, and technological change occurring so rapidly in others, that "knowledge generations" are of briefer and briefer duration. A physics professor or engineering professor who becomes a dean for three or four years may never effectively return to the classroom and research laboratory in her or his previous capacity. The same is true, although to a lesser extent, in other fields, and outside of academia as well as inside. A business person must keep up with the latest computer software capabilities as well as with the changes in tax laws; environmental impact study requirements mean that construction engineers, developers, and local politicians must learn at least the rudiments of a new field which itself is in constant flux. To the extent that the elderly become obsolete, they will be valued less.

It is not that getting older reduces the individual's cognitive capacity to absorb new information, but that the kinds of changes in thinking required by frequent readjustment in approaches will become unsettling. With age, the effort may not seem worth it.

Let me risk a personal experience as an example. As a child during the 1930s I was an avid baseball fan, and I remained in close contact with the sport until after college, when I lost interest. As time went on, new teams and eventually new divisions came into being; I made no effort to absorb this new information, even though it closed an avenue of discussion with my son. I assume that if I were really motivated, I could once again learn enough to rattle off the names and averages of players and teams, but it does not seem worth the effort.

I am suggesting that knowledge obsolescence in work-related matters can be like my knowledge obsolescence in baseball. Experience and what we like to call wisdom replace specific information. In some fields, however, experience and wisdom themselves are quickly outdated as technologies and practices change, and for an employee to go through several "outdatings" may prove emotionally difficult. This situation will occur somewhat with curve-squaring, but will be very much the case with any lengthy life-span extension.

But curve-squaring technologies will presumably result in considerably greater physical stamina and cognitive alertness throughout most of the life span. Thus, although early knowledge and values may become obsolete, the task of absorbing new information and understanding new values will be less difficult than with life-span extension. With the latter, the extremely long potential work life will permit even greater entrenchment in certain positions than exists today. More people will, in terms of the Peter Principle, be promoted to positions beyond their abilities, where they will remain. But with a much longer life and, I am certain, a much longer work life, these individuals, minimally competent for their present status and probably too anxious to move sideways, will remain indefinitely. Presently, this occurs for ten or even fifteen years; the possibility of it continuing for forty or fifty years is enough to make a supervisor or a subordinate sabotage the life-extending technology.

Whether the economy of a country is primarily capitalistic, socialistic, or communistic, this situation would be untenable. Further, it would be exacerbated by increased pressures from younger people for promotion. One reason that arbitrary retirement age regulations find favor among so many young persons is that they allow informed estimates of when particular positions will become open for them. These regulations also assure steady movement into and out of a work system. Presently, illness and death remove many people from the labor force before age 65 and keep even more people over 65 from attempting to reenter the working population. But with curve-squaring, illness and death are unusual, except in the year or two that marks the median life expectancy; and with life-span extension, illness and death, although more widely distributed, occur many years later.

It is possible that some new mechanism will develop to move people out of a job that has been held for a long time. There is also likely to be encouragement for entering entirely new careers once, twice, or even more often during a work lifetime. It is doubtful that laws will require leaving a position after X number of years, and equally doubtful that the economic system can handle early pensions as bribes to move people out. Pensions are used in many police and fire departments and in the military, but these funds still presuppose today's life expectancy. A lengthy extension to that expectancy cannot possibly be accommodated.

Other options are possible, such as small pensions or guaranteed annual incomes along with increased loans for small businesses; required sabbaticals, perhaps one full year after twenty years of work, in which to try a new career or job; and easily available leaves of absence for one-year periods, with return to the position guaranteed. A totally untried possibility would be to attach a maximum number of years to each position; after this time the worker would have to be changed to another position within a stipulated period. Although this could be accomplished without salary reduction, it may well be found unconstitutional and would not be popular. Obviously these options, which are adapted to large organizations rather than small ones, will not settle all the difficulties. In all likelihood, a variety of options will be used simultaneously.

One final option which will be discussed more fully in a later section, is an enlarged continuing education program to prepare people for job career changes. Indeed, life-span extension will virtually require this, while even curve-squaring technologies will give continuing education considerably more impetus than it has today. Without it, people who must wait a long time for jobs or promotions may become rebellious, bored, or both.

Until now there has been no mention of boredom and overfamiliarity with a specific job or even with a career. Most of us think of assembly-line workers as having routine and boring jobs, but my own discussion with school teachers, physicians, upper level management, and academic researchers suggest that no line of endeavor lacks people who are bored or who find their tasks routine.

There seems little doubt that, given ten or fifty more years at the same tasks, boredom and overfamiliarity will increase, while any sense of challenge will decrease. We do not know to what extent certain workers will find new challenges in their work or whether some tasks, in becoming routine, will permit more time for talking with friends, engaging in pleasant reveries, and like activities. Perhaps there is a point beyond which repetitive tasks lose their boring quality (although it is more probable that the tipping point will tip the individual toward total frustration).

This suggests that the value of work may diminish as the result of prolonged life or, at least, the value of any job or job line (that is, a given job and the possibilities for direct promotion). Work may become tedious for many more people than find it so today because they would be required to work many more years with no increased potential for upward or challenging sideways mobility.

What will happen to the importance of work itself? Given the much longer time during which men and women will work, jobs in general and careers will become more important, while any given job will become less important. The reduced import of specific jobs arises because the workweek will likely shrink to four days, people will move from job to job and probably from career to career more frequently, and a given job will be less important in terms of both the waking day and the work life. Conversely, work itself will become more important because it will encompass many more years and, overall, many more hours.

An alternative position can be argued: that work itself will become less important because other involvements and loyalties will become greater due to reduced working hours.

I sense that both positions are correct. One portion of the population, those who through education and skills are competent managers, scientists, and creative people, will find work more important. Their skills will be very much in demand, and they will be able to work as hard and as long as they wish, with very high earnings. The rest of the population, many of whom will be unemployed, will find work less important except as a means of financial sustenance.

Given a long work life and good health, the former group will accumulate additional skills and abilities, and their enjoyment of work will increase as will the demands on them. Moving from job to job or field to field will again enhance their worth on the job market, since they will bring much-needed new perspectives to the job situation. Conversely, those who do not like their work and whose skills do not warrant mobility into the former group will find work increasingly onerous and will turn increasingly to a leisure-oriented life.

Although some rotation would occur, it is obvious that the elite would guard their status and power, perhaps even to the extent of passing it on to progeny (or to others, in exchange for deference, continued power, wealth, or whatever is of value). These possibilities become very speculative, but they offer an example of possible interactions between life prolongation and other social forces and changes.

EDUCATION

There is little doubt that continuing education or lifelong learning, now often perceived as slogans by which adult education programs promote their images in the community, will be more common as life-span extension or curve-squaring become realities. This is already occurring in a limited way, as educational gerontology emerges as a strong subspecialty. The focus is on the older adult as learner and student. Even though older adults, given the prospect of longer life, may not then be perceived as appropriate subjects for gerontology, the general concept will survive. That is, formal education will not cease at 22 years of age nor at the completion of a baccalaureate or even doctoral degree.

Several factors will encourage the return for more education and training, whether through a sabbatical, released hours (time granted by management for employee education), or completely through the worker's resources. First, changing technologies and concepts will quickly cause skills and knowledge to become outdated. It will be increasingly difficult to apply earlier training and previously developed skills to new job requirements. Second, changing attitudes and values will require changes in social understanding. Just as racist or sexist personnel interviewers have become a liability to their organizations, other personal attitudes will become inappropriate. Since we often have difficulty in seeing our values, especially our prejudices, for what they are, there may be a required resocialization program. Third, a combination of boredom, overfamiliarity, and lack of challenge will encourage further education.

This education can comprise essentially four categories: (1) to improve and update skills for present jobs and career lines; (2) to develop skills in order to change jobs or careers; (3) to enhance general knowledge and understanding, in the tradition of liberal arts general education programs; and (4) to develop non-work-related skills, such as gardening, investments, photography, or carpentry, for both improved leisure and practical reasons.

People move back and forth between work and education, even in the present. With prolonged life, this move will accelerate. Also, given a much longer future, high school graduates may spend two or three years earning money, developing immediate job skills, traveling, or engaging in leisure activities. Thus, younger people would be entering the job market without higher education, while those middle-aged and older would be leaving the job market temporarily to acquire additional education and training.

In effect, education would have multiple functions: job-training, transition between jobs or careers, and preparation for leisure. As anyone who has attended college with students of a wide age mix can attest, people benefit from interacting with others of various ages. The relative docility of the young high school graduate and the reentering housewife will be replaced by the aggressiveness of more experienced men and women. The educational system will need to become more flexible and serve a wider mixture of demands than it does at present, or new systems will replace them. The increase in external degree programs of the last few years provides support for this position.

I believe that both public and higher education will become increasingly reluctant to innovate, as a function of the more static job market and the growing militancy of unions. Therefore, I predict a burgeoning of external degree programs or some comparable mechanism.

If life-span extension doubles the present life expectancy, predictions become considerably more difficult to make. We have had experience with educational programs for 75-year-olds; curve-squaring extends the number of years one may participate in educational programs by a decade or so, while increasing the numbers of persons involved. An educational program for 125-year-olds who have worked, off and on, for ninety-five years is quite another matter. The possibility of boredom is considerable: How many retraining programs can one individual go through without becoming totally bored? The only reports of people this age—and even these are questionable—emanate from communities where considerable time and effort are needed just to survive; also, I believe, religion and sacred values have high status in these communities. Present Western society has not retained traditional sacred values, nor are its people pitted against their environment to remain alive. On the other hand, we do expend much time and energy discussing the meaning of life and its purpose; intuition suggests that any society that replaces unswerving faith and essential hard work with discussion of meaning is ill-equipped to have its members live contentedly for 150 years. Indeed, Viktor Frankl has contended that meaning does not develop through attendance at "growth groups" but with participation in life through work, love, and suffering.

If, as I have speculated, work, particularly a given job or job line, becomes less important, education will become more important because it will provide ways out of the work tedium, offering opportunities for both upward and sideways mobility. In the past few years, the role of educational gerontology has increased in importance among gerontologists and those concerned with community education.

LEISURE

In some instances we can make sharp distinctions among work, education, and leisure. In other instances, the distinctions are questionable. A professor takes a sabbatical to study in a city that she much prefers to the one where she teaches; a company president attends a six-day seminar in Aspen; a hair stylist attends his state convention where he competes in some contests, listens to presentations, learns the newest techniques, and meets his old friends. How, in each of these examples, can we differentiate work, leisure, and education?

Most often, of course, differentiation is relatively easy. In spite of endless academic discussions about the importance of work for self-esteem, we appear to be moving toward a leisure-oriented society. This trend is likely to continue because of " ... the inevitable realization on the part of the employee that there is nothing sacred about working during the best years of life when he might go back to school, travel, or fish."[14]

Additional years of life will mean both more hours and years of work and more hours and years of leisure. Depending on political and economic pressures, one or the other will predominate. There will be a longer time to develop leisure interests—longer in terms of hours because I assume that the workweek will continue to shrink, and longer in terms of years because of increased life expectancy. These two forces will combine to produce an enlarged leisure industry, perhaps with more emphasis on personal creativity (for example, in arts and crafts) and competence.

Given more time, leisure will assume ever-greater importance, particularly if some of the earlier hypotheses about the shrinkage of the labor force come true. Today, a recently retired person may feel there is insufficient time to embark on either a new career or a fully-developed leisure activity. But with a better ability to predict the end of life, or merely a good chance of living for many years, involvement in specific leisure activities can have a good pay-off in the development of high competence and expert knowledge. Not only will well-developed work skills be well rewarded, but exceptional leisure skills will be highly valued and will bring considerable commendation and personal satisfaction. There is now enough time to learn a foreign language, play a musical instrument, and assume a leadership position in community political or social action groups. That is, there will be enough leisure time to develop depth and breadth of competence, leisure activities will offer an opportunity to become expert in a way that many, perhaps most, jobs do not and will not permit.

RETIREMENT

On very few matters does the middle-aged, middle-class professional display ethnocentrism more overtly than in evaluating work and retirement. In spite of substantial evidence that the majority of employed persons would welcome retirement, assuming that neither income nor social status would suffer, the psychological benefits of work are extolled not only by the rich and conservative, but also by the less rich and liberal. Nonetheless, one major longitudinal study of 1400 male workers found that over 90 percent wished to retire before or at the same age as they actually will be able to, and these figures hold for those in their twenties as well as those in their sixties.[15]

These pieces of information do not deny the deleterious effects of retirement on some individuals, but they explicate the evidence that, far from wishing to avoid retirement, the majority of American workers welcome it. It is not likely that retirement itself, even over many years, will create millions of angry, frustrated, militant older persons. However, low income, poor health care, inadequate housing, or strong feelings of relative deprivation may create exactly that.

There is no reason to believe that the present retirement age will remain in effect. In recent years, the previous age of 65 has inched downward to 62 for social security, and down to even younger ages for retirement from some public service and military positions. If present pressures on the social security system remain, and if the health of the elderly is improved through curve-squaring techniques, it is virtually certain that some movement will be made to alter the social security benefits program by encouraging later rather than earlier retirement. This has indeed been happening recently with new retirement-age legislation.

Even today, most retired persons over age 65 would be unable to return to work because of health or physical limitations.[16] If good health could be prolonged, some of these people would wish to continue to work. Of these, a portion could be bought off through higher pension benefits, but there is some question as to whether the economy could handle this. At the same time, a shrinking birthrate will, assuming it continues, reduce the numbers of young persons trying to enter the job market. (An unknown is whether the proportion of working women will continue to increase, thus putting more pressure on the labor market.)

Given the likelihood that arbitrary retirement regulations will be eliminated (there is already legal action in this direction), and that more people will work until later in life, we are still faced with the majority of persons who will wish to retire with adequate pension benefits. It is difficult to estimate how many more years of work the "average" worker will opt for, given good health and reasonable retirement benefits. If curve-squaring permits most persons to live to 90 years of age, I estimate that the median age of desired retirement will increase by, at the most, half of the increase in life expectancy. Thus, retirement will still come at 73 to 75, allowing fifteen or more years of life expectancy for retirees. And I suggest that earlier retirement is more likely to be demanded than later retirement, assuming adequate retirement income. This would mean that some very unpopular legislation might be necessary to keep people on jobs from which they wish to retire; this could be done, for example, by reducing social security benefits sharply for those who retire before a given age, rather than, as we do today, reducing them only for those who work beyond a certain age.

Life-span extension brings about another set of difficulties. Here the uncertainty of future life increases rather than decreases, so those who wish to assure themselves of a moderately lengthy retirement must risk erring on the side of a very lengthy retirement or else risk dying before they have enjoyed much retirement at all. Assuming the doubling of life expectancy, as I do in this chapter, I foresee a great desire to retire out of boredom, fatigue, and ennui. However, one might retire for six or eight years, then return for education for two or three years, then return to work for another 30 years, if the economy permits and politics implements.

CONCLUDING COMMENTS

This chapter has examined the possible effects of curve-squaring and life-span extending technologies on (1) the self, personality and the meaning of death, (2) the family, and (3) work, education, leisure, and retirement. The focus has been on values, both the valuing of the older person by himself and others, and the valuing of social institutions in view of changing life expectancies. An additional focus has been on the meaning of the changes for society and for the individuals that constitute what we globally refer to as "society."

When I began my study, I had few biases or preferences regarding the matter of curve-squaring vis-à-vis life-span extension. What impresses me at the conclusion, however, is that in virtually every section of the investigation, life-span extension appears to increase social, psychological, and economic difficulties, while curve-squaring either ameliorates the problems or leaves them no worse than before.

Therefore, I feel considerable urgency in making several recommendations:

1. Curve-squaring techniques should take precedence over life-span-extending techniques in terms of funding, efforts, and encouragement.
2. To the extent that life-span-extending techniques are funded and encouraged, they should receive support in increasing the rectangularity of the curves. They should not receive support if it appears that they will return the curves to the shapes of a century or more ago.
3. Policy decisions should receive input from a variety of sources, not just biological and biomedical sources. The sources should include—but not be limited to—philosophers, theologians, economists, behavioral scientists, health care professionals, geographers, social workers, housing experts, lawyers, and community members who lack the above skills but who do not represent specific community pressure groups.
4. Planning for the future should proceed slowly but should keep pace with biological research. Planners should not also be implementers, but should keep in close contact with implementers. Planners should develop a variety of contingency programs that make differing assumptions concerning demographic aspects, financial potential, and social forces.
5. The best thing at this point would be for a federal task force of leading scientists and nonscientists to be established to monitor what is going on both in this country and in other nations. I would also suggest that an international task force be established on these concerns, because they will be international concerns as soon as the technologies are developed.

These recommendations emphasize the importance of immediate contingency planning. I recall my childhood when Walter Reed and other biomedical scientists were extolled as heroes for having eliminated yellow fever. They fully deserved the admiration, and I

116   RICHARD A. KALISH

do not wish to detract from it, but it would have been useful had
some organization then begun to contemplate what was going to
happen sixty years later when the populations of previously yellow
fever-ridden countries expanded explosively.

We are now faced with a value-related set of concerns every bit
as important—and eventually more important—than the eradication of yellow fever. The considerations in this and accompanying
chapters need to be dealt with now by people who can plan flexibly
and bring their plans to the attention of those with the power to
implement them at the appropriate time.

NOTES

1. R. A. Kalish, "Death and Dying in a Social Context," in *Handbook of Aging and the Social Sciences,* ed. R. Binstock and E. Shanas (New York: Van Nostrand Reinhold Co., 1976), pp. 483–507.
2. H. Brotman, "Life Expectancy: Comparisons of National Levels in 1900 and 1974 and Variations in State Levels, 1969–1971," *The Gerontologist* 17 (1977): 12–22.
3. E. Becker, *The Denial of Death* (New York: Free Press, 1973).
4. R. A. Kalish and D. K. Reynolds, *Death and Ethnicity: A Psychocultural Study* (Los Angeles: University of Southern California Press, 1976).
5. D. Gutmann, "The Premature Gerontocracy: Themes of Aging and Death in the Youth Culture," *Social Research* 39 (1972): 416–448.
6. L. E. Duncan, "The Effect of Prolongation of Life on Health." Paper presented at the Center for the Study of Democratic Institutions, Santa Barbara, Cal., April 1970.
7. A. I. Goldfarb, "Socialization, Personality Type, and the Welfare of the Aged." Paper presented at the Center for the Study of Democratic Institutions, Santa Barbara, Cal., April 1970.
8. H. S. Abrams, "The Choice between Dialysis and Transplant: Psychosocial Considerations." Paper presented at the Institute of Society, Ethics and the Life Sciences, The Hastings Center, Hastings-on-Hudson, New York, December 11, 1976.
9. R. A. Kalish, "Four Score and Ten," *The Gerontologist* 14 (1974): 129–135.
10. H. Brotman, "Life Expectancy: Comparisons of National Levels in 1900 and 1974 and Variations in State Levels, 1969–1971," *The Gerontologist* 17 (1977): 12–22.
11. Kalish, "Four Score and Ten," p. 130.
12. B. L. Neugarten, "The Future and the Young-Old," *The Gerontologist* 15, no. 1, part 2 (1975): 7.

13. S. M. Golant, "Residential Concentrations of the Future Elderly," *The Geron-tologist* 15, no. 1, part 2 (1975): 16–23.
14. M. Kaplan, "Lifespan, Lifestyles, and Leisure." Paper presented at the Center for the Study of Democratic Institutions, Santa Barbara, Cal., April 1970.
15. D. J. Ekerdt, C. L. Rose, R. Bosse, and P. T. Costa, "Longitudinal Change in Preferred Age of Retirement," *Journal of Occupational Psychology* 49 (1976): 161–169.
16. National Council on the Aging, *The Myth and Reality of Aging in America* (Washington, D.C.: National Council on Aging, 1975).

5

Pain, Suffering, and Life-Extending Technologies

LAURENCE B. McCULLOUGH

The moral status of pain and suffering is not clear. Are they evils? Are they always to be avoided or, instead, sometimes endured? In dealing with the issue of active euthanasia, H. Tristram Engelhardt has written:

> Further, the choice of positive euthanasia could be defended as the more rational choice of a less painful death and the affirmation of the value of rational life. In so choosing, one would be acting to set limits to one's life in order not to live when pain and physical and mental deterioration make further rational life impossible.[1]

Thus, it would seem, we can argue that under some circumstances life becomes intolerable and death is no longer regarded as the enemy. Indeed, in the presence of overwhelming pain and suffering, death may be considered a positive good.

This argument has a counterpart that says that life in general can become of very low quality, even approximating an injury[2] or an evil.[3] As Seneca argued:

> For mere living is not a good, but living well. Accordingly, the wise man will live as long as he ought, not as long as he can. . . . He always reflects concerning the quality, and not the quantity, of his life. As soon as there are many events in his life that give him trouble, and disturb his peace of mind, he sets himself free. . . . It is not a question of

dying earlier or later, but of dying well or ill. And dying well means escape from the danger of living ill.[4]

We find, then, a variety of approaches and arguments about the moral status of pain and suffering vis-à-vis death. In an effort to sort through and evaluate the diverse approaches, this chapter first outlines basic moral positions and then examines whether and how each of these positions is consistent with a policy advocating life extension.

THE NATURE OF PAIN AND SUFFERING

A set of issues regarding pain and suffering must be outlined before the two tasks of this chapter can be properly engaged. They originate in the use of the terms *pain* and *suffering*. To begin with some remarks are in order about how these terms are used here and about the general character of pain and suffering. Then too, there is a serious philosophical controversy concerning whether a person can be mistaken about his own pain claims. There has been a great deal of discussion in the philosophical literature on this subject, focusing for the most part on issues in the philosophy of mind: the character of pain language and knowledge of other minds. These issues need not concern us directly, but the character of claims about (one's own) pain and suffering must be emphasized, as it is a persistent leitmotiv in the subsequent discussion.

David Boeyink, in his excellent piece on pain and suffering, defined pain as follows:

> Pain is the stimulating of some part of the body which the mind perceives as an injury or threat of injury to that portion of the body or the self as a whole.[5]

That is, "pain" denotes phenomena that are principally physical in origin. According to my colleagues in physiology,[6] this understanding is sound. The pain receptors in the body are typicallly activated, and transmit their messages to the brain, when bodily tissue has been damaged or when the body has been impinged upon in a way that is likely to damage bodily tissue. If we regard the pain receptors as integral to a body control system, then pain serves as a part of a "negative feedback system." Pain operates on the sensor side of th ·
feedback loop and warns us of injury or the threat of injury.[7] Be-

cause this threat may be to a part of the body or to the body as a unified organism, some pain includes an aspect of a life threat.[8] All pain, though, appears to involve tissue damage. Pain can also warn us when we have stretched our bodily capacities beyond their limits; the pain of swelling of some internal organs such as the intestine is quite severe and warns us of a threat to our continued well-being, such as the possibility of peritonitis from bursting of the intestine. On the other hand, the aching of the leg muscles after lengthy walking on concrete sidewalks does not customarily pose or include a life threat.

"Suffering" is reserved to denote phenomena that are principally psychic in origin. Following Boeyink, I here adopt the characterization of suffering offered by Daniel Day Williams:

> We ordinarily mean by suffering an anguish which we experience, not only as a pressure to change, but as a threat to our composure, our integrity, and fulfillment of our intentions.[9]

This definition is not to deny that pain is a mental state,[10] but to emphasize that, in contrast to pain—a mental state principally physical in origin—suffering is a mental state whose origin is principally, though not exclusively, psychic. Hence, we suffer at the loss of a loved one or in dread of some awful occurrence.

There is a point about the relation of pain and suffering that is worth making separately. As Boeyink puts it:

> Pain itself can be a direct cause of suffering, especially if that pain is very intense. It is here that pain and suffering are most directly related. There is, therefore, a great deal of overlap between pain and suffering insofar as both may coexist simultaneously in this cause-effect relationship. One can never be certain when pain will produce suffering. In one individual a slight pain is sufficient to elicit a response of suffering; for another an intense pain will yield little or no suffering.[11]

Relying again on my colleagues—this time in psychiatry—I want to add to Boeyink's remarks the following: surely it is true that pain can cause one to suffer. At the very least, pain distracts and irritates us; if it also poses a life threat, there follows the anguish of knowing that one might (soon) die from that which causes or occasions the pain. For the terminally ill, this is especially and poignantly true. The increase in pain caused by the advance of terminal illness often means that one is more firmly in the grip of the disease and that death has drawn even closer. Then too there is the concern, even fright, about pain we will have to endure, for example, consequent to extensive heart surgery. This kind of suffering can arrest our attention and, by fully absorbing our energies, overwhelm us.

> Under conditions when it becomes nagging and persistent, pain impairs the sufferer's ability to work and to think clearly, prevents his sleep, abolishes appetite, lowers morale, and may even destroy his will to help himself survive.[12]

In a recent essay, Irwin Lieb makes this same point in sharper detail.

> Pain can possess us. It can take our whole thought and have us give ourselves up to it, and it can happen then that there is nothing that we would not do to get relief from pain. It is only when we have control over ourselves or when we can come to have it, that we can ask how we ought to bear the pain we have. Then we can measure the portion we will let it have in our lives and decide how we will feel or express it. Prolonged pain can be a terrible discipline, though it seems that some people have learned how to live in it.[13]

Thus, pain and suffering as well while they arrest us, not always possess us wholly; in such cases they can teach us valuable lessons about the frailty of our lives, of how closely we live with death. This realization allows us to give measure to our lives and our ambition. We fail to appreciate pain and suffering unless we understand that we can learn from them even as they threaten us.

> For we have forgotten that the self must be transformed if we are to see the world as it is, and that the transformation into loving persons is not accomplished overnight by declaring our good intentions but by submitting patiently to the suffering that makes us real. We have impoverished our ethics by assuming that our lives can easily embody and reflect the good.[14]

As we shall see, not all views are like Hauerwas's. Others appear to invite us to think that pain and suffering render living pointless, devoid of meaning and full of torment (much like Harlan Ellison's character who had no mouth while having to scream). These varying views have significantly different consequences when brought to bear on their moral status vis-à-vis death. These differences are set out below.

A further problem in assessing the moral status of pain and suffering is that, unlike most knowledge claims, those about pain and suffering lack that public character that commands assent. After all, no one but myself can experience my pain or suffer as I suffer. Hence, it seems my claims are incorrigibly true.[15]

The point to emphasize here is not so much the incorrigibility of knowledge claims about one's own pain and suffering as that, in disputes about them, the one experiencing the pain and suffering is in a preeminent position to judge their severity and interference in his life.

> I do not suggest that the personal nature of feelings supports either the doctrine of the incorrigibility or the doctrine of alien unknownability, i.e., it does not indicate the feeler generally *knows* his feelings any better or more clearly than another, but it does, I think, establish the natural prerogative of the feeler, i.e., it does indicate that wherever there is a conflict of knowledge-claims concerning the nature of feelings between the feeler and another the testimony of the feeler has evidential priority.[16]

We are obliged, then, to take others at their own word in assessing how much pain is bearable. (Pain researchers face this very problem.) Of course, analgesic drugs may provide relief, or at least we hope they do. It is not clear, however, that we can always relieve pain. This is complicated by a peculiar feature of the experience of pain. Pain of continuing duration can cause one to become hypersensitive to further pain stimuli. That is, as the pain continues, its perception may actually increase in intensity. What began as a moderate pain may, without any increase in stimulus strength, become a very severe pain—hyperalgesia.[17] Thus, pain may take an increasing toll even as we seek to relieve it. Drugs used to alleviate pain often diminish the ability to think clearly, and so may increase suffering. We can sometimes hope only to "manage" pain, that is, interfere with and control it. But the one in pain is still preeminent in assessing its severity.

> Real pain cannot be distinguished readily from imaginary pain and the only true pain to the patient is his pain.[18]

In the case of suffering, this is not always the case, though it is the rule. We do know that suffering, say at the loss of a friend or loved one, passes. Unlike pain, suffering in its worst form is not unrelenting. These troubles will pass, we tell each other, even as they threaten to overwhelm us. But the severity of that suffering and its impact on one's life is not a "public" matter; what Bakan says about pain applies equally as well to suffering:

> The problem inheres in the fact that pain is "private." If one insists that the data of psychology be "public," then pain has to be ruled out as being beyond the enclosing limit. Pain is *ultimately* private in that it is lodged in the individual person, the person individuated in many relevant respects out of the larger telos. If we insist that science be guided by a canon of what the contemporary philosophy of science jargon refers to as publicity, there simply cannot be a science of pain which can do justice to the phenomenon.[19]

The upshot is that claims about pain and suffering will admit of a wide variety. The pain that accompanies a broken limb may temporarily overwhelm some and not others, and people have to be taken at their word about the severity of their pain. To argue that one should not succumb to this or that level of pain or suffering is to argue something new, that is, that one should be stronger and not so easily defeated by the vicissitudes of nature and human living. But how can one secure this argument? To what can one make appeal? Usually such arguments are based on what the good life is taken to be, the life that adheres to the Good. But we can, and do, disagree deeply on what the good life is. In a society of "unfocused values," to use Ramsey's phrase,[20] agreement on what constitutes the good life may well be impossible. Hence, we lack a common ground from which to instruct each other about what pain, suffering, and endurance are. This disagreement bears directly on alternate understandings of the moral status of pain and suffering vis-à-vis death.

There is however, a point on which the differing views seem to agree: that autonomy is core to the good life, the moral life, and that pain and suffering diminish it. It is this diminution of autonomy that is to be avoided. One might say that there are disagreements about the character of autonomy. I shall argue that it is possible to construct an account of the moral status of pain and suffering vis-à-vis death that is consistent with any reasonable notion of autonomy. But let us now turn to the various ways in which the moral status of pain, suffering, and death are to be understood.

PAIN, SUFFERING, AND DEATH

There are five basic positions on the moral status of pain and suffering vis-à-vis death. The common theme is autonomy and the issue that distinguishes them is the scope of autonomy: Should it be within the scope of autonomy to end one's life in the face of pain or suffering? By "end one's life" here I mean to include both active (positive) and passive (negative) euthanasia.

Gerald Dworkin has recently set out the central features of the concept of autonomy, including authenticity and independence.[21] The notion of authenticity must be here understood in an open-textured manner. Authenticity for the religious man turns on how well he approximates God's will in his life. The nonreligious man, by contrast, understands authenticity in terms, perhaps, of the extent to which he realizes the rational life in his own life. In this respect there can be considerable latitude in the way people will understand and use "autonomy."

The notion of independence, however, offers less latitude. Independence means control of one's life. Typically, and as used here, this means that we seek to avoid submission to the vicissitudes of nature and of our fellows. Instead, we seek to bring as much of our lives under our own control and within the domain of our own will as we can, by avoiding whatever diminishes our control. On this point the five positions all agree: Autonomy includes at least the notion of independence in the sense just explained. That is, autonomy in this sense has great, even absolute, value because independence is necessary for our experience of the world to be our own. When independence is diminished or minimized, we shrink as we lose a necessary condition for being a moral agent: control of and responsibility for self and environment. The five positions also agree that pain, suffering, and death are among the vicissitudes of nature and man that we all must face. Disagreement arises on the issue of the *scope* of autonomy in its aspect of independence. To repeat, at issue is whether it should or should not fall within the scope of autonomy-independence (in what follows, autonomy is always used in this sense unless otherwise specified) to end one's life in the face of pain and suffering, that is, when death becomes preferable to life.

GENERAL RIGHT TO DIE

The first position maintains that it falls within the scope of one's autonomy to end one's life when that life decreases in value. This is given expression as a general right to die. Hence, pain and suffering, anxiety, boredom, or even whim or pleasure could serve equally well as occasions for ending one's life. The right is *general* in that no special circumstances are required for it to obtain; it always obtains. This is in contrast to a *special* right to die, which obtains only in specified circumstances. The only restraint on this right is the presence of conflicting and binding duties, such as duties to family, promises, and so on. That is, although the right is general, it is not absolute. To end one's life falls within the scope of autonomy when one does not, by ending one's life, fail to fulfill duties to others to which one is morally bound.

What exempts one from fulfilling binding obligations such as those to family, friends, and so on, would principally be an inability to do so. Terminal illness, for example, renders moot obligations that cannot be fulfilled in the time left. In addition, some argue that life can become not worth living, in which case one would be freed from all binding obligations to others. Seneca, of course, is the outstanding classical representative of this position.[22]

To put it in more familiar language, when the quality of life has diminished to a point where life is no longer worth living, one can (even ought to) end one's life. In such circumstances, one can avoid further and continuing diminution of one's autonomy—a loss of value—by death. The submerged premise in this argument is that a low quality of life releases one from binding obligations to others. What is yet to be specified is what factors count in the diminution of the quality of life. Also, separate argument must be made for the submerged premise.

Clearly pain and suffering are leading causes of diminished autonomy. This point has been developed, as an extension of Seneca's (more general) position, by Engelhardt in his exposition of life itself constituting an injury.

> The suits for tort for wrongful life raise the issue not only of when it would be preferable not to have been born but also when it would be *wrong* to cause a person to be born. . . . The concept of tort for wrong-

ful life raises an issue concerning the responsibility for giving another person existence, namely, the notion that giving life is not always necessarily a good and justifiable action. Instead, in certain circumstances, so it has been argued, one may have a duty *not* to give existence to another person. This concept involves the claim that certain qualities of life have a negative value, making life an injury, not a gift.[23]

Engelhardt elsewhere in the same article seems to have clearly in mind such causes of the diminution of the quality of life as multiple and/or severe birth defects.

The main line of argument should be clear. That is, it should fall within the scope of autonomy to end our lives: Death is not absolutely disvalued. The only limiting condition is the potential conflict with outstanding and binding obligations. Otherwise, the general right to die obtains in all circumstances. Pain and suffering are among those circumstances, a fortiori. Indeed, they are among the circumstances most commonly appealed to in securing release from binding obligations to others, thus freeing one for the exercise of the right.

This first view holds that death is never to be absolutely disvalued. Consequently, anything regarded as a greater disvalue than death is to be avoided, even if this means ending one's life. In such a view, many things may be of greater disvalue than death. In contrast, two other views hold that death is, as a rule, to be disvalued. These views allow, however, that some diminutions of autonomy may become so great that they are seen as more evil than the disvalue of death. Hence, in special circumstances death is preferable, even permissible. These views may be regarded in terms of a limited, or special, right to die. Pain and suffering are included here, among the "special circumstances." In general, when pain and/or suffering achieve a sufficient level (or intensity or duration), it is justified to avoid them through death. This line of argument takes two forms: beneficent euthanasia (as defined by Marvin Kohl[24]) and benemortasia (as defined by Arthur Dyck[25]). These are taken up in turn.

SPECIAL RIGHT TO DIE: ACTIVE KILLING

Marvin Kohl's advocacy of beneficent, that is, active and kind, euthanasia may be taken as the paradigm of the second position on the moral status of pain, suffering, and death. Kohl's main argument is that we have an obligation to be kind. Chief among kind acts is the eradication of evil, which is defined as that which interferes with the control of our lives. A fortiori, it is an act of kindness to relieve others of the evils of pain and suffering. In some circumstances, typically in late stages of terminal illness accompanied by unyielding pain and suffering (though there is no reason, logically, to restrict the cases to terminal illness since pain and suffering are at issue whenever they occur), only killing someone will relieve them. It is, therefore, morally obligatory to end those lives in order to eradicate the evil of that pain and suffering. It is also morally permissible for those so tormented to suicide. This obligation and the corresponding right of the afflicted, of course, acquire sufficient authority only in the absence of conflicting and compelling duties.[26] In summary, pain and suffering can become great evils, greater than the evil of death. Indeed, pain and suffering of sufficient degree can bring one to view death as a positive good to be pursued, the good of eliminating the evils of pain and suffering. As this passage from "A Plea for Beneficent Euthanasia" puts it:

> To require that a person be kept alive against his will and to deny his pleas for merciful release after the dignity, beauty, promise, and meaning of life have vanished, when he can only linger on in stages of agony or decay, is cruel and barbarous. The imposition of unnecessary suffering is an evil that should be avoided by any civilized society.[27]

The underlying premise here is that autonomy ought to include control over the vicissitudes of pain, suffering, and death, and that death may be chosen as a means to eliminate pain and suffering. Kohl quite explicitly adopts this premise, as anyone advocating a position on active euthanasia must. He distinguishes two senses of dignity. It is the second sense that is relevant here.

> The heart of the matter, I believe, lies elsewhere. It has to do with dignity, the having of which roughly denotes the actual ability of a human being to rationally determine and control his way of life and death and to have this acknowledged and respected by others.[28]

Kohl means for the scope of autonomy to extend to include death, but only in the special circumstances of pain and suffering. More exactly, what is claimed is the freedom to take or initiate positive measures to cause the end of one's life—in short, a right to active euthanasia. This may take the form of unassisted or assisted suicide. This second position differs from the first principally in that it claims limited, not general, scope for autonomy regarding the control of death. Like the first, it argues that pain, suffering, and death are evils and that sometimes pain and suffering can become greater evils than death. When that occurs, the special right to die obtains and, in the absence of conflicting and strong obligations, the right creates a duty to eliminate the evil in question by ending life.

SPECIAL RIGHT TO DIE: PASSIVE EUTHANASIA

The third position differs from the second in that it denies that either assisted or unassisted suicide should fall within the scope of autonomy. That is, only negative or passive euthanasia is viewed as the acceptable alternative to pain and suffering. We may take Arthur Dyck's arguments as typical of those that advocate a special right to die but draw the line at suicide and killing. [29]

Dyck opens his argument with an attack on the advocates of active, or beneficent, euthanasia. His attack is centered on an uncertainty regarding the scope of autonomy, as evidenced in the widespread disagreement on the concept of human dignity in the sense meant by Kohl: control over the circumstances of life and death. In essence, he urges prudence regarding the nature and scope of that control. He does so because of a slippery slope of a logical character—as opposed to a psychological character, which depends on its predictive success for authority—that proponents of active euthanasia cannot avoid.

> The point of the wedge argument is very simple. Since killing is generally wrong, it should be kept to as narrow a range of exceptions as possible. But the argument for beneficent euthanasia . . . applies logically to a wide range of cases, and the reasons for keeping the range of cases narrow are not reasons on which people will easily agree. In short, arguments for beneficent euthanasia apply logically either to a narrow or wide range of cases. Whether beneficent euthanasia will be applied to a narrow range of cases does not depend simply on how kind a society is. It will depend also on the various notions that are held about what constitutes a dignified or meaningful human life.[30]

Since we cannot agree that the scope of autonomy should include suicide, we cannot urge, as a matter of policy, the practice of beneficent euthanasia and expect a consensus to form on its (moral) permissibility, much less on its character as a positive duty. The more prudential position is to advocate passive euthanasia. Hence, pain and suffering are still taken to be evil; the greater the pain and suffering, the more it is to be avoided. When pain and suffering become greater evils than the evil of death, one avoids them only *by refusing treatment* that will sustain or even save one's life. In short, one chooses a course that is reasonably certain to end in death but does not end one's life by direct means. What Dyck says about pain applies to suffering, as well:

> There is widespread agreement among those who oppose beneficent euthanasia but who believe in mercy that pain relief can be offered to patients even when it means shortening the dying process. . . . This means that one does not knowingly give an overdose of a pain reliever, but rather concentrates on dosages that are sufficient for relief of pain, knowing that at some point the dose administered will be fatal.[31]

These two positions, beneficent euthanasia and benemortasia, agree with each other and with the first position on a central point: Life can be shortened in order to avoid the evil of pain and suffering when that evil is taken to be greater than that of death. They disagree on what means are morally open to secure the goal of a shortened life. Both, too, are open to the same attack. There are no guidelines for assessing the degree of evil that pain and suffering must assume before measures to shorten life are permissible or obligatory. In short, the moral status of pain, suffering, and death remains unclear. Examining this issue more closely, one finds that only extreme pain and suffering ("extreme" or "overwhelming" is defined below) qualify as sufficiently evil or of sufficiently negative value to justify life-shortening procedures. In all other cases of pain and suffering, I shall argue, the morally proper course of action is to endure, thus enhancing and enriching the scope of one's autonomy.

AUTONOMY AS A MEASURE OF THE MORAL STATUS OF PAIN AND SUFFERING

The fourth position begins with an attempt to understand the moral status of pain and suffering. This is made in terms of autonomy. Pain, suffering, and death are among the vicissitudes of man and nature, those evils that befall us either by fate or at the hands of our fellows. The issue for autonomy involves bringing as many of the vicissitudes of nature and man under our own control as we can. In this way our autonomy is made rich and its scope increased. As we control some aspect of our life, we deepen and enrich our experience of the world and extend the scope of our independence by avoiding unnecessary minimizations of it. This is, for autonomy, the good to be sought. That is, one can claim a broader scope for autonomy over the vicissitudes that befall us, from the least to the ultimate (death), only in a stepwise fashion. Pain and suffering fall between the least and ultimate vicissitudes.

The picture for the evil of pain and suffering versus the evil of death is different, for what must be allowed for—and is often claimed—is that the evils of pain and suffering can be greater than that of death. What is needed is some way to determine when that is the case. Moreover, in light of the difficulties regarding the incorrigibility of pain claims, what is needed is a nonarbitrary way to assess the evil of pain and suffering. Without some limiting condition or touchstone, it is impossible to assess the moral status of pain and suffering in a reliable fashion. The touchstone required here is provided by autonomy. On the basis of an analysis grounded in autonomy, we can arrive at an objective understanding of the moral status, that is, one that avoids the difficulties of the subjective character of the experience of pain and suffering.

I propose autonomy as the measure of the moral status of pain and suffering: it is only when pain and suffering make autonomy in the sense of independence impossible that they are greater evils than death. Thus, even though we may respond to similar stimuli differently or to the same stimulus differently over a period of time, we can usually cope with and manage that pain and suffering. Differences in degree of pain and suffering would not count, since they overwhelm us totally only in rare instances where the minimization of autonomy is extreme and irreversible. In such cases, we are completely helpless before the power of pain and suffering. Only then do they become more evil than death, the final overwhelming of our independence. As a rule, pain and suffering should be endured, as they provide an opportunity for enrichment and deepening of the moral life. To claim, as do the first three positions, that one should avoid pain and suffering by choosing death is, in effect, to submit to these lesser vicissitudes while at the same time claiming control—in a non-stepwise fashion—over the ultimate vicissitude, death. One therefore claims a false autonomy; one's independence has scope but lacks depth. Such a position succeeds only at the price of adopting a broad and at once impoverished understanding of the nature of autonomy. Consistent with the requirements of the concept of autonomy, the fourth position argues, one should accept and endure pain and suffering, except, as noted, when it is impossible to do so.

> It is the accepted rather than the deserved or undeserved character of pain which is most important for the achievement of *personal* well-being or redemption. In it one makes an active response to pain and disease through an exercise of one's will. The acceptance of pain, rather than seeing it as an unnatural and unnecessary intruder that threatens or takes control of the person, yields a greater degree of personal integration with the freedom to control one's own life. In addition, if the pain is accurately viewed as deserved, one can in this acceptance develop a sense of responsibility for that pain, or more correctly, for the disease or injury that causes the pain.[32]

This position differs from the second and third in that it restricts the negative value of pain and suffering and views them uniformly in a more positive light. They are thus understood as opportunities to enrich our experience, to learn more fully the lessons of finitude.[33] Thus, we are able to give proper measure to our lives. This position is also more consistent with the logical character of the stepwise extension and enrichment of our independence, which the first position overlooks entirely. On balance the fourth position seems to be, in terms of autonomy, the most coherent account of the moral status of pain, suffering, and death. It may also be—in the sense of demanding—the most difficult position in that it calls us to test ourselves at the price of great torment and anguish. It is a counsel whose burden is not easily taken up.

It should be noted separately that this position does not rule out the special right to die. It is consistent, in this view, to maintain that in the face of overwhelming pain and suffering—as this has been defined—it is permissible to end one's life. As "overwhelming" is understood here, this advocacy of euthanasia—whether active or passive—is not uncomplicated. First, it does restrict logically the class of cases concerned and does meet Dyck's objection to active euthanasia. Second, since overwhelming pain and suffering in effect means that one is wholly consumed by the pain and/or suffering, provision would have to be made in advance for the course of action willed by the dying person. By definition, overwhelming pain and suffering make it impossible for one so afflicted to choose rationally any course of action. Hence, this view creates an additional burden

for those who care for the terminally ill, that is, making clear to
such patients that the prognosis includes the likely prospect of overwhelming pain and suffering and that they must decide a course of
action prior to its onslaught. Then too, those who care for patients
who do not yet experience this degree of pain and suffering but still
face the prospect of them must be willing to support the patients as
they do battle with these dread opponents.

DEATH AS AN ABSOLUTE EVIL

The last position is uncomplicated, at least at first glance. It
holds that death is the greatest evil, than which there could be no
greater. It follows, therefore, that one must always avoid death, no
matter what the price. The counterpart to this view is that life possesses absolute value, and death absolute disvalue, regardless of circumstances.

The difficulty with this position is that the value of life and the
evil of death are, for a view like this, difficult to define consistently.
The principal approach, it seems to me, is to maintain that death is
evil because it represents the full stop, our ceasing in all ways to be.
One way to interpret this kind of view is in terms of autonomy:
Death robs us of our independence in a final and irrevocable way.
As the final irreversible submission to the vicissitudes to nature and
man, it is always to be avoided. Consequently, to end one's life ought
never to fall within the scope of autonomy, for this is to bring down
upon oneself ultimate ending, which is irrational.

This sort of position fails to appreciate that death is not the only
robber on the scene. Our independence can be finally shattered in
other ways as well. Chief among these, obviously, are pain and suffering. As the preceding reflections teach, these can overwhelm us
and in the end so occupy us that they destroy the possibility of all
other experiences. Such, I am given to understand, is the nature of
the pain that accompanies the late stages of brain cancer. Competing in horror with these ravages is the dread terror that descends
upon those afflicted with cancer of the larynx. As this disease grows
progressively worse, the throat is further and further constricted until it becomes impossible to breathe. Anyone who has ever come
close to drowning can recount vividly the power with which the terror of suffocation can seize and wholly occupy one.

This last position, then, can succeed only by ignoring the

inescapable realities of our experience and knowledge of pain and suffering; one presumes that few are willing to hold such a view.

This completes the consideration of the basic ways in which the moral status of pain, suffering, and death have been and may be addressed. Of the five, it was argued that the fourth is the most adequate; it provides an objective account of that status, if one takes as a starting point autonomy, upon which all five positions build. It remains now to discover which of these positions is consistent with a policy to avoid death by the adoption of life-extending technologies.

PAIN, SUFFERING, AND LIFE-EXTENDING TECHNOLOGIES

The five positions are considered here under the presumption that we could know in advance that a certain life-extending technology would be accompanied by pain and suffering. The issue in question is whether it is consistent for advocates of the position under consideration to adopt such a technology, or to adopt a public policy in pursuit of realizing that technology.

LIFE EXTENSIONS AS OBLIGATORY

Let us begin with the clearest-cut case, the fifth position. For those who maintain that death is always to be avoided as the absolute enemy, since it is the greatest evil, it is perfectly consistent, perhaps even logically obligatory, to advocate a policy of life extension, even if the pain and suffering that accompany the life extension are very great indeed. After all, nothing—so the argument would go—is worse than death. This position is subject to serious objections, as we saw. In addition, it appears to be an extreme position, rarely found in our society. Hence, there is little prospect that it will provide the basis for the development of a public policy on life extension.

GENERAL RIGHT TO DIE PERMITS LIFE EXTENSION

A more interesting conclusion follows from the first position, the general right to die. The general right to die obtains in all circumstances and the only limiting condition is the presence of conflicting and binding obligations to others. In the absence of that limiting condition, any circumstance or, equally, no circumstance is an occasion for the exercise of the right. It would be consistent for one holding this view to advocate a policy of life extension since, in essence, pain and suffering would be irrelevant to a decision to do so and to a decision—later—to end life. So far, the two extreme positions, that death ought always and that death ought never to fall within the scope of autonomy, are consistent with advocacy of policies favoring life extension.

ACTIVE KILLING PRECLUDES LIFE EXTENSION

The second position, that in favor of beneficent euthanasia, is not consistent with a policy of life extension. Here the difficulty regarding the moral status of pain and suffering in this account asserts itself. We could never be sure, in advance, that the pain and suffering expected to accompany the extension of life would not be worse than death. Consequently, for any such plan of extending life, the advocates of this position would have to maintain:

1. We ought to extend life by x number of years by adopting technology A.
2. Attending the application of technology A will be a certain chance of a certain amount of pain and suffering.
3. That pain and suffering is to be assumed more evil than death.
4. It is obligatory to eliminate such evil, even by killing.
5. Hence, beneficent euthanasia is justifiable, even obligatory.

We would have, on the one hand, a policy of extending life and, on the other, a policy of shortening life. If it is correct—as it seems to be—to interpret beneficent euthanasia as a policy of shortening life, it is plain that there is a contradiction between premises 1 and 5. That is, the position on the moral status of pain and suffering held by the advocates of beneficent euthanasia commits them to holding that longer life is not worth the cost, whether that life were somehow extended or not, since longer life is not more valuable than the evil of pain and suffering.

The problem here is whether premise 3 must be assumed. It seems so. After all, how could we tell how bad the pain and suffering would be in advance? Dare we find out? Better to find ways to end life painlessly and, on the whole, to eliminate pain and suffering before we adopt any life-extending technology. Moreover, what life-extending technology could ever promise convincingly to be free of inevitable pain and suffering? It is this unanswered question, especially, that justifies the inclusion of premise 3. Hence, the understanding of pain and suffering by the second position prohibits its advocates from adopting a policy of extending life by pursuing technologies that might inflict pain and suffering. Because an objective account of pain and suffering cannot be provided by this position, no clear decision procedure can be established on the basis of which one could determine in an objective manner whether or not to adopt a method of life extension that involved pain and suffering.

PASSIVE EUTHANASIA PRECLUDES LIFE EXTENSION

The advocates of benemortasia are not much better off and for the same reason. Their position on extending life can be represented as follows:

1. We ought to extend life by x number of years by adopting technology A.
2. Attending the application of technology A will be a certain chance of a certain amount of pain and suffering.
3. That pain and suffering is to be assumed more evil than death.
4. In the face of such pain and suffering it is justifiable to withdraw life-sustaining *and* even lifesaving (there is no logical reason to exclude this addition) treatment.
5. Hence, benemortasia, passive euthanasia, is permissible, even obligatory.

Here, too, there is an inconsistency. On the one hand, we shall spend enormous effort to extend life; on the other, we shall fail to sustain that very life because of the pain and suffering that accompanies it. This is, in effect, to advocate the lengthening and the shortening of life at once. The third position fails to be consistent with a policy of life extension for the same reason that the second position fails.

It seems that for both positions on the special right to die—that advocating beneficent euthanasia and that advocating benemortasia—it would be logically inconsistent to advocate at the same time a policy of life extension. No clear decision procedure allowing the decision to adopt a life-extending technology involving pain and suffering is available. This is because the end product, extended life, is regarded as less valuable than the evil of pain and suffering that must be absorbed at the cost of that additional life. That is, death is not to be avoided at the cost of pain and suffering, whether that death occurs now or falls within a longer, life span or life expectancy. Furthermore, and here the inconsistency is most plain, a policy of life extension (under the stated presumption) could conceivably be understood as a policy of *inflicting* pain and suffering on people. Such a policy could not be tolerated, logically, by the advocates of either beneficent euthanasia or benemortasia.

ENDURING OF PAIN AND SUFFERING FAVORS LIFE EXTENSION

This leaves the fourth position, which says that, as a rule, pain and suffering ought to be endured for the sake of fuller and broader autonomy. This position has two parts. The first maintains that pain and suffering should, as a rule, be endured. The second deals with the exceptions to this rule, that is, those rare cases where pain and suffering overwhelm us. In such cases, pain and suffering need not be borne. For the second part, the extension of life would be inconsistent under the stated presumption, *but only with an added stipulation*. It would have to be shown that the expected pain and suffering would indeed be overwhelming and not simply present in the application of the technology in question. In the absence of such a demonstration, the technology could consistently be adopted. Doubt concerning the accompanying pain and suffering can be defeated, since overwhelming pain and suffering are rare. Hence, premise 3 in the third and fourth positions need not be adopted, and the root of the previous unclarity is eliminated.

The difference between this position and the two advocating a special right to die is the presumption here in favor of the lesser evil of pain and suffering and the greater value of life. The positions on beneficent euthanasia and benemortasia presume the opposite. They are forced to this stand on the moral status of pain and suffering by their lack of a firm and objective standard for assessing the evil of pain and suffering. This disadvantage does not characterize the position that urges us to endure pain and suffering. Moreover, with the standard of autonomy as the measure of the evil of pain and suffering, it is clear that overwhelming pain and suffering can be assumed to be very rare; it is difficult to defeat our ability and drive to control our lives, particularly to battle pain and suffering and so force them to submit to our will. Therefore, it is not difficult, or impossible, to predict in advance that any life-extending technology would be acceptable vis-à-vis its attendant pain and suffering. Positions lacking an objective standard are unable to predict confidently and so must assume, prudently, that the pain and suffering will be unacceptable.

There is a final point to be made here. The strength of the fourth position turns on the pain and suffering being *accepted*, that is, accepted as inflicted upon us. When that pain and suffering is *sought*, that is, self-inflicted, the argument diminishes in force. There appears to be no moral defense of masochism. The difficulty that remains for this position vis-à-vis life-extending technologies is whether their adoption under the stated presumption—knowing that pain and suffering are part of the package—is a species of masochism. The way out, a way of which I am not yet fully confident, is to argue that what is principally sought is increased life and the opportunity for new experiences and not the pain and suffering. Indeed, the desire for the first two would seem to displace any possible desire for the third. In this way the charge of masochism can be avoided. How this argument is finally to be displayed is not clear. Until it is made clear, however, this position remains open to a serious and perhaps fatal objection, leaving the field only to the extreme representations of the moral status of pain and suffering, the first and fifth positions.

SUMMARY

I have attempted to display what I take to be the basic positions on the moral status of pain, suffering, and death. Further, I have argued that in terms of autonomy in the sense of independence, one position stands out as the most coherent account of autonomy and the moral status of pain and suffering. I then examined the consistency of each view with a policy advocating the adoption of life-extending technologies, under the assumption that such technologies would be accompanied by pain and suffering. The extreme views succeed, two views fail, and the position that I had earlier defended appears to succeed. The extreme views, however, had earlier been shown to be flawed, in their account of either autonomy or the moral status of pain and suffering. So, as a basis for argument concerning the adoption of policies advocating life-extending technologies, there remains only the view that pain and suffering should be endured. Only in such a view is the concept of autonomy most fully embodied. This view is urged, therefore, as the most attractive basis for the discussion of the relative values of avoiding pain and suffering and avoiding death by the adoption of life-extending means.

To show how each of the five positions differ in their implications for policy decisions, we shall consider the following case. It illustrates how, depending on how one assesses the moral status of pain and suffering, one can arrive at quite different responses to the same problem. Suppose it is possible to slow down, and in a significant number of cases to disrupt, the aging process by means of a chemotherapeutic intervention. Suppose, further, that this intervention is accompanied by considerable pain and partial disfigurement, in the form of hair loss. Should we fund research and implementation of this technology?

The first position, that death is never to be absolutely disvalued, leads to the conclusion that it is permissible to commit the funds to this cause. After all, it will add to our experience and enjoyment of the world to live longer than we do at present. The pain and suffering may or may not be relevant; it depends on how bad they become. Of course, more life may turn out to be so much tedium, in which case it would surely not be worth living. It may also not be tedious. In short, one gets no definitive answer on the question from this view.

The fifth position, that life is absolutely to be valued and death disvalued, leads to the conclusion that this technology should be adopted, no matter how horrible the pain and/or suffering caused. Indeed, all life-extending technologies are to be adopted. The difficulty is that this view is indiscriminate; it gives no final guide to choosing *among* methods of life extension—only a method of choosing for them rather than against them.

The second and third positions, beneficent euthanasia and benemortasia, yield similar answers and can be treated together. This technology, so the supposed case goes, will be accompanied by a certain chance of some pain and suffering. But how bad will that suffering be? That depends on your view of pain and suffering. Since neither position provides a final, objective basis for assessing the moral status of such pain and suffering, one must, out of prudence, conclude that the technology might not be permissible. It is certainly not preferable to a technology that is free of pain and suffering. The technology in question might be acceptable; it might not. In short, no clear decision is forthcoming. What these positions seem to suggest is that it would be permissible to invest in the development of this technology to the point where the pain and suffering become intolerable. But one cannot say in advance what that point will be; it may be reached quickly or not at all. Hence, these positions, like the first, give no final guidelines for this or similar cases. They do help us, though, in deciding among classes of life-extending means. Those that will be free of pain and suffering will be permitted. Better, then, to invest uniformly in these. This will, of course, require sacrificing very promising means of extending life that happen to involve pain and suffering.

The fourth position does not suffer this ambivalence. According to this view, there are two classes of life-extending technologies. The first are accompanied by overwhelming pain and suffering, and death is to be avoided only at the cost of finally compromising our autonomy. These are not to be pursued. The second class includes all technologies accompanied by less than overwhelming pain and suffering and those free of pain and suffering. These can be adopted. The case considered here appears to fall within the latter class. The pain and suffering will be bad, but endurable, and they will accompany a technology that will expand the scope of our autonomy by bringing the aging process under our control. Hence, one can decide clearly to adopt and fund this and similar life-extending methods.

It is important to emphasize again the distinct advantage of this position: It provides a clear decision procedure for choosing among life-extending technologies, as well as grounds for choosing for or against such technologies. The only kind of case that remains involves competition between life-extending technologies and other technologies, especially those that relieve pain. Consider, for example, the following. By investing large sums of public moneys, the government could develop and install air (crash) bags in all automobiles in this country. This action, studies show, would save 5000 lives annually. On the other hand, this same sum of money could be invested in a program to relieve those stricken with arthritis, thus relieving the suffering of one million people annually, but saving no lives. On the view I advocated, the pain and suffering to be relieved are not as great an evil as the death to be avoided by the use of air bags. Arthritis is a minor, if persistent, diminution of autonomy; death is the final and extreme one. Hence, the funds should be spent on the air bags, with consequent results for life extension through avoiding accidental death in automobiles. If the choice is between life-extending technologies and other technologies designed principally to relieve pain and suffering, where the pain and suffering to be relieved are not overwhelming, the choice will be for life extension. Overwhelming minimizations of autonomy are to be avoided; the rest are to be endured.

The claim of death on us as a society is that death is the final and irreversible minimizing of autonomy. Thus, it is clearly reasonable to invest in life-extension programs. But pain and suffering can also, though not as a rule, minimize our autonomy to the point that death appears to be the only way to avoid that minimization. It is this evil of pain and suffering, determined on objective grounds, that serves as a moral constraint on policy regarding life extension. These constraints are most clearly appreciated from the position that pain and suffering are, as a rule, to be endured. I offer this position, therefore, as the basis for discussing public policy regarding life-extending technologies.

NOTES

1. H. T. Engelhardt, Jr., "Ethical Issues in Aiding the Death of Young Children," in *Beneficent Euthanasia*, ed. M. Kohl (Buffalo, N.Y.: Prometheus Books, 1975), p. 182.
2. H. T. Engelhardt, Jr., "Ethical Issues in Aiding the Death of Young Children," passim.
3. M. Kohl, "Voluntary Beneficent Euthanasia," in *Beneficient Euthanasia*, ed. M. Kohl (Buffalo, N. Y.: Prometheus Books, 1975).
4. Seneca, "On Suicide," from *Epistula Morales*, in *Moral Problems in Medicine*, ed. S. Gorovitz (Englewood Cliffs, N. J.: Prentice-Hall, 1976), p. 376.
5. D. Boeyink, "Pain and Suffering," *Journal of Religious Ethics* 2 (1974):86.
6. See A. Guyton, *Textbook of Medical Physiology* (Philadelphia: W. B. Saunders and Co., 1976), pp. 662–664.
7. Ibid. The other portion of the feedback loop is evidenced when action is taken to remove or eliminate the source of the pain or to alleviate its intensity.
8. This is contradistinct to the views apparently maintained by D. Bakan, *Disease, Pain, and Sacrifice* (Chicago: The University of Chicago Press, 1968).

9. D. Boeyink, "Pain and Suffering," p. 86.

10. This could be process, state, or whatever. The point is that minds do indeed experience pain, typically as a result of bodily change. Whether one wants to call pain a mental state, process, or whatever, is not, for present purposes, a central issue.

11. D. Boeyink, "Pain and Suffering," p. 87.

12. D. Bakan, *Disease, Pain, and Sacrifice*, p. 68.

13. I. Lieb, "The Image of Man in Medicine," *Journal of Medicine and Philosophy* 1 (June 1976): 172.

14. S. Hauerwas, *Vision and Virtue* (Notre Dame, Ind.: Fides Press, 1974), p. 96.

15. D. Browning, "The Privacy of Feelings," *The Southern Journal of Philosophy* 3 (Spring 1965): 55.

16. Ibid., Browning's emphasis.

17. A. Guyton, *Textbook of Medical Physiology*, p. 664.

18. D. Boeyink, "Pain and Suffering," p. 87.

19. D. Bakan, *Disease, Pain, and Sacrifice*, p. 61, emphasis added. "Telos" denotes the unifying principle of personal life.

20. P. Ramsey, *The Patient as Person* (New Haven, Conn.: Yale University Press, 1970).

21. G. Dworkin, "Autonomy and Behavior Control," *Hastings Center Report* 6 (February 1976): 23–28.

22. Seneca, "On Suicide," p. 376.

23. H. T. Engelhardt, Jr., "Ethical Issues in Aiding the Death of Young Children," p. 186. Engelhardt's emphasis.

24. M. Kohl, "Voluntary Beneficent Euthanasia," pp. 130–141.

25. A. Dyck, "Beneficent Euthanasia and Benemortasia: Alternate Views of Mercy," in *Beneficent Euthanasia*, ed. M. Kohl (Buffalo, N. Y.: Prometheus Books, 1975), pp. 117–129.

26. M. Kohl, "Voluntary Beneficent Euthanasia," p. 125.

27. M. Kohl et al., "A Plea for Beneficent Euthanasia," in *Beneficent Euthanasia*, ed. M. Kohl, p. 234.

28. M. Kohl, "Voluntary Beneficent Euthanasia," p. 133.

29. What must be assumed by anyone who makes such an argument is the correctness of the distinction between acting and refraining. One must be able to show a morally relevant difference between active and passive euthanasia. This complicated issue cannot be taken up here. Its importance for the success of this position, however, cannot be overstated.

30. A. Dyck, "Beneficent Euthanasia and Benemortasia: Alternate Views of Mercy," p. 121.

31. Ibid., p. 125.

32. D. Boeyink, "Pain and Suffering," p. 90.

33. H. T. Engelhardt, Jr., "The Counsels of Finitude," in *Death Inside Out*, ed. P. Steinfels and R. Veatch (New York: Harper & Row, 1975), pp. 115–128.

III

NATURAL DEATH
AND DYING

Natural Death: A History of
Religions Perspective

FRANK E. REYNOLDS

The obvious empirical fact that human life ends in death has been a
focus for reflection in all kinds of cultures—primitive, Western, and
Eastern. In many cases such reflection has led to the development of
mythical and philosophical conceptions that affirm that "in the beginning" human beings were either actually or potentially immortal,
but that mortality became the destiny of men through the actions of
a divine being, through a primordial happenstance, or through an
action taken by the mythical ancestors. In other cases, however,
such reflections have led to the quite different conclusion that mortality has been man's natural fate from the outset.

DEATH AND THE HUMAN CONDITION

In primitive traditions, the emphasis on a lost immortality has
been expressed in many diverse ways. In a fascinating study of
mythologies of death, which focuses on African traditions but takes
into account materials from primitive religions in India, Indonesia,
and the South Sea Islands as well, Hans Abrahamsson has provided
a variety of examples.[1] In many of the myths, divine beings play an
important role by setting in motion the process through which death
becomes established in the world; in certain instances they actually

introduce death, often as a punishment for a religious or moral transgression. In other instances death is introduced through an event characterized primarily by its absurdity. The most common of all African myths concerning the origin of death recounts that in "in the beginning" God sent two messengers, one a chameleon whose task was to bring the word that men would be immortal, and the other a lizard whose task was to inform men that they would be subject to death; as it happened, the chameleon tarried along the way, the lizard arrived first, and from that time forward death became the natural fate of men. In still other cases, death is introduced by a demon or death-being against whom an unsuccessful struggle was waged. But whether emphasizing a divine action, an event of transparent absurdity, or the victory of a being who personifies death, these accounts all reflect a strong nostalgia for the condition or possibility of immortality that has been lost.

In many primitive mythologies, the mythical ancestors play the primary role in bringing death into the world. Sometimes they bring death because of their weakness—for example, their inability to maintain a prohibition against sleep. Sometimes they do so because of their ignorance—for example, they make an uninformed choice or strike a bargain whose full consequences they do not recognize. Sometimes they bring death upon themselves and their progeny by committing a basic moral transgression such as making a vengeful attack on a relative. In some cases they make a conscious decision to accept life-with-death rather than another possible mode of existence; they choose a life that includes death but also the propagation of offspring rather than one without death but also without sexuality or descendants.[2] Like the myths that emphasize a divine action, a primordial happenstance, or the victory of a personified form of death, those that focus on the actions and choices of the ancestors also reflect a certain nostalgia for the immortal condition or its possibility, which pertained at the beginning of time. But in these myths, particularly those that depict a conscious human choice, the attitudes are often profoundly ambivalent, and in some cases even suggest a positive valorization of human mortality. Abrahamsson devotes one entire chapter to a consideration of myths in which men desire death, including accounts in which death appears in the world because men seek relief from disease and old age, become bored with the routine of existence, or fear the imminent threat of over-population.

In spite of the preponderance of primitive myths affirming that in the beginning men were immortal or had the possibility of immortality, the alternative perspective is not completely absent. Leo Frobenius has recorded a Kasai myth that clearly affirms that from the very beginning death was a necessary and integral aspect of the human condition. It is interesting to note that the myth further asserts that without the presence of death, life would lose its zest and meaning.[3]

In the so-called higher cultures in the Western and Eastern worlds, these two major perspectives concerning the origins of death appear in clearly recognizable forms. The idea that mankind has lost an original capacity for immortality is, of course, basic to all three of the Abrahamic traditions (Judaism, Christianity, and Islam). All of them share, though with significantly different interpretations, the ancient Israelite mythology that gives a preeminent place to the story of Adam and Eve and includes other mythic episodes conveying a similar message of a primordial transgression and a divinely prescribed punishment of mortality.[4]

This kind of interpretation is also present in the religious traditions of the Eastern world, particularly in India. Consider the intriguing myth preserved in the vast Hindu epic, the Mahabharata. In the beginning, the great God Brahma created the world and generated beings to populate it who were not subject to death. Soon, however, the number of beings had increased to the extent that no one was able to breathe; what is more, the goddess of the earth was beginning to sink down into chaos. Unable to find a solution, Brahma became frustrated; his frustration gave way to wrath, and this wrath produced a great conflagration that destroyed the entire cosmos. At the behest of the god Siva, who pleaded the cause of the unfortunate beings who had been killed, Brahma repressed his anger and restored them to life. But, in order to prevent a recurrence of the problem that had caused his frustration, he provided that all of those who were born should also die. From the pores of his body the goddess of death appeared and, after a long period of asceticism, during which she cultivated the necessary detachment, she took up her task of preserving the world by bringing to an end the lives of those whose time had come. Moreover, in order to assure that the goddess of death would bear no guilt for her actions, Brahma instructed her to inflict each of her victims with desirous attachments and the sinful wrath that comes with the loss of worldly pleasures.[5]

The "higher" cultures of both East and West also provide many prominent conceptions of death as an original and necessary aspect of the human mode of being. This understanding of the essential and inevitable relationship between human nature and death has been articulated with great poignancy in the wisdom literature of the ancient Near East, has received classical biblical expression in the Book of Ecclesiastes, and is even reflected in a few passages in the Koran.[6] It has appeared in very different forms in the philosophical traditions of the Graeco-Roman world (for example among the Epicureans and the Stoics) where, in some cases, the natural necessity of death was not only recognized but extolled. Among biological and medical theorists in the tradition of Aristotle, Galen, and Avicenna, a closely related conception of natural death constituted an assumption that went practically unchallenged.[7] In the modern Western world this kind of perspective has come to the fore not only among philosophers but in the popular consciousness as well.[8]

In India and China, too, there has been strong emphasis on the essential and inevitable link between human nature and death. In India, classical philosophical traditions of Hinduism such as Vedanta and Samkhya, as well as the mainstream of Buddhist thought, have been dominated by a cosmic vision in which life and death are two aspects of the same process; this process is conceived as a painful cycle of birth and death in which men have been entrapped from the very beginning.[9]

In China, man's full involvement in the perennial cosmic process of alternation between life and death has been consistently affirmed, though in the Chinese context the understanding has been more "this-worldly" and humane, and the evaluation more positive. Among the Confucians, for example, the most common goal has been the acceptance of the implications of human finitude with equanimity, whereas in certain versions of philosophical Taoism (notably in the thought of Chuang Tzu), man's participation in the process has, on occasion, been affirmed with almost lyric enthusiasm.[10]

THE POSTPONEMENT OF PHYSICAL DEATH

The recognition that physical death either came into man's life by virtue of a primordial event or is an inseparable aspect of his nature is common to practically all religious and cultural traditions. However, this recognition has seldom been taken to imply that death should be passively accepted. On the contrary, in every viable society about which we have any knowledge, efforts to ward off or postpone death have played an important role.

Again, there are two typologically different conceptions. The first distinguishes the ultimate cause of death from the proximate causes that determine the mode and timing of its appearance in each instance. By mitigating the latter, a *temporary* postponement of death is possible. In the second conception, this distinction between causes is not made or considered relevant. The ultimate cause of death can be mitigated or obviated in such a way that a more or less *permanent* postponement of death is possible. Although the boundary lines between the two perspectives may sometimes be blurred, the typology helps organize many diverse kinds of materials.

The perspective distinguishing and focusing on death's proximate causes and seeking, by counteracting these, to postpone death temporarily, is socially and culturally universal. Thus, the ways in which various proximate causes have been conceptualized, interrelated, and dealt with are fantastically variegated. But in spite of the great amount of obvious diversity most of the major themes can be discussed under three rubrics—namely, physiological causes and correlated medical and alchemical practices, magical causes and magical means of defense, and religio-ethical causes and religio-ethical activities deemed supportive of life.

The recognition that at some level certain physiological factors operate as causes of death is self-evident, and all types of societies attempt to mitigate these by basically physiological means. Though little attention has been given to the physiological conceptions and medical practices of primitive peoples, there are enough casual references in the ethnological literature to suggest that efforts are

made to prolong life through proper diet, the use of natural herbs
and drugs, the proper physical treatment of sickness and injury, and
so on. And certainly each of the great classical traditions has
developed its own style of medical practice and has perceived the
medical task as involving prolongation of life.[11]

Certain alchemical and related traditions carried the concern to
postpone death by influencing its proximate physiological causes
much further. Taoist adepts in China tried to do this by purifying
the body and by producing and absorbing vitalizing substances. In
the medieval Western world, Roger Bacon argued vigorously that
through contacting a perfectly purified substance such as gold or the
renowned philosopher's stone, or by ingesting substances in which
the vital principle or innate moisture of living things was concentrated, a man could be freed from the ravages of old age and his span of
vital life extended by a century or more.

In most human societies, magical influences have also been
recognized as an important cause of individual deaths. Mircea
Eliade has maintained that the predominant conviction among
primitive peoples is "that man, though no longer immortal, could
live indefinitely if only a hostile agent did not put an end to his life."
He goes on to explain, "As the ancestors lost their immortality
through accident or demonic plot, so a man presently dies as he falls
victim to magic, ghosts or other supernatural aggressors."[12] Thus, in
most primitive societies shamans and other practitioners ward off
evil forces in order (among other things) to protect the community
from death and, more specifically, to postpone death of their
patrons. Moreover, the belief that life can be extended by warding
off the evil influences of magic and demonic spirits has persisted in
both Eastern and Western cultures up to the present time. The
officiants and other representatives of each of the great religious
traditions such as Christianity, Islam, and Buddhism have devised
various rituals and chants specifically designed to serve this purpose;
local practitioners on the fringes of these great traditions have
provided similar services often recognized as even more potent and
effective. Even today, right in the centers of modern, supposedly
rationalist culture, the belief that men's lives are threatened by
magical forces persists in many quarters, as does belief in the
efficacy of magic to ward them off.[13]

If, in many cultures, wrongful or religiously inappropriate

actions have been identified as the ultimate cause of the entrance of death into the world, proper ethical and religious actions have been identified as effective means for postponing death. In various theistic contexts in primitive cultures, in the Western world and in India, a proper relationship with the deity has been considered a key element in preserving health and postponing death. Through proper obedience and/or devotion, the wrath of the deity may be averted and his protection assured. Similarly, in the less theistic or nontheistic religions of the East, acting in harmony with the cosmic law (Dharma, Tao, and others) is commonly advocated as the most appropriate means of warding off death. Even in a supposedly otherworldly religion like Theravada Buddhism, proper ethical and religious action is considered efficacious; for example, the acquisition of merit through venerating the Buddha or giving alms, the accumulation of positive karma through proper moral behavior, and the avoidance of the destructive karma generated by immoral action, are all invoked as effective means of delaying man's encounter with death.

These are basically individualistic ways to utilize ethical and religious actions in the struggle against death, yet a more social or communal emphasis has also been prominent. In a number of traditions, it is simply assumed that, when a community maintains a proper relationship to its god or to the cosmic order, the well-being of its members (including their prospects for longevity) is increased. Particularly intriguing and explicit is a pattern of beliefs developed in the Indian traditions and especially in Buddhism. When the moral and religious condition of the community is strong, the gods are beneficent: the rains fall at the appropriate time, the earth is productive, the plants produce medicines that are effective, and the life span of men becomes marvelously long. But when religion declines and immorality runs rampant, the gods grow angry, the rains do not fall at the proper time, the earth becomes barren, the medicines the plants produce are no longer potent, and the life span of men becomes horrendously short. Thus, the myths clearly suggest, if society improves the religious and moral quality of its life, the death of its members may be postponed and their chances for longevity greatly enhanced.[14]

Man's perennial concern with evading death has, in certain times and places, led to a second and quite different perspective.

Within the history of religions, a number of conceptions make no significant distinction between ultimate and proximate causes, and the more or less permanent postponement of death is recognized as a possibility, at least for a few selected individuals.

One major theme from this perspective involves the simple maintenance of ordinary physical life. In some cases, this maintenance of life is acquired through heroic deeds or is granted to heroic figures by divine intervention; we have the indefinite postponement of death attained by the semi-divine Herakles of the Greek tradition, by Utanapischtim, the Mesopotamian hero of the deluge, and by Enoch and Elijah in biblical tradition. But in other cases, an indefinite maintenance of life is associated with the adoption of a radically different style of living; certain Taoists in China believed that if one performed no personal actions out of harmony with the natural cosmic order (Tao), no personal energy would be expended, no vital force lost. Life would remain undiminished and death would never occur.[15]

A second major theme is continual rejuvenation. Its most famous expression involves the search for a fountain of youth that provides the waters of life through which full vitality can be restored.[16] But many other traditions might also be cited. The pre-Christian Celts recounted stories of a Land of Youth where one might be continuously rejuvenated by certain foods or a magic cauldron; many ancient Chinese believed that death-preventing mushrooms could be obtained in the Islands of the Blessed. In India, numerous stories tell of men's youth being restored by the transfer of magical power from a saint, the magical transfer of life from one mortal to another, living in a particular holy place, or hearing the recitation of an especially sacred text.[17]

Finally, certain ancient Chinese traditions have maintained that permanent postponement of death can be obtained through the transmutation of the mortal body into a more subtle physical body not subject to decay or degeneration. Joseph Needham has recently suggested that the massive efforts of many successive generations of Chinese to find immortality derived from a unique set of religious and historical circumstances. When the idea of immortality entered the Chinese consciousness, probably from an Indian or Central Asian source, it confronted a world view in which other-worldly realms were neither conceivable nor desired; furthermore, the conception of man's being as constituted by two or more souls whose unity was absolutely dependent on the continued presence of the physical body, was firmly established.[18] The foreign ideas concerning immortality were then domesticated into the specifically Chinese "cult of the *hsien*," in which the goal of physical immortality was zealously sought.[19] However one may evaluate this historical argument, it is clear that the ancient Chinese developed a marvelous array of sophisticated respiratory, dietary, gymnastic, sexual, alchemical, and correlated religio-ethical techniques aimed at transmutating their mortal bodies. Moreover, these techniques, originally aimed at attaining an almost ethereal mode of existence in the natural world, eventually assumed a popularized form intended to extend the more mundane aspects of normal social experience indefinitely.[20]

DEATH AND HUMAN FULFILLMENT

The belief that human fulfillment should be sought through the indefinite postponement of physical death has appeared on the periphery of a variety of cultures and, has come to occupy a very central position in the particular case of ancient China. However, throughout history, most men have adopted a very different attitude, one emphasizing a distinction between deaths that constitute a serious affront to human nature and those that do not. In addition to the more or less descriptive ambiance of natural death, then, there is also a more normative ambiance.

In focusing on the normative distinction between unnatural and natural deaths, the notion of cultural models of a meaningful life or life cycle immediately comes to the fore. Such models exist in every significant social group; a death that destroys the possibility of living out a relevant model is unnatural and abhorrent, whereas one that culminates or follows the realization of such a model is natural and at least minimally acceptable. Obviously, the identification of particular deaths as either natural or unnatural is often difficult and sometimes impossible, not only because there are degrees involved in the realization of cultural and personal goals, but also because in each society there are a variety of relevant models. Still, this distinction seems to have been recognized in one way or another in all types of human societies.[21]

In virtually all societies, premature death due to disease or to arbitrary and adventitious violence has been considered the preeminent form of unnatural death. To be sure, each group has made an effort to account for such deaths within its own system of meaning. In many primitive societies—and in many "advanced" ones as well—such deaths are attributed to witchcraft and sorcery. In theistic milieus, such as those provided by Judaism, Christianity, and Islam (and to some extent by Hinduism as well), these deaths may be explained as the inscrutable will of the deity or as a mode of divine punishment for sin. In the Confucian environment in China such deaths were often attributed simply to an arbitrary and incomprehensible fate. In the Hindu and Buddhist contexts they may be understood as the inevitable working out of the law of karmic retribution. For example, a Thai Buddhist text that Mani Reynolds and I have just translated discusses four ways of death, two occurring when a man's life span is completed and two occurring in a clearly unnatural manner. In both instances of unnatural death, the ultimate cause is identified in karmic terms. In the case of an undramatic death that occurs when a person "ought not to die," the root cause is identified as the premature exhaustion of the relatively positive "reproductive" karma that gave rise to the particular life. In the case of a violent or accidental death, the cause is a special kind of "destructive" karma that the individual generated through heinous deeds committed during his lifetime or in a previous existence.[22] As interesting as the diversity of cultural explanations is the fact that at another level there has been another kind of response; in almost all traditional societies there has been widespread belief that because the natural human aspirations of the prematurely deceased individual have been frustrated, his soul or spirit is likely to be angry and must be propitiated lest it return and vent its hostility in the land of the living.[23]

In contrast to unnatural deaths characterized by the negation of basic human potentialities, deaths that are recognized as natural assume the realization of a cultural or religious model of human fulfillment. In each case there is a common understanding that, if an individual lives his life properly and fully, his death is divested of its negative meaning and its destructive power. However, the specific forms and contents of the various models are as diverse as the societies that have produced and maintained them.

Though premature deaths due to illness and arbitrary or adventitious violence have been considered the most unnatural deaths, early death and unnatural death cannot be simply equated—consider the cases of the Huron Indian or Japanese samurai warriors who die as heroes, or of the Hindu ascetics who, after attaining an experience of enlightenment, go off to the Himalayas to die.[24] On the other hand, the great majority of cultural models that have led to the attainment of normatively natural deaths have involved at least the completion of what the society considered an ordinary life span. Thus W. Lloyd Warner describes the Australian aborigines' conception of the life cycle of the male members of the tribe as a process in which birth is a fall from a preexisting state of pure spirituality, childhood is a period of completely profane and unspiritual existence, the adult individual becomes more ritualized and sacred as he moves toward death, and death is the reattainment of a purely sacred and spiritual mode of being. [25] To cite another primitive example, in Malakula it is assumed that a full lifetime is required to gain a proper knowledge of the realm of the dead and to make the vast number of sacrifices necessary to generate sufficient spiritual power to assure a proper postmortem existence.[26] Probably the best known example of a fully articulated life cycle is that of classical Hinduism, according to which the major segment of a man's life is divided into a stage of studentship, a stage of household responsibilities, which comes to an end when he "sees that his skin is wrinkled and his hair is white and sees the son of his sons" (Manu 6:2), and two subsequent stages specifically devoted to increasingly austere preparations for death. Finally, in our own time, Erik Erikson has developed an extremely influential conception of the life cycle that involve eight different stages of development. The cycle culminates in a stage in which the individual builds on all the previous stages to achieve a kind of integrity and transcendence that can divest death of its destructive force.

Various religious and cultural traditions have also generated ways of understanding the specific actions through which a normatively natural death is achieved and what it involves. Perhaps the most common view has emphasized the acquisition of an attitude in which a man identifies himself and his destiny with a more or less empirical reality transcending his own individual ego. This perspective often enjoins the sublimation of personal aspirations in the life of a community—sometimes the family, sometimes the nation or people (as in much of the Judaic tradition and, with different connotations, in contemporary Maoist thought), and sometimes the human community as a whole. In still other cases, this perspective has emphasized an identification with the cosmic order itself. In the ancient Hindu Brahmanas, men are enjoined to follow a regimen of ritual practices designed to culminate in the identification of various aspects of their being with their cosmic counterparts—that is, the eye with the sun, the breath with the wind, and so on. In certain phases of the Taoist tradition in China and the Buddhist tradition in Japan, the goal has been to slough off false ideas of the individualized ego and realize true identity with the Cosmic Tao or the Buddha Nature that constitutes the true reality of all things.[27]

A second common way of understanding how a natural death can be obtained affirms the effectiveness of religious and ethical action in achieving a favorable rebirth. In certain primitive traditions and among the Chinese this view has included the belief in postmortem existence as an ancestor whose continued vitality is maintained by the veneration and offerings of his descendents. In other cases, notably but not exclusively in various primitive contexts as well as in Hinduism and Buddhism, the emphasis has been on the attainment of a temporary rebirth in a heavenly realm or a rebirth in a favorable position in the human world. On the other hand, in a number of orientations, including especially Christianity, Islam, and certain forms of theistic Hinduism and Pure Land Buddhism, the goal has been conceived in terms of a permanent resurrection or rebirth in the Kingdom of God, a Buddha Land, or a similar kind of paradise.

Finally, a third mode of understanding how a natural death can be achieved involves beliefs and practices aimed at freeing man from his bondage to existence, and attaining immortality. In the West, this kind of view has been associated with Plato and with certain phases of the Gnostic tradition, in which it is held that each man possesses an immortal soul that can be set free from his mortal body. In the Eastern world, it has developed in one way in the Upanishadic and Vedantic literature of Hinduism. Here, the key element is the recognition of the identity between the true being inherent in every man (the Atman) and the ultimate reality, which is unchangeable and immortal (the Brahman). Indian Buddhism has developed still another way; the crucial affirmations have been that the soul (the Atman) has no real existence and that immortality or nirvana may be experienced by those who practice the "path of action," which is grounded in this insight. Within these various perspectives it is sometimes said that the goal of immortality may be obtained in the midst of life, and that physical death is thereby divested of all its negative meaning and power.[28] In other cases—for example in the Phaedo and the Tibetan Book of the Dead—the moment of physical death is seen as the occasion when those who have properly prepared for the attainment of immortality enjoy a unique opportunity to achieve the final breakthrough.

SOME POSSIBLE IMPLICATIONS

In the great majority of traditions we have considered, man's struggle against death has involved aspects of the human endeavor that, in our modern modes of thought and forms of social and professional organization, have come to be divided into a number of carefully isolated segments, notably into two segments labelled religion and medicine, along with a third intermediate kind of practice called psychotherapy. It is perhaps true that in the struggle to postpone death, the medical aspects have traditionally been in the foreground, but we have noted the important presence of religious dimensions as well. Similarly, in the struggle to achieve a normatively natural death, the religious aspects have been especially prominent—but it is also true that medical efforts to maintain health and acquire longevity have been recognized as an integral and necessary part of the total process. I am well aware of the considerable leap that is required to move from recognition of historical interdependence between religion and medicine in the struggle against death to any policy decisions that recognize the need for more contemporary cooperation between the two associated professions; however, the possibilities that might be realized as a result of such a leap deserve more serious attention than they ordinarily receive.

My second observation, not unrelated to the first, is that the two major modes of man's struggle against death—the efforts to postpone it and the efforts to achieve a normatively natural death—have, in the great majority of traditions, been perceived as mutually supportive. On the one hand, the postponement of death has been at least partially justified as providing a more extended life span during which to pursue the goal of a normatively natural death. On the other hand, most of the practices and attainments associated with efforts to achieve a normatively natural death have been recognized as supportive of longevity as well. There need be no conflict between contemporary proponents of medical efforts to secure a meaningful prolongation of life on the one hand, and contemporary proponents of natural death on the other.

Finally, I would like to recount a myth that presents a kind of eschatological vision in which some of the complexities inherent in the relationship between the postponement of death and the achievement of a normatively natural death are recognized and then resolved in a fascinating and highly suggestive synthesis. Composed in northern Thailand, probably in the late fifteenth century, this myth has traditionally been recited at an important annual festival closely associated with the popular hope that in the future another Buddha—the Buddha Maitreya—will come into the world and establish an ideal society.[29] According to the myth, the Future Buddha, asked about the time of his coming, responds by describing the cycle of degeneration and renewal to which human society is subject. Because of the evil propensities of men, he declares, society will become more and more degenerate in every respect, and the life span of men will decrease from the present one hundred years all the way down to ten. (As the account proceeds, the listener or reader at first suspects that Maitreya will make his descent into the world at this point, but he does not and the prophecy continues.) Following a terrible period of viciousness and destruction— a tiny remnant of people repent of their evil ways; they begin to practice morality and meditation; as a result, the conditions of life improve and the life span gradually increases. As time goes on, the process accelerates, and men's lives become filled with joy and happiness, diseases are virtually eliminated, and the life span becomes so marvelously extended that the reality of old age and death, as well as the causes of death, are all but forgotten. (Again the listener or reader suspects that Maitreya may now make his descent into the world, but again he fails to do so and the prophecy continues.) As men become accustomed to this paradisiacal mode of existence, their forgetfulness concerning the cause of sickness and death leads to a decline in the practice of morality and meditation; disease and death again make their appearance and the life span begins to decrease. As the decline proceeds, however, a certain situation is reached in which, though life is still very long (80,000 years is the figure given!), satisfying, and full, disease and death are sufficiently imminent that men again begin to contemplate their cause; they become aware of the true character of existence and open to the possibility of breaking completely out of its cycle and attaining the even higher goal of nirvana. It is at this point, Maitreya announces, that he will make his entrance into the world, preach his Message, and establish the Ideal Society.

NOTES

1. H. Abrahamsson, *The Origin of Death: Studies in African Mythology* (Uppsala: Studia Ethnographica Uppsaliensia, 1951).
2. For a fascinating discussion of this theme as it is expressed in the Indonesian myth of the ancestors' choice between the stone and the banana, see M. Eliade, "Mythologies of Death: An Introduction" in *Religious Encounters with Death: Studies in the History and Anthropology of Religion,* ed. F. Reynolds and E. Waugh (University Park, Penn.: Pennsylvania State University Press, 1977).
3. H. Abrahamsson, *The Origin of Death: Studies in African Mythology,* p. 73.
4. For an excellent discussion see W. Hermann, "Human Mortality as a Problem in Ancient Israel," trans. J. Price, in *Religious Encounters with Death: Studies in the History and Anthropology of Religion.*
5. This myth is more fully recounted and interpreted in J. Long, "Death as Necessity and Gift in Hindu Mythology," in *Religious Encounters with Death: Studies in the History and Anthropology of Religion.*
6. For the Koranic references see A. Welch, "Death and Dying in the Qur'an," in *Religious Encounters with Death: Studies in the History and Anthropology of Religion.*
7. See the discussion of the Graeco-Roman philosophers and the biological and medical theorists in G. Gruman, *A History of Ideas about the Prolongation of Life* (Philadelphia: American Philosophical Society, 1966).
8. An interesting discussion that draws on the history of Western philosophy but focuses on the "post-Christian" position of Hegel is presented by H. T. Engelhardt in "The Counsels of Finitude," in *Death Inside Out,* ed. P. Steinfels and R. Veatch (Harper & Row, 1975), pp. 115–128. The emergence of the dominant modern view and its popularization is traced in a rather flamboyant way in I. Illich, "The Political Uses of Natural Death," in *Death Inside Out,* pp. 25–42, and with greater historical sensitivity and focus on the American scene in G. Davidson, "In Search of Paradigms: Death and Destiny in Seventeenth Century

North America," in *Religious Encounters with Death: Studies in the History and Anthropology of Religion.*

9. These traditions are discussed in the chapters on the orthodox and heterodox philosophies of India in F. Holck, ed., *Death and Eastern Thought,* (Nashville: Abingdon Press, 1974).

10. For a more extended discussion see F. Reynolds, "Death and Eastern Thought," in *Encyclopedia of Bioethics* (New York: Macmillan, 1978).

11. Writers who are better informed on the subject than I have maintained that in the West, for example, the idea of prolonging life did not enter into the practice of medicine until the early modern period. (See I. Illich, "The Political Uses of Natural Death," in *Death Inside Out,* pp. 25–42). However, the difference may be terminological; whereas the practitioners of the older medicine in the West (and in various primitive and Eastern traditions as well) may not have claimed or striven to postpone death for those "whose time had come," they certainly did conceive of their task as one of postponing deaths that might, apart from their intervention, have come prematurely.

12. M. Eliade, "Mythologies of Death: An Introduction," in *Religious Encounters with Death: Studies in the History and Anthropology of Religion.* Those who refer to this passage should observe that whereas Eliade employs the term *natural death* in his discussion, he gives it a quite different connotation than we have chosen to emphasize; in his discussion it is quite clear that he is contrasting deaths attributed to natural causes with deaths attributed to supernatural causes.

13. In a more extended discussion of the modern situation, it would be interesting to consider the appropriateness of including among the successors of the traditional shamans and magicians not only peripheral cults and idiosyncratic beliefs, but also the various psychoanalytic and psychotherapeutic traditions that play such a central role in the modern cultural experience.

14. One version of this myth is recounted in *Dika Malai Deva Sut* (Bangkok: Thambanakhan Press, 1971).

15. This interpretation of the relevant texts depends on the translation of the Chinese term *wu wei* as "no action out of harmony with the Tao" rather than as simply "nonaction." On this point see J. Needham, *Science and Civilization in China,* Vol. II (Cambridge: Cambridge University Press, 1956), pp. 68–70.

16. See E. Hopkins, "The Fountain of Youth," *Journal of the American Oriental Society* 26 (1905): 1–67.

17. In these cases, the distinction between a temporary and a permanent postponement of death is not made; however, since the rejuvenation can presumably be repeated, it seemed appropriate to include references to them at this point in the discussion.

18. This latter conception is dealt with in detail by D. Smith in "Chinese Conceptions of the Soul," *Numen: International Review for the History of Religions* 5 (1958): 166–179.

19. J. Needham, *Science and Civilization in China,* vol. 5, part 2 (Cambridge: Cambridge University Press, 1974), pp. 71 ff. It is perhaps not inappropriate to call attention to the fact that the distinctive religio-historical factors to which Needham attributes the rise of beliefs and techniques concerning physical immortality in ancient China have quite obvious parallels in the modern Western context.

Note the presence of conceptions of immortality and resurrection derived in this case not from a foreign source, but from our own philosophical and religious heritage—the dominance of a world view in which other-worldly realms have no meaningful place, a conception of the human person that makes it all but impossible to conceive of the continuation of an individual's life apart from the preservation of his physical body. Each of these points is explicitly emphasized in R. Veatch's defense of the contemporary search for physical immortality in "Natural Death and Public Policy," in *Death, Dying, and the Biological Revolution* (New Haven, Conn.: Yale University Press, 1976).

20. For an excellent discussion of these two modes of physical immortality and their interaction see Ying Shih-Yu, "Life and Immortality in Han China," *Harvard Journal of Asiatic Studies* 24 (1964–65): 80–122. Those who refer to this article will observe that in contrast to Needham, who uses the terms *other-worldly* and *this-worldly* to distinguish non-Chinese views such as those of Indian Buddhism and Christianity from the indigenous Chinese perspective, Ying Shih-Yu uses these same categories to differentiate the more ethereal ideal sought after by the early Chinese recluses from the more mundane conceptions of physical immortality later disseminated at the popular level.

21. It should be noted that the two types are not exhaustive, and that there are deaths that do not fit into either category—for example, the death of a retarded child not capable of realizing the basic life model of his culture, the death of an old man who has missed his opportunity to realize this model, and so on.

22. See the section "Kamma and the Process of Death" in the chapter "The Realm of Men" in F. Reynolds and M. Reynolds, trans., *The Three Worlds of King Ruang* (Berkeley: Berkeley Research Publications, 1979).

23. In this connection it is interesting to note that there are certain traditions in which the tendency to propitiate spirits of this kind sometimes leads to their establishment as more permanent local deities. For a myriad of examples see the discussions in W. Elmore, "Dravidian Gods in Modern Hinduism," *University Studies*, 15, no. 1 (Lincoln, Neb.: University of Nebraska Press, 1915), and H. Whitehead, *The Village Gods of South India*, 2d ed., rev. and enl. (Delhi: Sumit Publications, 1976).

24. For an excellent discussion of the meaning of death suffered by a captured Huron warrior, see G. Davidson, "In Search of Paradigms: Death and Destiny in Seventeenth Century North America," in *Religious Encounters with Death: Studies in the History and Anthropology of Religion*.

25. W. Warner, *A Black Civilization: A Study of an Australian Tribe* (New York: Harper Bros., 1937).

26. J. Layard, *Stone Men of Malakula* (London: Chatlo and Windus, 1942).

27. For an excellent discussion see W. LaFleur, "Japan," in *Death and Eastern Thought*, ed. F. Holck.

28. It has often been assumed that once a man attains such immortality he acquires a certain control over his physical death. For example, the early Buddhist scriptures emphasize that the Buddha, if he had chosen to do so, could have postponed his death or parinirvana until the end of the cosmic era.

29. The text in question is the Phra Malai Sutta. For the Zhar text of one version of the myth see *Dika Malai Diva Sut*.

7

Natural Death and Public Policy

DANIEL CALLAHAN

Four images of death stay fresh in my mind. The first is that of an old friend who died at the age of sixty-one of cancer of the liver. He knew at least two months beforehand that he was going to die, as did his family and friends. During that time, he received a constant stream of visitors. They knew and he knew they were taking their leave. He was a model of gaiety and hospitality; it is hard to imagine how any dying person could have put people more at ease. When his time came, his family and many of those friends were at his bedside in his home and not in a hospital. Without any significant pain, he slipped into a coma some six hours before he died. Until then he was fully lucid. I arrived ten minutes after his death. I wept, as did everyone else there, but I could not feel that his death was "untimely"; one could only hope to die with equal grace, encircled by friends and family.

That kind of image invites sentimentality. It was almost too perfect a death, and those of us prone to take a dark view of the world tend to be skeptical of such perfection, even when we witness it with our own eyes. But I *did* witness it, and the image is fresh and powerful. Naturally his death was easier for me—a friend—to bear than for his family, who lived with him day-in and day-out; their sense of loss was greater than mine. Yet, however great their sadness, I had no sense that they felt his death was wrong. I might add that he left his wife healthy and financially secure, his children grown and self-sufficient, and his business affairs in order.

My second image is that of the funeral of the 20-year-old son of another friend—a bright, attractive, promising boy who died unexpectedly of a coronary caused (it was learned during the autopsy) by an undetected congenital heart defect. It was an unbearable funeral. I have never been able to think of *anything* good to say for that death.

My third image is that of the death of my own son, Thomas, at the age of six weeks. The cause of death, also unexpected, was that catchall phrase "crib death." Alive and well one hour, dead the next. While I certainly was devastated at the time, and even now miss Thomas, I find it hard to know what to *think* about his death. It seems in some sense wrong that he died, but then again, his attachment to others in the world was tenuous, he felt (as far as we know) no pain in his dying, and he had had no chance to develop hopes or goals. His death was hardly a routine event in our lives, but I do not know what kind of event it was in his.

My fourth image is that of the death of a very elderly patient in a chronic care facility, a death preceded by a long period of physical and mental decline, with the last few years of life marked by almost total isolation, certainly from others but seemingly from self as well. In this particular case, the isolation did not come from staff insensitivity. The time had long passed when it was possible to do more than care for the body of the patient.

I mention these images for several reasons. I believe it impossible for anyone to consider the concept of "natural death" totally free of one's personal images of death, particularly those witnessed firsthand. Moreover, given the varied forms death can take, we are each likely to have rather different images.

I have witnessed at least one death that seemed to me (intuitively at any rate) to be a "natural death," at least one that seemed wrong and "un-natural," at least one that did not easily fit into either class, and one that seemed to have come much too late. That there can be so many images of death points to the problem in attempting to define or characterize the notion of "natural death." Any socially significant definition will and must be affectively colored, evoke different private images, and take its point of departure from certain powerful cognitive-emotional exemplars.

A DEFINITION OF NATURAL DEATH

My goal here is the immodest one of proposing a definition of natural death that will be at once rationally persuasive, emotionally satisfying, socially advantageous, and politically attractive. It will have to be a stipulative definition since, so far as I know, there exists no commonly accepted meaning; it is a popular rather than a technical phrase.

Why define and gain cultural support for the concept of natural death? First, we must do so because such a concept is becoming socially, economically, and politically imperative. Without one we will not, for instance, be able to specify rational limits to the aspirations of medicine, limits to the kind and extent of medical research and care individuals can legitimately ask of society, and limits (quite apart from economics) to the medical care that ought to be invested to keep people alive. Second, a concept of natural death is psychologically imperative in order that we may know, as individuals, what it is right and reasonable to hope for; the alternative is both spiritual and psychological chaos. Third, a concept of natural death is a moral necessity, in order that we may gain an idea of what we owe, as human beings, to those who are going to die.

I mean by "death" more the event of death than the process of dying. I would like to make a total separation between the event and the process but have never found that to be altogether possible. My definition of "natural death" is this: the individual event of death at that point in a life span when (1) one's life-work has been accomplished; (2) one's moral obligations to those for whom one has had responsibility have been discharged; (3) the death will not seem to others an offense to sense or sensibility or tempt others to despair and rage at human existence; and finally, (4) the process of dying is not marked by unbearable and degrading pain.

Each part of this definition requires some explanation. By the accomplishment of one's life-work I mean primarily vocational or professional work. Some obvious problems present themselves. The paradigm of a life's work is the pursuit and attainment of a particular goal, but some goals are obviously more easily achieved than others. It is easier to become president of a bank than to discover the cure for cancer, and easier to gain leadership of a national political party than to achieve perfect world justice. Some life goals, that is, focus on limited and finite projects; others may transcend the grasp of any one individual, either because of inherent difficulty or because they depend on the joint effort of many individuals, no one of whom has full control.

One might, by this criterion, say that a person who died before achieving the long-sought bank presidency died (in his terms) prematurely. Yet if, for lack of talent or luck, that person, prior to death, had lost any chance of achieving the goal—and further time would not restore the opportunity—it would not be possible to label the death premature; more life would not have helped. If there is disappointment in such a life, its reason has nothing to do with death. For someone whose life-goal is the perfectly just society, a goal perhaps beyond reach regardless of how much time is invested, death prior to its achievement cannot really be called premature or untimely either. There is no way of knowing if a longer life would have made any difference. How long does a person have to live if his ambition is to see a permanent eradication of war?

The model of life-work as seeking some specific goal is by no means the only one possible. Much more common is the vocational aim of simply doing a certain kind of work, where the dominant motive is the satisfaction of the process itself. A person becomes a shoemaker or a physician because he prefers the activities that go with those roles. In that sense, such people have achieved their goals when they first undertake the activities. If it is their ambition to do such work *forever,* then I suppose one could call their deaths, after a year or two hundred years, premature. In that event nothing but immortality would suffice; a longer life span would only stay the day of reckoning, not do away with the problem.

The second element of my definition also requires examination. When I speak of having discharged one's moral obligations, I have in mind primarily family obligations, particularly to one's children. Obligations to children are very special and inescapable. The death of a parent when children are still wholly dependent on him or her is easily and rightly seen as particularly sad and wrong. Yet if the children are grown and are self-supporting and self-directing, it is fair to say that the parents no longer have special obligations toward them; they have done their work. We may be sad when an elderly person with grown children dies, but rarely (save in very special cases) feel that the children still *need* the parents as parents for their own welfare.

Of course, there are other kinds of obligations as well. Wives and husbands, by virtue of marriage, take on mutual obligations. An ideal of many if not most marriages is to plan so that the death of one will not mean the ruination or impoverishment of the other. A premature death then is one in which, for lack of time, a spouse has not been able to provide the basis for at least the material security of the survivor. If that has been accomplished, however, or if the society does not allow the death of a spouse to undercut all future social security of the survivor, then it becomes possible to imagine situations in which spouses have discharged their obligations to each other. This is hardly to deny that the survivor may severely and permanently grieve the death of the other. But that possibility does not seem to be sufficient to call the death wrong or untimely.

There is still another set of obligations. What about the situation in which a person undertakes voluntarily to bear the burdens of others or to work for their improved welfare? A premature death in that context is one in which death occurred before the chosen obligations could be discharged. There are a number of difficulties in evaluating this kind of situation. First, though a person may undertake voluntary obligations, it is not evident that an inability to discharge them is an evil. There is loss on the part of those who would have benefited and whose sense of obligation was thwarted; yet, since the obligation was voluntary, it could not easily be claimed that its beneficiaries had any right to it. The death of their benefactor cannot be counted as an injustice. Second, some voluntary obligations are finite and time-limited, others open-ended and infinite. It is one thing to take responsibility for the welfare of an orphan, and quite another to take responsibility for the welfare of all orphans. More time may help in the first instance, but (assuming one can even talk sensibly about obligation toward all orphans) no amount of time is likely to assure the second goal, if for no other reason than that more children destined to become orphans will continually be born.

The third aspect of my definition, that a given death will not seem to others an offense to sense or sensibility, or elicit feelings of rage and despair at human existence, brings us to some fundamental problems about death itself. The death of an elderly person who has lived a rich and full life is apparently not, in any society, counted as an evil, symptomatic of a deranged and cruel universe. It may well be that mankind has simply rationalized that kind of death; since it cannot be helped, it might as well be accepted. There is no way to determine if that is the case. Nor is there any way to determine whether, as many (though not all) elderly testify, their proclaimed readiness to die is rationalization. One can only point out the brute fact that in the eyes of neither themselves nor others is death an evil. But the main reason given in both cases for that judgment is that they have lived a life, have done what they can, and thus are not victims of malevolent divine or natural forces. This seems especially true if they have, in their own eyes and those of others, completed their life's work and discharged their moral obligations to others. It is not that life has lost a purpose because of that, but rather that life's *main* purposes—self-realization and assistance to others in self-realization—have been achieved.

That point may be underscored by thinking of the death of an elderly person, not at the time of death or immediately thereafter, but in distant retrospect. I speak from limited experience here, but I have never heard anyone recall with bitterness, or sharp regret, the death of an elderly person who lived a full life, and whose death occurred twenty, thirty, or forty years previously. I remember sadness thirty years ago at the death of my 80-year-old paternal grandmother. But I do not now feel sad that she is dead, nor do I know any of her children—my father, uncles, and aunts (who were much closer to her than I was)—who are still sad that she is no longer alive. That many of them are now dead and their lingering sadness, if any, is buried along with them, only adds to the difficulty of imagining her death as an evil. If an event was evil, as opposed to sad, it should be possible to look back even now and identify what made it evil.

Finally, I have added a special stipulation that natural death should not be marked by unbearable and degrading pain. Pain, whether physical or psychological, can destroy personality, sense of self, and the ability to relate to others; it separates a person not only from himself but from others as well. Without further argument, I will assert that it is impossible for a death amidst pain to be in any sense acceptable to either the victim or those around him.

IS DEATH AN EVIL?

In explaining my stipulative definition of natural death, I have provided a variety of arguments in support of the cogency of its various parts. In general, they stem from the observation that hardly anyone seems to consider the death of an elderly person, after a full life, as an evil; moreover, there seem to be intuitive considerations to support this common feeling. That kind of death is, then, my paradigm of a natural death.

The obvious premise behind my definition, assuming all the criteria are met, is that such a death is not an evil. To make that case, which can be done only in part here, it is necessary to specify what I mean by evil. Death could not, in my paradigm, be called a moral evil in the narrow sense of the term, that is, in the sense that rights have been violated, a social injustice done, or clear obligations defaulted; no person or persons did wrong to the one who died. I believe there is a broader sense of evil, however, that emphasizes the absurdity and irrationality of life itself, where nature, fate, or some other implacable and uncontrollable power victimizes hapless human beings, forcing them to be born and to die in a world not of their choosing. One might call that "metaphysical" as distinguished from "moral" evil.

I admit to an enormous ambivalence about whether human life as such, and the inevitable death which goes with it, is a metaphysical evil. Paul Ramsey, Robert Morison, and Leon Kass have most recently wrestled with that question, and Robert M. Veatch has added some points.[1] I will not try to join that argument directly, but will highlight some important confusions it has revealed. One confusion was introduced by Paul Ramsey, who tried to argue "the contradiction death poses to the unique worth of an individual human life."[2] But Ramsey does not really defend that proposition. To do so, he would have to show that to be worthy, an individual human life is one in which death has no part. He does not show that, and he does not even try to show that. Instead, he contents himself with arguing that death is a threat to human life, an enemy of life. That is a very different matter from demonstrating that both the threat and the reality of death remove from human life some of its value and worth. One can acknowledge that "there is grief over death which no human agency can alleviate,"[3] without thereby accepting the notion that, because people do and must die, an absence of worth is thus displayed.

Kass very effectively points this out, but he then makes the further case that death itself cannot be judged an ultimate evil: *"Death is natural and necessary and inextricably tied to life.* To live is to be mortal; death is the necessary price of life. . . . When we 'buy' life we 'buy' death."[4] The general thrust of Kass's argument is that since death *is,* it cannot be considered an ultimate evil. He does not really ask whether this is a good situation for humans to be born into, that is, metaphysically good. His use of the metaphor "buy" betrays that omission. One does not "buy" life, as if it were some voluntary transaction knowingly and freely entered into; one has no choice about being born or about dying. If ever there was a forced sale, it is this one. Indeed, life is a "bitter-sweet bargain,"[5] in which the ultimate transaction was not of our choosing.

What is finally missing in Kass's account is the centrality of human individuality and subjectivity in human life. Kass appears to see dwelling on that part of human nature as somehow harmful to the more important quest for larger truth about human life.[6] I will here point out only one basic problem with that tack. Let us agree for the sake of argument that death is the price of life, and that life and death are inextricably and necessarily related. We then "see nature as it is."[7] But if that is our goal, what else can we discern about nature as it is, and particularly human nature? It seems obvious that we will at least see the hard fact that people want to live and not to die; that drive also seems an inextricable and inescapable part of life. I did not "buy" that drive, nor was I given an opportunity to bargain about its strength.

Thus, even if we are wise enough to accept the necessity of death, we will have an internal war on our hands between that hard won wisdom and our own unchosen psychic makeup (seemingly a generic and not individuated, idiosyncratic part of human nature) that makes us want to live. The paradox (or, if you will, the sheer perversity) of this situation can best be seen by rephrasing a passage of Kass's. "Death," he says, "is necessary not just in the sense of 'unavoidable,' which it is also for the individual, but in the sense of 'indispensable.'"[8] Consider this rephrasing: "A drive for life is necessary, not just in the sense of 'unavoidable,' which it is for the individual, but in the sense of 'indispensable.'" I believe that to be a true

sentence; if Kass's sentence is true as well, it is no wonder that we
have trouble figuring out the meaning of life and death.

In expressing his worries about the social wisdom of installing a
concept of natural death, Veatch is driven back, as one must be, to
the question of whether death is an evil. He considers two options,
the rationalist and the social-eschatological cases for life. The first
rests on the premise that, as an individual, I do not want to be dead,
that is, nonexistent; I can have an "anticipatory regret of my non-
existence."[9] But Veatch rejects this line of argument on the ground
that a desire for continued life does not prove that it is desirable. He
rests his own convictions on the social-eschatological case for life, by
which he means the persistent Western eschatological vision of perpetuation. A central part of that vision is the conquest of the evil of
death—"life shall prevail and death shall be no more."[10] Veatch's
initial case would be stronger if he had distinguished between religious and secular eschatological visions. While a great part of the
Western religious tradition, at least the Christian, has seen the overcoming of death as a legitimate part of human aspiration, this is by
no means the case with the major secular eschatologies. Neither
Marxism nor other variant socialist eschatologies appear to hanker
for the perpetuation of individual lives. It is the perpetual life of the
just community, a community of people who live and die, that is
sought.

In the end, Veatch does not confront directly the proposition
that "life is indeed a good and death is an evil."[11] In fact, by posing
the problem that way, as if a belief in the goodness of life necessarily
entails the judgment that death is an evil, he gets off on the wrong
foot. Though he tries in his discussion of death as a relative rather
than an absolute evil[12] to rectify that narrow posing of the question,
he never solves his own problem; if anything, he makes it worse. He
contends, for one thing, "that death is fundamentally incompatible
with the ideal human community."[13] But nowhere, other than invok-
ing the very general Western eschatological vision, does he define
the ideal human community. (I would not want to be forced to
specify that either. It is not at all clear to me what, even as an inchoate vision, such a community would be like or what would be particularly good about it. Self-evidently, it would be good in that no
one would fear death; beyond that feature, however, I am hard
pressed to think of any benefits it would bestow.) The very notion of

a "human community" is bound up with what we presently know of human communities: life and death, hope and fear, parents and children, the succession of generations, being young and growing old. The removal of death would entail a totally different kind of human community; not being able to imagine what that would be, I cannot judge whether it would be desirable. Moreover, how could anyone presume to know enough about such a community to give its advantages the benefit of the doubt?

An equally serious difficulty arises in Veatch's attempt to hold that "immortality is a desirable goal (but) some deaths may be preferred to a painful and dehumanizing struggle to that goal."[14] Veatch asserts that these two values are not incompatible, but nowhere tells us why. The most he says is that "to hold death as an evil and still feel that individual deaths are acceptable may be a tragic view of death . . ."[15] But that hardly deals with the problem. What is meant by a "tragic view of death"? That life is absurd, that things do not come out right? If nothing else, there are some logical puzzles in his position. If life is inherently good, he cannot say that some people are better off dead. If not all life is good, it cannot be concluded that life as such is good; it all depends on what kind of life one is talking about. If death is an evil, it is not less of an evil simply because some people find life unbearable or degrading. What is finally missing in Veatch's position is some account of what makes life good and what makes death evil. Lacking that, it is impossible to find any coherent reason why life as a permanent state is better than death as a permanent state.

THE IMPLICATIONS FOR PUBLIC POLICY

Defending my definition of natural death (and the paradigm of death it draws upon) as a basis for public policy involves considering the implications (1) for those whose lives have reached the stage where, if they died, their deaths would be considered "natural," and (2) for those whose lives are threatened with premature or untimely deaths. However, an important qualification is in order. A public policy based on a concept of natural death is not a wholly formal policy. The most absurd manifestation of such a policy might be, for instance, a federal or state definition of natural death, followed by a rigorous attempt to conform law, regulation, and practice to the

definition. Enamored as I am of my own definition, it would strike
me as pure Orwellianism for a legislature or a committee to deliberate formally about whether a given person did or did not meet the
criteria, and thus to decide whether to extend further medical or social asssistance. The most to be hoped for is a broad social consensus, dipping deeply into what Philip Rieff[16] has called "the cultural
unconscious," which will push society toward rough limits of any desire to conquer death or greatly extend the human life span. That
would leave considerable room for dissent and variation, as well as
considerable leeway for dealing with particular cases.

The most important social implication of my definition is that it
does not lend itself to the language of rights. As I have defined it,
there could not be a "right to die a natural death." Given the
subjective nature of life-goals, no society could guarantee their
realization. The most that could be guaranteed would be the
provision of those minimal materials necessary for the realization of
any human goals—food, clothing, shelter, education, and decent
health care. Nor could a society, at least in the foreseeable future,
guarantee that a person would live long enough to discharge all
family obligations; quite apart from diseases that can kill people
early in life, accidents, suicide, and other misadventures are unlikely
to be banished. Neither could a society guarantee that there would
be no deaths of the kind that lead people to fear their own deaths or
wonder about the rationality and benignity of the universe. The only
aspect of a natural death that society might conceivably guarantee,
though who knows when, is total freedom from pain and degradation; that is, perhaps, a technological and cultural possibility.

If a natural death could not, given its combination of subjective
and objective elements, be a legal or social right, could it at least be
a moral right? No, for if it is impossible to imagine ways in which
societies could fulfill such a right, it is no more possible to imagine
that individuals, in their lives together, could have a duty to insure
the natural death of another. The same contingencies that make it
impossible for society to have meaningful duties with respect to the
natural death of its citizens, make it impossible for individuals. How
can it ever be said, for instance, that I have a duty to see that my
neighbor achieves his life-goals, whatever they might be?

If, then, the language of rights, duties, and obligations cannot
appropriately be used in the case of natural death, the concept itself

stands revealed for what it is: a quasi-utopian ideal—that, while it admits of frequent empirical realization, will remain an ideal. It would cease to be such only when all or most people have a good chance of dying such a death, and that possibility still seems far distant. It is, nonetheless, a meaningful ideal, precisely because my paradigm case of the death of an elderly person has, more than once, been historically realized.

To note that a natural death is an ideal, and that it cannot be a right, is to defuse concern that the political acceptance of such a concept would open the way for abuse. Veatch has expressed this concern, observing how easy it would be for a society to turn a *right* to natural death, if such were affirmed, into a *duty* to die a natural death. But that move could come only—which is not to say it would not—by virtue of an almost total lack of reflection on the nature of a natural death. More pointedly, there would have to be a prior potential for abuse for a society to seize upon natural death as a pretext to rush people into the grave.

Are there not, however, even in my ideal, the seeds for abuse? An implication of my definition might be that those who have lived a full life, and whose death would be called natural should it occur at some point in that realized life, would be less entitled to expensive and socially marginal high-technology medical support than those who have not reached that stage. I do not think that would be an unfair or an unreasonable outcome, at least as a broad result. But how far should that be pushed? Not very. Without trying to fully develop the case here, it strikes me as reasonable for a society not to invest large amounts of money in expensive life-extending therapies for those who have lived full lives, particularly when, as is true in this country, there are many others in the society who need that money more—if they are even to live out their lives.

At the same time, in order to achieve the ideal of a death not marked by unbearable pain or degradation, supportive care of the elderly—care designed not necessarily to extend their lives, but to make those lives as comfortable and carefree as possible—ought to be fully financed. This would cost money that could be spent otherwise, but it is doubtful that people could tolerate life in a society, however fine the other social conditions, where they would have to anticipate abandonment in old age. That would be a fearful cloud under which to live. The point about acceptance of the concept of a natural death as I have defined it is not that it would condemn the elderly to neglect and mistreatment; on the contrary, it could not even be conceived as an ideal unless the conditions of old age were tolerable. The forces of nature, finitude, and mortality are quite enough for the elderly to cope with; at a minimum, society should not make matters worse.

Another social implication of my definition is that society would eschew any quest for immortality or for a significant extension of the human life span. If it is possible to die a natural death, as it is, and to hold out the ideal that most people could die such a death, there seems no reason to seek immortality. The ideal of a natural death presupposes that one has lived a full life, that completion of that kind of life is not an evil. Only those will be left dissatisfied who say that, given all the conditions for a natural death, such a death would still be an evil. The only plausible reason I see for such dissatisfaction rests on a broader complaint about the nature of reality— the problem of metaphysical evil, which sees us born into a world not of our choosing, with the best to be hoped for being a natural death. But that moves into the question of religion. While I do not accept it, the Christian belief in the resurrection of the body seems to make more sense than a quest for earthly immortality, the former at any rate presupposes a transcendent reality it does not pretend to understand.

If the quest for earthly immortality makes no particular sense, the same will be true of any significant attempt to extend the average life span. No case has yet been presented for an average life of 100 or 150 years being significantly better than one of 75 years. More of the same is not, by itself, a good argument. One might as well contend that the plays of Shakespeare or the sonatas of Beethoven are flawed by the fact that they come to an end. If a full and complete life can be lived in seventy-five years, what is the advantage of a few additional decades? If it could be shown that a natural death is more easily attained with a longer life span, that would be a persuasive argument, but I do not believe that life span is at present the major obstacle to a natural death.

Improvement in medical care, the eradication of the most common diseases, and general living conditions appear to bring a gradual increase in the average life span. The biblical three score and ten is now well exceeded in Sweden where the life expectancy for women is 79. The main problem for medicine is to deal with those remaining diseases and conditions that stand in the way of a full life. A by-product of that effort will be a longer life for most people. If, along the way, medicine finds better ways of coping with the conditions that often make old age a burden, well and good; research on aging is a valid and potentially fruitful area. The possibility of a natural death will then be enhanced. But until some good reasons have been presented why a longer life per se is good, as distinguished from a long life where life's evils have been minimized as far as possible, there is no public policy case to be made for the investment of one cent in efforts to extend it.

NOTES

1. P. Ramsey, "The Indignity of 'Death With Dignity,'" pp. 81–96; R. Morison, "The Dignity of the Inevitable and Necessary," pp. 97–100; and L. Kass, "Averting One's Eyes, or Facing the Music?—On Dignity and Death," in *Death Inside Out*, ed. P. Steinfels and R. Veatch (New York: Harper & Row, 1975), pp. 104–114; R. Veatch, "Natural Death and Public Policy," in *Death, Dying, and the Biological Revolution* (New Haven, Conn.: Yale University Press, 1976), pp. 277–305.
2. Ramsey, "The Indignity of 'Death With Dignity,'" p. 81.
3. Ibid., p. 96.
4. Kass, "Averting One's Eyes, or Facing the Music?—On Dignity and Death," pp. 101–114.
5. Ibid., p. 113.
6. Ibid., p. 103.
7. Ibid., p. 110.
8. Ibid., p. 113.
9. Veatch, "Natural Death and Public Policy," p. 294.
10. Ibid., p. 296.
11. Ibid., p. 292.
12. Ibid., p. 302.
13. Ibid.
14. Ibid.
15. Ibid., p. 303.
16. P. Rieff, *The Triumph of the Therapeutic* (New York: Harper & Row, 1966), p. 137.

Further Reflections on Natural Death and Public Policy

JAMES F. CHILDRESS

The issues involved in natural death and public policy are important and complicated. I want to identify and clarify some of them, particularly in response to the preceding chapter by Daniel Callahan. I shall test some definitions and criteria of natural death and assess their policy implications.

MAKING AND TESTING DEFINITIONS

Although Callahan views his definition of natural death as stipulative, there are some reasons for thinking that it is more reformative. While my suggestion may appear to be merely a terminological quibble, it has, I think, an important point. Consider the following sorts of definitions and the tests that are appropriate for each one. First, we might offer a *reportive* definition, indicating how people ordinarily use a term or phrase such as "natural death." To test it we would only need to determine whether people actually use the term or phrase in a particular way. Second, we might offer a *stipulative* definition, indicating how we use a term to facilitate communication; the test is its usefulness in a particular discussion. Third, because of the inconsistency or ambiguity of ordinary usage, we might offer a *reformative* definition, which recommends that a term or phrase be used in a certain way. Several tests are appropriate for such definitions: Is the definition clear? Does it illuminate the subject? How does it relate to other concepts?

Callahan indicates that "natural death" as a nontechnical phrase has no commonly accepted meaning. Thus, a reportive definition would not be helpful although ordinary usage is relevant to both stipulative and reformative definitions. After insisting on the importance of a definition of natural death, Callahan recommends a particular definition that he hopes will "gain cultural support." His definition is thus reformative and is subject to various tests.

A definition of natural death, according to Callahan, should be "rationally persuasive, emotionally satisfying, socially advantageous, and politically attractive." Such a definition, he contends, meets three basic needs: to set rational limits to medical aspirations, expectations, and the prolongation of life; to enable individuals to handle spiritual and psychological questions; and to indicate morally what we owe to those who are going to die. It is not clear that a definition of natural death is essential for these limits or that it will in fact establish them. Given its ambiguity in common usage, the phrase "natural death" may not be susceptible to clarification and reformulation so as to provide a meaningful interpretation of limits. Part of the difficulty stems from the notorious ambiguity of "natural," which is both descriptive and prescriptive. Furthermore, one concept cannot do all our moral and political work. Too much is involved in moral and political discourse about limits to be resolved by clarification of one concept. Conceptual analysis is essential, but it can only take us so far.

THE CRITERIA OF NATURAL DEATH

Perhaps Callahan does not intend to present the meaning of natural death, but rather to offer the criteria for determining when a death is natural. His four criteria are: (1) one's lifework has been accomplished; (2) one's moral obligations have been discharged; (3) the death does not offend the sense or sensibility of others or tempt them to despair or rage; and (4) the process of dying is not marked by unbearable or degrading pain. Callahan intends to concentrate on death as an event, not as a process, and he emphasizes the temporal aspects, asking whether the event of death is premature, especially in relation to accomplishing one's life-work and discharging one's moral obligations. Thus, the first two criteria are the most important; the third criterion appears to depend on the first two. The fourth criterion does relate to the process, but in most medical settings, pain can be controlled. Since we can generally manage pain and even provide care to alleviate suffering, we should concentrate on the first three criteria.

Callahan's criteria invite numerous questions. Are they offered as necessary and/or sufficient conditions of natural death? As they stand, they have a greater prospect for being considered necessary than for being considered sufficient. While we might say that a death that does not meet these criteria is not "natural," some deaths that meet the criteria may not be considered "natural." Suicide under some conditions could satisfy the criteria, but it is not clear that Callahan or anyone else would want to speak of suicide as natural.

The example of suicide also raises the question of whether Callahan can emphasize event over process in the criteria of natural death. The one criterion that relates to process—how death comes about—is pain. Nevertheless, considerations of how as well as when are important in ordinary usage, and even if Callahan does not take ordinary usage as the final arbiter, he apparently does not consider suicide or a violent death at the hands of others natural. Consider the following example. A healthy 65-year-old man, whose wife has died and whose family has grown up, is now ready to retire from his position as president of a bank. He devoted his life to becoming president of the bank and to making the bank the best one in his state; he has no other interests. Now, suppose that after his retirement he (1) kills himself, or (2) is shot by a sniper as he is taking a walk. In either case, he dies instantly with no pain. Whether his death is by his own or by someone else's hand, it could be said to meet Callahan's criteria for a natural death. Of course, Callahan could respond that such a violent death of a healthy person would offend others' sense or sensibility or tempt them to despair. But he would still need to add to or modify his criteria since it is the *process* rather than the event of death in this instance that offends people or tempts them to despair (if indeed it is empirically true that people react this way).

Another example makes a similar point. Imagine that a general who has no family and lives for fighting in battle is killed on the battlefield. He dies with his boots on, suffering no pain. It is difficult to imagine that his death would offend people or tempt them to despair. Yet would it be appropriate to call this general's death natural? "Natural" seems to have at least as much to do with process as with timing. While Callahan could hold that the process of dying determines whether a death is "good" or "bad," and the timing determines whether it is "natural" or "unnatural," he still needs to indicate why the experience of pain falls under the latter.

Yet another question is whether these criteria are objective or subjective, whether they are applied by the spectator or by the agent/patient. Clearly the criteria depend largely on the way spectators or observers respond to the deaths of others—what they think, feel, and say about them. But how the observers respond could depend, for instance, on (1) whether they think the deceased person had in fact fulfilled his or her obligations, or (2) whether the deceased person *thought* he or she had fulfilled those obligations. Since we distinguish having an obligation from recognizing that one has an obligation, the observer might perceive obligations that the agent does not recognize or thinks have been discharged.

Some of the ambiguities in Callahan's discussion of moral obligations may be clarified by a distinction between an *obligation to do something* and an *obligation to another person*.[1] This distinction is not a separation, for often we have obligations to perform certain acts because of our obligations to other persons. Nevertheless, it is a mistake to think only of obligations to perform certain acts, which can then be clearly and completely discharged. Not all our obligations to other persons can be discharged, for they cannot be specified in advance as "Do X, Y, and Z." The moral life requires imagination, for there may be several obligation-meeting actions, not all of which are obligatory. For instance, what do obligations between parents and children or between spouses entail? Often in a family setting, we are concerned with obligations that connect with what ethicist Gene Outka calls "relational norms," which "locate certain relatively definite sorts of *relations,* often involving roles and expressing generally what are taken to be fundamental rights and obligations."[2] Faithfulness between husbands and wives is one example of a relational norm that does not definitely specify what will count as fulfillment. Because we cannot reduce relational norms to certain specific acts as though the latter exhaustively express the former, we cannot indicate a point in time when such relational obligations are fulfilled. What it means to be a "father," "mother," "husband," or "wife" cannot be reduced to specific, definite obligations to be fulfilled at certain points in time.

Even if we can check off some completed obligations (such as seeing that one's children get an education), many obligations persist. Callahan's language of discharging obligations suggests that their force can be extinguished. Another party or the law may discharge an agent from a contractual obligation, or the agent may discharge this obligation by performance. Callahan's view that an obligation's binding force may be cancelled by performance does not take account of more general obligations, such as respect or care for one's spouse, that cannot be fulfilled short of death. They are never completed so that one has nothing else to do.

I have appealed to distinctions between having and recognizing obligations, between being under an obligation to someone and being obligated to do X, between obligations to act in certain general ways (such as caring) and obligations to act in definite ways (such as educating one's children). All these distinctions suggest that Callahan's view of discharging obligations, particularly to one's family, needs to be clarified and perhaps modified. A dying person may conceive his or her obligations quite differently from a spectator, but either of them could insist that some obligations are never discharged. Such an insistence, which can be defended, would mean that Callahan's second criterion for a natural death could never be met.

When we ask whether the criterion of accomplishing one's life-work is objective or subjective, we encounter similar difficulties, although Callahan seems to acknowledge them more clearly in relation to life-plans than obligations. Whether it makes sense to speak of finishing a life-work or realizing a life-plan depends on the nature of the work or plan. If it focuses on unlimited projects, is dependent on the collaboration of others, or involves an activity done for its own sake rather than to achieve a goal, there may be no way to say "It is finished." Death at any time might seem premature and unnatural. But Callahan tries to avoid some of the implications of the subjectivity of life-plans by appealing to the observer's more objective standpoint. For instance, if X had no chance to become bank president because of a lack of talent or missed opportunities, Callahan would not say that X's death was premature by the first criterion, even if X still thought that he had a chance to gain this coveted position. Callahan does not accept X's viewpoint as determining our interpretation of X's death as natural or unnatural. If a person's goal is unattainable, then "death prior to its achievement could not really be said to be premature or untimely either." It is not clear how Callahan handles the person who has no life-plans or goals.

Callahan's emphasis on the subjectivity of obligations (which is even greater than he recognizes), the subjectivity of life-plans, and the subjectivity of the experience of pain poses some difficulties for his position. After all, one of his main reasons for developing a notion of natural death is the need for specifying "rational limits to the aspirations of medicine, limits to the kind and extent of medical research and care individuals can legitimately ask of society, and limits . . . to the medical care that ought to be invested to keep people alive." Without a concept of natural death, he contends, we will be unable to specify those limits. Yet by stressing the subjective elements in the criteria of natural death, he weakens those limits. Subjective life-plans and obligations (the latter conceived in the broader terms that I suggested) are open-ended and provide no rationale for limits. They do not yield clear and helpful distinctions between premature and natural deaths which can then serve as rational limits for our policies. Consequently, Callahan is forced to invoke some idea of reasonableness—death is natural, or not premature, when a reasonable life-plan has been completed and reasonable obligations fulfilled. Like the notion of the reasonable man in law, Callahan's conception is an attempt to achieve some objective standard. Its vagueness, however, still precludes a clear statement of the limits that he thinks a concept of natural death—and only such a concept—can provide.

Finally, the third criterion (the responses of observers) really depends in most settings on the other three. Whether a death will offend the sense and sensibility of observers, or tempt them to despair, ordinarily depends on whether these other criteria are met. The third criterion is thus derivative and perhaps even dispensable. How does Callahan conceive the relationship between criteria 1, 2, and 4 on the one hand, and criterion 3 on the other? Do 1, 2, and 4 indicate why people are offended and tempted by some deaths but not by others? Does Callahan imply that whenever 1, 2, and 4 are met, the third one will be met also? Or when a death is deemed unnatural because it does not meet the third criterion, does it necessarily fail to meet at least one of the others as well? These questions need careful attention.

POLICY IMPLICATIONS

Despite Callahan's contention that a concept of natural death is necessary for appropriate public policies, he is primarily concerned with a very general cultural level: "The most to be hoped for is a broad social consensus, dipping deeply into what Philip Rieff has called 'the cultural unconscious,' which will push society toward rough limits of any desire to conquer death or greatly extend the human life span." Because of his emphasis on social consensus and the cultural unconscious, Callahan's language of images and ideals is especially fitting. Indeed, he attempts to develop powerful images and attractive ideals that can help forge a consensus in part by connecting with the cultural unconscious. Undoubtedly, a cultural consensus and its unarticulated premises significantly shape what is desired and what is politically possible. But before we can evaluate the significance of the concept of natural death for public policy, we need to have Callahan's views of the relations between the unconscious, culture, and policy, as well as his understanding of social change.

Short of an altered culture, what are the relations between Callahan's concept of natural death and public policy? I very much agree with the policy implications that he sees in his concept of a natural death. He stresses that it is reasonable for a society not to give priority to expensive life-extending technologies, that we ought to provide care for the elderly to prevent pain and degradation, and that society should "eschew any quest for immortality or for a significant extension of the human life span." But to present acceptable policy implications of a concept of natural death is not to show that the concept itself is essential to those conclusions, which might well be defended on quite different grounds. For instance, a coherent interpretation of justice in allocation and distribution could lead to the same conclusions without the intermediary notion of natural death, which, as we have seen, has tremendous shortcomings.

Callahan holds that the "most important social implication of (his) definition is that it does not lend itself to the language of rights." There could not, he continues, be a "right to die a natural death." His point hinges in part on the subjective nature of life-goals, whose realization no one or no society can guarantee. It holds, however, only for one sort of right—a right to be enabled or empowered to be or do something, such as a right to be supported so that one can die naturally (that is, meeting Callahan's criteria). Because some of the criteria (accomplishing life-plans, for example) are subjective, society cannot guarantee their realization. But another sort of right is more negative, stressing noninterference. A society could recognize the sphere of privacy, liberty, and self-determination and could hold that one has the right to what one takes to be a natural death (that is, one that meets one's own criteria of a "natural" death). This could give rise to a right to commit suicide or a right to refuse treatment.

Finally, a difficulty in recent discussions of natural law may illuminate Callahan's dilemma. After Nazi Germany, many attempted to revive natural law as a basis for criticizing and resisting states, laws, and policies. Some commentators even insisted that a doctrine of natural law is logically or, at least, psychologically indispensable for criticism and resistance. While these needs stimulated a revival of natural law thought, they have not been met by several recent interpretations of natural law. The personalistic, historical, and flexible versions are less helpful in discriminating criticism and resistance, for they do not appear to provide an objective standard. In a similar way, Callahan insists that we cannot develop adequate limits for policies without a concept of natural death. While a more traditional biological understanding of natural death might have provided such limits, Callahan's subjective version (even with its modification in the direction of objectivity) falls short. He wants to call on the power of the concept of natural death but refuses to arm it for victory. As a result, it is a weak ally.

NOTES

1. See A. I. Melden, *Rights and Right Conduct* (Oxford: Basil Blackwell, 1959).
2. G. Outka, "Character, Conduct, and the Love Commandment," in *Norm and Context in Christian Ethics,* ed. G. Outka and P. Ramsey (New York: Charles Scribner's Sons, 1968), p. 44.

Is Aging a Disease?

H. TRISTRAM ENGELHARDT, Jr.

Any attempt to decide whether aging is a disease must be undertaken with the knowledge that the question is not an empirical one. It is not like asking, How many legs do cats have? Deciding whether any particular state of affairs is a disease requires an antecedent judgment about how we will use concepts. That is, it is more like asking whether octopods have eight legs or eight arms. All empirical questions can be transformed in that fashion because all our judgments of and experiences about the world presuppose certain antecedent conceptual decisions insofar as we wish to make judgments about those experiences and compare them (for example, most of us have already decided to call both the front and back limbs of cats "legs"). This is particularly the case with respect to the concept of disease, which presupposes judgments about what human beings should be like and should be able to do. Though everyone might agree that angina is an element of a disease and teething is not, each judgment would still turn on a decision about what is proper to humans. Namely, one would be deciding that the pain of angina is part of a disease because it serves no basic human good or goal, while the pain of teething is part of a process that does.

Similarly, to decide that the physical limitations that one would accept as normal for a 95-year-old are not normal for a 25-year-old is to make judgments concerning normal or proper expectations for human beings. Such decisions involve more than simply describing the world. After all, IQs of 140 are rare and statistically abnormal.

They are not abnormal in the sense of being diseases. A disease is not simply unusual, it also violates some expectations concerning the human condition. The word *abnormal* thus has at least two senses that are relevant here: unusual (for example, an IQ of 140) and improper (for example, arteriosclerosis). To put it another way, two senses of "normal" are relevant here: not statistically deviant (an IQ of 100), and a state considered proper to humans (for example, plaque-free coronary arteries). Finally, we must also be aware that we have a whole set of words indicating ideas that grade one into another: illness, disease, disability, deformity, and so on. These concepts function in different ways. Here I use *disease* to identify a physical and/or psychological state of affairs held to be dysteleological (for example, arthritis, circumscribing one's ability to be active), deforming (for example, vitiligo), or causing pain.[1]

We may be motivated by a number of considerations to pose the question of whether aging is a disease. We may have a straightforward conceptual puzzle. That is, we might be struck on the one hand by the disabilities associated with advancing age and their similarity with disease processes, or, on the other, by the universality of aging, which makes us reluctant to call it a disease. Part of this reluctance may be bound up with the connection between aging and death, and the realization that death plays an important role in the natural economy, reducing the number of the old to make room for the young. We may be seeking to determine whether conceiving of it as disease would give us better control over our own condition. Disease concepts do perform social functions. As Talcott Parsons has indicated, calling people sick puts them within the sick role and confers on them the attention of the medical profession.[2] We might hope to ameliorate the condition of the aged by calling them "sick" and thus recruiting the forces of the medical professions and the biomedical sciences (compare "Alcoholism and drug addiction are not moral failures but diseases for which treatment should be sought, not punishment given" with "Aging is a disease; the aged should not be abandoned as useless but given treatment so that they can resume or maintain their roles as useful members of society"). But we might also have the very opposite intention; we might be struck by what we would take to be vain and ludicrous attempts to postpone aging and wish instead to counsel acceptance of old age and death by terming aging normal, not a disease.

BASIC CONCEPTS

In order to answer these questions about aging as a disease, we must begin by sorting out the different senses and usages of concepts found in such questions and in possible answers. For example, there is a distinction between growing old and aging. One must distinguish becoming chronologically older from becoming progressively debilitated. One might be old but not aged, or growing older but not appreciably aging. Speaking of aging as a disease calls up that congeries of physical and psychological debilities usually associated with growing older. Further, treating aging as a disease does not necessarily imply an intent to postpone death. There is a difference between extending life expectancy and extending useful life. To decide to treat aging as a disease should then imply an interest in extending useful human life by decreasing the period of the human life cycle prior to death that is characterized by limitation of physical and psychological functions that are consequences of various debilitations associated with growing older. Treating aging as a disease does not necessarily imply a wish to increase human life expectancy or increase the human life span.

To speak of aging as a disease would, among other things, require some notion of its being improper. This sense of impropriety cannot be based on aging being unusual. Most people grow old; it is far from unusual. An exception is "premature aging" where it occurs in an individual prior to its usual occurrence in other humans. The sense of "unusual" is then specified in terms of the length of life lived. Aging is, in that sense, found to be improper by reference to the usual expectation of function associated with particular periods of life. Allied to this sense is the notion that aging that could have been postponed, but was not, is premature. Here, the availability of technology could expand expectations. Thus, if the loss in cardiovascular reserve that usually attends aging could be prevented, such loss could be considered a disease. It would no longer be a "normal" element of life, especially if it could be easily forestalled (that is, required preventive measures could be readily performed). Another sense of aging being premature lies behind the social force of the question whether aging is a disease: One is concerned that aging cuts short life projects that humans believe they ought to be able to complete.

As humans come to recognize that technology may be able to postpone aging, or elements of aging, certain forms of loss of function due to aging may no longer be accepted. Menopause, for example, may come to be viewed as a disease long before there is acceptable treatment for it.[3] This criterion for judging certain forms of aging to be premature is most interesting in that it turns on the ability of humans to transcend the particular limits of human nature. It points out that what is premature or natural for humans depends in large measure on what they will accept. Man, in this sense, becomes self-creative, and human nature (in the sense of the usual physiological and psychological lineaments of function) is seen as plastic before human goals. Thus, not only postponable aging, but also aging that should be postponed, can be viewed as premature. Here one imposes judgments as to what should be the lineaments of a healthy human life. Premature aging is thus aging that (1) occurs before the aging of one's cohorts (for example, presenile dementia, Alzheimer's disease, would in this sense involve "premature" aging), (2) could have been easily prevented, and (3) involves becoming unable to do the things one still wants to do even if that aging occurs at a statistically usual point in human chronology. Premature aging is consequently an ambiguous concept that turns on a blend of the expected scope of human abilities at different points in human chronology (statistically achievable expectations), the element of aging that can be postponed, and the scope of one's own life projects, which may differ from the usual. When a society as a whole wishes a different range of abilities than is statistically expected at a particular age, raised expectations are likely, forcing questions whether aging is a disease or whether debilities associated with growing old, such as widow's hump, senile vaginitis, loss of youthful attractiveness, should be considered disease states.

Use of disease language in general, and particularly with respect to aging, thus turns on notions of life-projects and the scope of abilities that should normally be open to humans. Even imagining a population in which most persons had a duodenal ulcer or a myocardial infarction at the age of 40, one could still call those events improper, that is, diseases. Those states of affairs would restrict the set of expectations that humans might want to have as a part of their life-projects. More generally, treating aging as a disease would imply that humans want the expectation of being able to live out their lives with relatively little circumscription of physical, intellectual, and social activities. Calling aging a disease is a way of identifying a set of expectations with regard to activities: self-reliance, freedom from pain and infirmity, and realization of the goods and values usually open to humans.

One must avoid hubris and distinguish between aging that can be postponed and aging that cannot. Terming as disease only aging that can be postponed, and excluding aging that one would like, but not be able to postpone, can avoid arousing unsatisfiable expectations. After all, the disease concept is in great measure a construct, and it is reasonable to restrict its scope from futile projects (there is no point in flogging the Bosporus). One does best by employing the concept of disease in as socially useful a fashion as possible. For example, it is likely that treating postponable aging as a disease will be helpful in recruiting the young to care for themselves so as not to be aged when old, while calling unpostponable aging an illness or disease will lead only to increased frustration.

Any sensible (likely to result in helpful consequences) use of "aging as a disease" must be made with regard to finite life-projects. Judgments of the scope of aging as a disease must involve a finite sense of the life-projects open to humans (that is, death must be accepted as inevitable since humans are contingent beings and over the long run will cease to exist). Further, if one does not raise the issue of the postponement of death (an issue this chapter treats only in passing), then one is asking about postponing aging only within an already accepted human life span or life expectancy (for example, a human life span of about 120 years or a life expectancy of 70 years). Put within such confines, there is already an acceptance of finitude, and the question is whether it would be useful and consistent with our other general concepts of health and disease to call aging a disease. The question becomes that of extending human capabilities within an already accepted scope of human life. One might note in passing that this question may in the end be much more attractive than the issue of postponing death, which might increase life span or life expectancy without increasing the capabilities of the aged. The question of aging as a disease is one of the quality of life; the question of postponing death concerns the quantity of life. These questions are best distinguished even when they cannot be separated.

THE UTILITY OF THE "DISEASE OF AGING"

To call something a disease is to place it in a certain social context. Not only does it legitimize the use of the sick role by those afflicted, but it also recruits social investment in research to ameliorate the condition (the "disease"), to provide therapy, and to advance therapeutic concern. Moreover, in a society becoming increasingly appreciative of the ways in which we may be responsible for the development of our diseases (by smoking, failing to do regular exercise, overeating, and so on), the use of disease language tends further to indicate that individuals are responsible for acquiring diseases (including becoming aged), insofar as they fail to do things to prevent them. This recognition of the ways we influence our own destinies represents an increasing appreciation of human responsibility for the human condition. Before humans could adequately control disease or birth, the advent of both sickness and children was considered the punishment or gift of Providence. The appreciation of our own control over our lives has radically changed such perceptions, making diseases and parenthood questions of human responsibility. Conceiving of aging as a disease would likely (insofar as conduct while young would influence the rate of aging) make aging also a question of human responsibility.

In short, we will not discover if aging is a disease in the same way we might discover if the world is round or if an infectious agent is responsible for a type of cancer. We are rather asking how we wish to use the concept "disease," and what attitudes we wish to have toward aging. In particular, disease concepts function socially through validating sick roles (for example, malingering versus "true" illness), directing research monies, and authenticating the place of society's older members. That is, a claim that aging is a disease would be supported not by acquiring empirical information, but by considering the coherent employment of disease language or by arguing the social utility of the labelling. The social impact of this usage could be considered in global terms or in terms of particular arguments that treating certain aspects of the aging process as a disease would, given presently available therapy, cause more damage than benefits (for example, consider the factors weighed in arguments for and against estrogen replacement for postmenopausal women: increase in the sense of well-being and prevention of widow's hump and senile vaginitis, versus possible increased likelihood of carcinoma). Though empirical information is used, it is judged in nonempirical terms. ("How much increase in well-being is worth what increase in risk of cancer?" is not an empirical question.)

However one answers the question of whether aging is a disease, it will be couched in either conceptual cr social terms, which is to say that there is no final answer because our use of disease language and our interests may change.

CALLING AGING A DISEASE

The similarity between aging and conditions usually called diseases is fairly strong. The fact that the four cardinal aspects of the sick role (as described by Talcott Parsons) can be applied to the state of being aged suggests that aging can be called disease: (1) one is exempted from usual social responsibilities in a way not unlike the excuses based on sickness; (2) the aged person is not considered immediately responsible for his or her state (as is the malingering person), but is held (as is the case with sickness) to be in a state imposed by natural processes (that is, one not due immediately to his or her volition); (3) insofar as research focuses on postponing aging or reversing its processes aging, like sickness, is something to treat or avoid; (4) the aged person, as the sick individual, becomes the one who should seek the help of the health care establishment. Moreover, aging is easily considered a dysteleological and disaesthetic state often accompanied by pain and explainable in terms of pathophysiological and psychopathological laws. It is an illness in a much stronger sense than other states of debility which, though treated by medicine, are not considered diseases (for example, the pain of childbirth); it is not part of a process leading to a generally embraced goal. In short, aging can be construed as a state of affairs that should be treated as a disease not unlike illnesses in general. Aging as a disease identifies a disagreeable state or condition that appears within the sick role and is amenable to medical treatment.

The distinction between unpostponable and postponable aging is important in considering the language to apply to the phenomenon. Many current judgments turn on the avoidable versus the unavoidable debilities of age. To say "He is in good health for a man of 95," probably means (in part) that he has none of the avoidable debilities of old age, but only those that are unavoidable for his age. Using a different set of criteria to judge the health of a 25-year-old vis-à-vis that of a 95-year-old appeals to hidden judgments as to what debilities are avoidable or likely to be avoidable by each. Such differences in judgment turn in part on what is usual for persons in those age groups (so that to be unusually debilitated is to be pathologically aged). But the usual, though easily avoided, debilities constitute another group of conditions that could have been avoided and were not. That is, one may also mean that though most 95-year-olds have disabilities of a certain kind, they need not. Those treatable and/or preventable states would count as diseases even if widely distributed.

At this point, it is worth introducing an important caveat: The word *aging* includes a widely disparate group of human disabilities. One has some notion of what the word means, but it is imprecise. It seems to include disabilities such as presbyopia, loss of physical and psychological stamina and abilities, specific changes consequent upon menopause, the end states of general wear and tear such as the abrasion of teeth, and so on. To ask whether aging is a disease may then be a plea for assurance that it is proper to take responsibility for one's destiny, including vigor in old age. This may in part be a displaced religious question concerning the propriety of arrogating to one's self a power once attributed to the deity: setting the scope of human vigor. Or one may be asking very general social questions about the impact of successful treatment of the aged on our social structure: how to reformulate social security, how to provide an interesting life for the old but vigorous, how to change our notions of life-projects for vigorous 80-year-olds, and whether eliminating debilities of old age would be worth the burden of these social changes.

On the other hand, instead of these general questions, one may have in mind the treatment of particular debilities. As mentioned, this sort of issue has recently been raised concerning the treatment of menopause. Consider statements such as "[A] menopausal woman is . . . not normal; she suffers from a deficiency disease with serious sequelae and needs treatment."[4] Or the assertion, "We believe the menopause and the menopausal state to be a disease so insidiously blended with chronologic aging that there is a tendency for it to be overlooked and neglected."[5] Such assertions (1) isolate a universal occurrence and term it a disease, an improper or undesirable state, a deviance from that human norm which nature nowhere achieves (that is, all women who live long enough become postmenopausal); (2) label as disease a debility closely bound to aging; yet (3) attempt to distinguish the debilities of menopause from those of aging generally (perhaps with the presupposition that menopause, if identified with aging, will in some sense be conceived of as normal—though how it differs from other debilities associated with aging is not explained). We see, thus, in this consideration of menopause the isolation of one element of aging as a disease. This is probably a paradigm of how elements of aging will be, and can usefully be, considered diseases as they become avoidable or postponable.

To appreciate the significance of such moves, we should attempt to see what evidence counts against them. What is most unusual about calling such states as menopause diseases is their universal occurrence. One would be hard pressed to find non-aging-related instances of universal disabilities or deficiencies that are called diseases (the inability of humans, unlike many other mammals, to produce vitamin C is not considered a disease, although a rodent usually capable of producing vitamin C might be considered diseased if it became dependent on exogenous vitamin C). The response to this objection is twofold: (1) One understands aging to be a disease in that other members of the population, that is, the young, do not have the debilities of the aged. Considering aging as a disease requires observation of the population over time, not at one time-age point. (2) Unlike other animals, humans (at least some of them) have the unique ability to transcend in thought their present predicaments.

Thus, should human capabilities be radically enlarged, present restricted capabilities would count for future humans as states of debility, indeed disease. To repeat, judgments about whether states of affairs are diseases turn upon expectations concerning the human condition that can and do change. Many human expectations, though, are not likely to change, and some things are likely to continue to be appreciated as diseases. But that need not be the case, and is not the case, with respect to all human conditions, as changing attitudes attest (for example, attitudes toward homosexuality, alcoholism, drug abuse, and so on).

POSTPONING DEATH

Finally, in addition to being able to treat aging, postpone its consequences, and, at least as a logical possibility, eliminate it by preventing its limitations prior to death, it is possible that life expectancy, life span, or both may be extendable. Given the distinctions I have advanced, that would not strictly count as treating aging. Perhaps these will be extended, but without any impact on the time at which the ravages of aging appear (that is, the innovations would simply increase the years spent with the limitations of aging). With respect to this possibility, the concept of aging as a disease is a reminder of the danger of simply postponing death. Death is often portrayed as the old man's friend precisely because it means release from pains and problems.

Should both aging and death be postponable, problems of balances will have to be faced. Are there extensions beyond which life itself becomes boring? Could problems of boredom be solved by freely allowing suicide? What resources can be expended on postponing death without impoverishing the quality of life? Whatever the answers, they will be determined by an appeal in part to the amount and extent of aging humans will accept as the natural course of life—the extent to which aging will be considered a disease.

CONCLUSIONS

What, then, is the answer to the question, Is aging a disease? I suggest it is that aging can indeed be considered a disease, that in many respects it has already begun to be so considered, and, considering our increasing ability to understand its processes biologically, it is likely to be more and more frequently considered a disease. Our interests concerning the concept of disease will lead us to place aging, or at least many of the debilities of aging, under it.

It is worth stressing, however, that the efficient treatment of aging will have social consequences similar to those attendant upon our control of diseases that once caused high infant mortality rates. Postponing the limitations of old age will probably engender social pressures on a par with the population explosion; postponing the average age of death will add its own problems of population in-

194 H. TRISTRAM ENGLEHARDT, JR.

crease. When we suppress high senile morbidity rates, we will face the problem of extending the opportunity to live out life-projects and of giving expanded life-projects to meet expanded abilities. Should we be able to treat aging successfully as a disease, we will face startling and wide-ranging social consequences as a result.

NOTES

1. A distinction between "illness" and "disease" should probably be drawn, with "illness" identifying a constellation of signs and symptoms recognized as pathological (for example angina), and "disease" identifying that constellation of signs and symptoms that constitutes an illness when combined with an explanation given in terms of the laws of pathophysiology or psychopathology (for example coronary artery disease). See H. T. Engelhardt, Jr., "Ideology and Etiology," *The Journal of Medicine and Philosophy* 1 (September 1976): 256–268; and Lester King, "What Is Disease?" *Philosophy of Science* 21 (July 1954): 193–203.
2. T. Parsons, "Definitions of Health and Illness in the Light of American Values and Social Structure," pp. 165–187 and "Illness, Therapy and the Modern Urban American Family," pp. 234–245, in *Patients, Physicians and Illness,* ed., E. Jaco (Glencoe, Ill.: Free Press, 1958); "The Mental Hospital as a Type of Organization," in *The Patient and the Mental Hospital,* ed., M. Greenblatt, D. Levinson, and R. Williams (Glencoe, Ill.: Free Press, 1957), pp. 108–129; and *The Social System* (New York: Free Press, 1951), pp. 428–479. For a summary see M. Siegler and H. Osmond, "The 'Sick Role' Revisited," *Hastings Center Studies* 1, no. 3 (1973): 41.
3. See A. Barnes, "Is Menopause a Disease?" *Consultant* 2 (June 1962): 22–24; also R. Kistner, "The Menopause," *Clinical Obstetrics and Gynecology* 16 (December 1973): 106–129.
4. R. Wilson, R. Brevetti, and T. Wilson, "Specific Procedures for the Elimination of the Menopause," *Western Journal of Surgery, Obstetrics, and Gynecology* 71 (May-June 1963): 120.
5. Ibid.

IV

ETHICAL ISSUES IN
LIFE-SPAN EXTENSION

10

Justice and Valuing Lives

ROBERT M. VEATCH

Our society is currently debating the question of which life-extending technologies ought to get priority for research and development. Technologies exist or are projected that will cure specific diseases, replace failing organs with prostheses (such as the artificial heart or kidney), and regenerate tissue. We have several theories for understanding and modifying the life span itself. Implicit or explicit resolution of the controversy over life valuation will be required for choosing among these competing technologies. Among the most crucial policy questions are:

1. How much priority should be given to increasing life expectancy ("squaring the curve" or increasing the chance of reaching current normal life span) as compared with extending the life span?
2. How much priority should be given to diseases of the young as compared with those of the elderly?
3. If private market mechanisms or government policy planning techniques de facto make life span increase or curve-squaring techniques available only for the rich, is that ethically acceptable, or does justice require that they be available to everyone or to all people of a certain age group regardless of ability to pay?

Before looking at specific alternative theories for placing value on lives, two preliminary distinctions must be made. First, we shall have to address the question, Value to whom? A life may be considered valuable to an individual, but have no great value to other individuals or to society as a whole. Some theories of valuing lives assume that value to society or aggregate value is the relevant consideration; others may be uninterested in value to society, considering instead value to the individual, some social group, or the one paying the bills.

Second, we must keep clear the distinction between what is value and what is right. To say that action X produces more desired consequences than action Y is not necessarily to say that action X should be chosen or is a more right action than Y. According to some theories of normative ethics, in order to establish that X is more right than Y, it is sufficient to show that it produces, on the whole, better consequences. John Stuart Mill, Jeremy Bentham, and G. E. Moore, for instance, held this view.[1] This position—consequentialism or utilitarianism—is, however, rejected by many others, including Immanuel Kant and N. D. Ross.[2] (For two helpful summaries of the debate see J. J. C. Smart and Bernard Williams, and Michael Bayles.)[3] Thus, even if we were to decide that a particular group of lives is valuable, it is still an open question whether they ought to receive unique priority in matters of choosing among life-extending technologies. In the discussion that follows I shall examine alternative theories for giving priority to lives for public policy purposes. We shall see that in some cases lives are considered "valuable" according to some theory of value. In other cases, lives are thought to have a justified claim independent of their presumed value.

Much of the work of economists and policy analysts on the value of life is devoted to calculating the cost of medical and safety interventions designed to save lives and to determining the value of human life implicit in intervention decisions. Often debates focus on the proper method for making those calculations and what might be called "problems of accounting." Richard Zeckhauser and Donald Shepard see considerable evidence that expensive life years are being saved before less costly ones. They reveal errors in accounting, in estimating benefits and costs, and in double counting or failing to count relevant data.[4] Jan P. Acton shows that various methods of estimating the value of a human life are based on different conceptual foundations and, at times, lead to widely disparate estimates of the value of particular lives.[5]

As one trained to study and be interested in the ethical foundations and implications of public policy alternatives, I am in no position to question the empirical data or even the economic formulas on
which their calculations are based. Rather, I wish to examine the
valuing of lives controversy at a different level, that of exploring the
basic premises of the life-valuing enterprise itself. I shall argue that
regardless of the method of calculating the value of a human life
and the costs of alternative programs for adding years of life, it is a
mistake to base a public policy on an estimate of the value of life-
years in the aggregate or abstract. Public policy should focus on
ethical claims that cannot be captured in such estimates: on the fairness of the distribution of life-years, the quality of the life-years
with special attention to relief of suffering, and whether disease and
death that shorten lives are in some sense the responsibility of the
individual or are beyond individual control.

In the first part of this chapter I examine what seem to me in-
surmountable problems with the methods currently being proposed
for determining the value of life for public policy purposes. I argue
that they all involve aggregating benefits and harms, as if distribution were of no policy consequence. In the second portion I suggest
some alternative priority principles for deciding among policies for
lifesaving.

PROBLEMS WITH COST-BENEFIT APPROACHES

Acton summarizes three general methods of determining the
value of a human life using cost-benefit methods.[6] Use of political
precedent, livelihood saving, or willingness-to-pay measures will, at
least potentially, make a difference. Examination of past political
decisions tells us something about what people, through their representatives, value. At least it tells us to what they give priority whether or not it is valued. It could be, for instance, that political representatives are making allocation decisions not entirely on the basis
of what lives are valued, but also on other bases—a sense of need or
justice, compassion, or political opportunism. The proposals are
methods for telling us what is getting priority, but not necessarily
methods for telling us what is valued. The willingness-to-pay and
human capital approaches, however, move us closer to substance.[7]
They begin to tell us about what is relevant when deciding how to
value lives, that is, the individual's subjective willingness to pay for a

change in his chances of survival and his economic productivity, respectively. Both are essentially economic theories of value and measure value in dollar terms.

There are some problems with these economic formulas, though. First, they are at times incompatible. For instance, according to the willingness-to-pay approach, at least up to a certain point, the older one becomes, the more valuable life becomes (because, subject to willingness-to-borrow, one is generally willing to pay more to avoid death risk since one has higher income levels). On the other hand, in human capital terms, the older one becomes, the less valuable life is, to the point that at retirement (at least for males who tend not to be involved in nonmonetized domestic labor) life is "worthless."

There are also moral problems in the formulas. Using willingness-to-pay or human capital formulas, males will tend to be more valuable than females, the rich more valuable than the poor, whites more valuable than blacks, urban dwellers more valuable than farmers. According to these schemes, it would be rational (perhaps morally required) to target research on prevention of death to diseases that have a uniquely high incidence in upper income, white, urban-dwelling males.

THE PERVASIVENESS OF AGGREGATING MEASURES

As bases for determining priorities for health research, these schemes may present even more fundamental moral problems. Using economic values of various human lives is useful primarily because it permits aggregation of risks and benefits for purposes of comparing policy proposals. The literature on the theory and use of cost-benefit analysis (see Eckstein; Drake, Keeney, and Morse; Prest and Turvey; McKean; Sewell, Davis, Scott, and Ross; and Dorfman [8]) and its application to health care (illustrated by the work of Klarman; Bailey; Taylor; Zeckhauser; Bay, Flathman, and Nestman; Pauker and Kassirer; Williams; and Roberts [9]) makes clear that measuring aggregate net benefit over harm is the objective. The literature reporting or summarizing the data (see Held; Buxton and West; McNeil et al.; McNeil and Adelstein; Neuhauser and Lewicki; Schoenbaum et al.; Longmore and Rehahn; Bush, Chen, and Patrick; Komrower; Mushkin; Steiner and Smith; and The Advisory Committee on Inborn Errors of Metabolism to the

Ministry of Health [10]) all use aggregate economic indicators such as cost per death averted, per year of life extended, per test performed, or per case treated, as the method of choosing among alternative life-extending technologies.

Zeckhauser and Shepard list six different potential measures of outcome: life expectancy in years, infant mortality rate, days of disability per capita, number of acute conditions per year, days of work loss per person in the currently employed population, and days of school loss per person of school age.[11] There are clear differences in what these indicators measure. Minimizing one, such as days of work loss per person, would probably not minimize another, such as infant mortality rate. There might be some correlations in certain programs, but not necessarily. What is crucial, however, is that all, no matter how they differ, are aggregate measures, averaged and expressed in per capita terms. They aggregate individual effects by summing the results of individuals and dividing by the number of individuals in the population. In doing so, important information on the distribution of the effects is lost. If we were to calculate projections of these aggregate indicators, we would not know whether the effects were distributed evenly or clustered with substantial impact on a small segment of the population. We would not know, for instance, whether days of work loss were the result of voluntary risk-taking (a skiing accident, for instance,) or of a genetic disease over which the individual has no control. If this information is considered in any way relevant to the policy choice, it is a meaningful loss in the process of data manipulation to produce the measures being used.

Aggregate measures may not tell us anything about the qualitative dimensions of the life-years added, although this is more of a problem with some measures, such as life expectancy in years, than others. Days of disability per capita or days of work loss per person would help to fill in the qualitative picture. Thus the combination of the measures tells more than any one alone.

More sophisticated "social indicators" developed over the last decade measure not only health, but education, nutrition, housing, political participation, and even cultural events.[12] A classic utilitarian would have to adopt a more complex set of indicators of value than strictly economic measures.

The proposal discussed by Zeckhauser and Shepard[13] to adjust for quality of life-years added by any health or safety policy intervention, provides a rough estimate of the quality of life these broader social indicators measure. It is certainly an improvement over cruder measures of average life-years added. The quality adjusted life-year (QALY), however, is still an aggregate measure. Zeckhauser and Shepard make clear that the individual marginal QALYs that would result from a proposed policy intervention should be aggregated. They say, "We would argue that individuals' QALY streams should be aggregated using their personal weights. . . . The appropriate measure for the output of a health-promoting program is the *total gain* in discounted QALYs it provides to all members of the population." [14] Later they reiterate that "the only information we need carry forward on the benefit side is the summary statistic computed to reflect our preferences: discounted QALYs saved." [15] Their goal is maximizing benefit in the aggregate by making the most efficient lifesaving decisions, efficiency being measured in terms of maximum improvement in their sophisticated but aggregating statistic. [16]

The willingness-to-pay measure discussed in more detail by Acton is also an aggregating measure. Individual expressions of willingness-to-pay are to be summed to determine the aggregate value of a proposed program. According to Acton, "By approving only programs such that people are willing to pay, *in the aggregate*, more than the programs cost, we can make a strong case that society *as a whole* gains." [17]

It is not clear however, why it is assumed that the goal of the policy is a gain to society "*as a whole*," if by that Acton means improvement in some selected group of aggregate indicators. In fact, it is not clear to me that the goal of public policy should be to maximize anything in aggregate, whether the aggregate be a crude measure such as years of life added, or a more sophisticated aggregate social indicator made up by combining several individual measures of social welfare, or total QALYs.

The principle underlying such a commitment must be that the goal of public policy is to maximize total social utility, to do what will be economically or more generally socially beneficial. We should, to use the utilitarian formula, produce the greatest good for the greatest number.

J. Vaupel makes the case that more emphasis should be given to early death, that is death between the ages of 15 and 65. [18] Although it is not stated explicitly, I believe that utility-maximizing is his implied principle. His arguments in defense of concentration on early death have that character. He argues, for instance, that "an individual who chooses an unhealthy life style (leading to an early death) imposes costs on other people," disrupting families and friendships, creating sizable medical expenses, and depriving society of members who support citizens under 15 and over 65.[19] In contrast, he characterizes individuals over 65 as consuming more than they produce.[20] Early deaths produce aggregate disutility—they "lower the average U.S. standard of living."[21]

I am not quite convinced that this is generally the case. Deaths of infants and the elderly are often very costly in human as well as economic terms. The death of the 55-year-old from a quick heart attack or automobile accident may be much less costly than a prolonged death from chronic kidney failure with senile dementia in an older person. I am willing to concede, however, for purposes of argument, that Vaupel is correct—that concentrating on deaths of those in their prime would be utility-maximizing. It still seems very much an open question whether concentrating on them is right as a matter of public policy.

Vaupel asked students to rank interventions in such a way that the students' own value of life could be calculated based on willingness-to-pay. I responded myself to the questions Vaupel put to his students and discovered that I placed a dollar value on my own life approximately five times that which his median student considered his life worth. Reflecting on my relative incomes now and when I was a student, I discovered that I now earn approximately five times as much. It strikes me as extremely implausible and morally outrageous that anyone should consider that my life is five times more valuable now or that it would be worth five times as much to prevent my death simply because my income has increased during the natural course of my career. Any formula based on personal estimates of how much one would pay to avoid a certain risk of death accepts the status quo distribution of incomes in our society. Accepting it may be efficient—it may be utility-maximizing—yet I am still convinced that it is not just and is not right.

JUSTICE, LIBERTY, AND INDIVIDUAL RIGHTS

Aside from economists, a few policy analysts, and a distinct minority of philosophers, very few in our society accept the principle that the objective of public policy is to maximize anything in the aggregate. Our tradition speaks of individual rights—rights to life, liberty, and the pursuit of happiness—even in the face of maximizing aggregate utility. I accept that tradition. Dollars saved or happiness produced in aggregate is not sufficient. A policy that concentrates on preventing deaths of individuals where it would contribute most to increasing QALYs in aggregate, or where there is the most aggregate willingness to pay, or where deaths will be most averted in the age group of 15 to 65, must be tested by the principle of maximizing aggregate measures of utility.

That aggregation process itself is morally suspect, at least according to many normative ethical theories. The Kantian maxim that the individual is to be treated always as an end and never only as a means would not permit a policy under which one individual or group (say the middle-aged) would benefit at the expense of another (say the elderly), even if the net benefits far outweighed the risks or harms.

Cost-benefit analyses may be very useful for determining how to maximize certain aggregate indicators such as the GNP or the increase in the average life expectancy as a result of various interventions. It is still very much an open question, however, whether maximizing anything in the aggregate is ethically right.[22]

Without abandoning economic measures of value, we might choose other policies of distribution. A maximin strategy, for instance, would strive to maximize the economic position of the least well-off members of society, not necessarily the aggregate economic well-being measured by GNP or some other aggregating measure. It is possible that rearranging resource commitments so as to maximize the welfare of the least well-off will, in fact, lead to a decrease in total welfare as measured by GNP or other aggregating measure. John Rawls's contractarian theory of justice is a contemporary revival of a nonutilitarian distributional principle.[23] His work, which is receiving great attention, provides a challenge to the use of cost-benefit techniques.

The Rawlsian maximin position is not the only plausible alternative to aggregate-maximizing cost-benefit analysis. Egalitarian theories of justice, such as those developed by Barry[24] and applied to questions of health care delivery,[25] would take as one policy objective the maximization to equality in distribution of relevant goods. In mathematical terms, the claim is that justice requires the minimization of the standard deviation of the well-being of individual citizens. Of course, justice may not be the only policy objective. The commitment also is to equality of distribution, *ceteris paribus*.

Burton Weisbrod has suggested reporting costs and benefits in disaggregated form.[26] This method would provide the means of superimposing distributional concerns on the data once the cost-benefit analysis has been performed. These distributional concerns could also be taken into account in the initial stage, that is, when setting the objectives to be evaluated by the cost-benefit analysis. All of these proposals, however, require superimposing the criteria of justice or fairness on the data at one point or another.

OTHER INHERENT PROBLEMS

The exclusion of the ethical claims of justice, equality, and liberty is not the only problem in cost-benefit approaches to establishing a value of life. There are other objections to the use of economic and broader aggregating social indicators. Whether one considers only economic or broader social goods, schemes that permit meaningful manipulation of data require some common scale of measurement. This is often dollars, although any generalized medium would do. (In fact, there are reasons why money is not linearly related to aggregate good—because of decreasing and increasing utility of dollars spent in various ways.) Whatever the scale, schemes permitting manipulation of aggregate data have the characteristic of quantifying goods often thought to be nonquantifiable. They reduce all goods to a common denominator. If the denominator is money, they monetize fundamental goods thought to be valued in such ways that their quality is lost when converted to a common, quantifiable scale.

Related to this problem is the underlying question of the value of systematic, structured planning. Economic and broader social indicator schemes permitting manipulation of masses of data are attractive precisely because they permit a systematic, rational analysis and comparison of alternatives. But systems analysis, rational centralized planning, and quantification are not value-neutral. They are attractive to holders of certain value orientations. Independent of whether systematic and rational centralized planning produces better or worse policy recommendations than, say, intuition, is the more fundamental question of style. It is not necessarily irrational to risk choosing a policy with lesser overall utility in order to adopt a more spontaneous, casual, "romantic" mode of policy choice.

There are two bases for this evaluation of the planning process itself. First, one might hold that systematic, centralized planning is acceptable in principle, but that error is so likely in its application that it is better, in the long run, not to adopt it. If it were likely that only certain goods would be quantified and, therefore, nonquantifiables would be systematically overlooked, and if those nonquantifiables were thought especially important, it would be rational to eschew the approach and avoid the potential policy error. One might, so to speak, trust one's intuitions more than the calculated answers. The problem is especially acute with complex systems for policy analysis because, as they become more complex, only those with special skills (and therefore possibly special biases) would be available to perform the analysis. If, for instance, one feared that those who choose to make careers out of quantifying complex policy choices had a unique commitment to quantifiable goods over and against nonquantifiable ones, then one might, as a matter of strategy, prefer that the experts in systematic policy analysis not perform their calculations.

On the other hand, one might object, in principle, to systematic data-based analysis of policy problems as contrary to a sense of human freedom or spontaneity, as overly rationalistic, or as an effort to reduce to conscious analysis choices better left to less precise modes of reflection. The author personally finds that attitude unacceptable; he finds responsible, conscious, systematic policy decision making not only good in principle, but part of being a responsible member of the human community. But it is sobering to realize that a basic life-style choice is at stake here. One cannot systematically or rationally prove that systematic, rational policy analysis is a preferable style of living in a social community.

Both the willingness-to-pay and the human capital formulas for determining the value of lives are interesting from the standpoint of health policy planning because they provide data for such policy techniques as cost-benefit analysis. Whenever the cost of a decrease in risk of a particular death threat is less than the projected benefits determined from the value of the lives in question, the implication is that the investment in that research or treatment is "worth it." Or, to be more accurate, health policy planners ought to invest in that research and treatment which is projected to increase benefits the most. It should be clear, however, that a shift in the method of valuing lives will radically change the policy conclusions.

SPECIFIC PROBLEMS WITH THE HUMAN CAPITAL APPROACH

The human capital or livelihood approach at first seems to increase the importance of adding extra years to life: The more years one is productive, the more human capital. Yet it is clear from the formulas that only productive years would count. The formulas should choose among alternative life-extending technologies on the basis of the more productive years for the dollar. These may be curve-squaring years or life-span-increase years. Life-span-increase years would have to be coupled, however, with an increase of the age of retirement. Since this is a likely outcome of a significant change in life-span in any case—because it would be necessary to keep the worker-dependent ratio the same—it may be a plausible assumption.

The real challenge to the human capital approach must come from the question, Is it really morally relevant for public policy that the years added through a life-extending technology are productive in the economic sense used by Rice and Cooper? Their economic calculations of human capital produce strongly counterintuitive implications. Men are much more valuable than women, whites more valuable than nonwhites; children with diseases that will predictably strike them down before they enter the labor force are worthless, as are all retirees (except those engaged in domestic labor if we monetize that in our calculations). Yet if life has moral importance independent of labor productivity or in addition to it, then use of the human capital or livelihood formulas may lead to inappropriate judgments and confuse rather than inform our policy choices.

SPECIFIC PROBLEMS WITH THE WILLINGNESS-TO-PAY APPROACH

Acton criticizes the human capital approach on the grounds that it lacks a satisfactory normative justification.[27] He argues, I think with good reason, that the approach is not conceptually sound. People are not machines; the value of life is not equal to the value of labor. He goes on, however, to advocate the willingness-to-pay approach, which seems open to the same attack. If it is conceptually unsound to equate the real value of a life with the value of the labor that life will produce, it is also unsound to conclude that there is any necessary relationship between what I would pay for a program to add years of life and what society *ought* to pay for that program. It should be granted, as Acton argues, that individual preferences count,[28] but this cannot mean that they are all that count.

The willingness-to-pay formulas of Schelling and others seem to have the same implications for life-extending-technology choices that they do for other policy choices: they select in favor of those with more ability to pay. No clear priority is given to curve-squaring over life-span-extending technologies, but some balancing of the two would result. If the allocation basis were private investment decisions, the balancing would be done by individuals. If it were done by a government agency aggregating willingness-to-pay decisions through surveys or other data-gathering techniques, the balancing would reflect the average willingness-to-pay of the target group. Such aggregating techniques might minimize, but would clearly not eliminate, the discriminatory impact. Furthermore, there is no necessary reason within the approach why a poor person's willingness-to-pay should be averaged with a rich person's. In fact, the direct implication seems to be that decreasing the chances of a particular death for a wealthy person is more valued than the same decrease in risk for a poor one. Aggregating would cost us what should be seen as important data for those seeing willingness-to-pay as important or relevant to the policy choice.

There have been some suggestions to account for distributional considerations. Willingness-to-pay could be measured for instance, in terms of percentage of income rather than dollars.[29] It seems plausible, though, that high income individuals might be willing to pay not only a greater amount, but a greater percentage of income to obtain an expensive life-saving technology. There is no reason why percentage of income is a fairer measure than dollars. Marginal percents are not much more comparable in different income groups than marginal dollars.

The use of total willingness-to-pay as a measure of which life-extending programs should be chosen also creates problems when considering conditions for which all are not equally at risk. Programs to treat genetic conditions, at least those that manifest themselves early in life, would be of no interest to those who do not have the condition; presumably their willingness-to-pay for decreasing their risk of it would be low. Analysts might ask instead, how much one would pay to reduce the risk to one's offspring. This would arouse the interest of a rational, self-interested adult who was planning to have children and who could not eliminate the possibility that they would be affected with the genetic disease. For many such diseases, however, we can know with certainty whether our offspring are at risk through pedigree analysis, genetic screening, and, if necessary, prenatal diagnosis. From the standpoint of self-interest, one should be willing to pay little or nothing for programs to prevent such diseases. One might have a self-interest in avoiding the witnessing of suffering around him, but this does not seem to be the real moral basis of a commitment to health programs designed to affect a condition one is virtually certain not to have.

The willingness-to-pay approach faces a similar problem when evaluating programs designed to affect conditions occurring predominantly in special ethnic or economic groups. I cannot see that it is relevant if sufferers from sickle cell disease (who might be low income on average) would pay less to remove a death risk than sufferers of ulcers would pay if it were true that ulcers tended to afflict only high income individuals. If certain diseases such as hypertension and Tay-Sachs disease, or mental conditions needing or appearing to need prolonged private psychoanalysis, cluster or appear to cluster in particular ethnic or socioeconomic groups, total willingness-to-pay measures will be distorted. It cannot be morally decisive that the total or per capita willingness-to-pay for diseases affecting the rich is higher than for those affecting the poor. Which programs ought to be supported, what society ought to be willing to pay for, cannot depend totally on what individuals are, in fact, willing to pay for.

Acton acknowledges that the willingness-to-pay procedure has been questioned on the grounds that it depends on income distribution. He writes off the objection without confronting it, however, claiming simply that the problem, which has not been solved by critics, is to devise an alternative benefit measure that satisfies such objections.[30] We have suggested some marginal improvements such as measuring willingness-to-pay in terms of percentage of incomes rather than dollars, but the real problem is the assumption that a *benefit* measure is required rather than some criteria for determining what is right independent of aggregate benefits. Acton's conclusion is that both the livelihood-saving approach (with its known drawbacks) and an imperfect, crudely measured willingness-to-pay methodology are clearly superior to the total lack of formal analysis.[31] I am not sure that is the case. If I had to choose between methods known to be not only crude, but flawed in their conceptual foundations because they systematically exclude considerations of justice, liberty, and other dimensions of rightness on the one hand and my intuitions on the other, I might often choose my intuitions.

ALTERNATIVE APPROACHES TO VALUING OF LIVES

Acton fairly accuses critics of not offering alternative approaches. It is unfair for those dissatisfied with aggregate-maximizing policy analysis devices, such as utilitarian economics and many forms of cost-benefit analysis, to simply throw a broadside, saying that dollar values cannot be placed on human life, and leaving policy planners with no alternative priority principles. I suggest four alternatives, each of which has its advocates, before attempting to construct a set of priority principles for selecting among alternative health and safety policies designed to add life-years to certain members of the society.

THE "ALL-LIVES-ARE-OF-EQUAL-VALUE" POSITION

The first and most obvious challenge to the economic and other aggregating methods for determining the value of lives is to retreat to the claim that all lives are of equal value—all men are created equal. Of course, the well-rehearsed argument is that obviously all men are not equal or that, even if they were, they would soon be very unequal because of different opportunities and life choices. The equally well-rehearsed response is that men—and women—are equal in what really counts: They are equal as members of the human community, or of the Kingdom of Ends, to use Bernard Williams's Kantian phrase. According to Williams:

> The respect owed equally to each man as a member of the Kingdom of Ends is not that owed to him in respect of any empirical characteristics that he may possess, but solely in respect of the transcendental characteristic of being a free and rational will.[32]

The policy implications of this understanding of the value of a human life are complex. It may be that theoretical principles of justice or equality cannot be applied directly to policy questions such as how health resources ought to be allocated. This seems to be the position of Rawls.[33] Yet, for some, this notion of the equal value of life can and should be applied.

One possible application would be that each life is to be given equal value and, therefore, variables such as future earnings, willingness-to-pay, their social correlates (sex, race, religion, and so on), and age are irrelevant. The objective of policy from this perspective might be to relieve the suffering of those who are suffering most, or increase the chances of survival for those most likely to die within a given period, without regard to whose suffering or life is involved.

An alternative application might be to conclude that each person, during his lifetime, ought to have an equal maximum health expenditure (at least at public expense). This is the principle behind proposed lifetime limits on national health insurance.[34] It would result in a quite different policy choice. In both cases, however, the starting point is that all lives—for purposes of health policy—are of equal value. To use the image of a graph, graphing age against the value of lives at particular ages would produce a straight line.

The implications of the all-lives-are-equal position depends a great deal on how one applies the egalitarian principle. Does it mean that everyone is entitled to an equal dollar expenditure on health, an equal access to the resources needed to be healthy, an equal maximum amount of health care, or an equal claim to the health care needed to provide opportunities for a level of health equal, as far as possible, with other persons' health? I have gone on record defending the last alternative.[35]

The methodology used to defend that conclusion resembles the Rawlsian original-position method, although the conclusions are somewhat different. In order to establish a moral principle for structuring basic social practices, we might ask ourselves what rational, self-interested people would choose as a guiding maxim, provided they were ignorant of what their station in life would be. If they knew general facts about human psychology, including preferences and values, and the facts of the natural sciences, but had no knowledge of what their particular situation in life would be, what would they choose? Rawls claims that rational people would choose first, liberty compatible with like liberty for all, and second, social and economic inequalities arranged to the greatest benefit of the least advantaged, and attached to offices and positions open to all.[36] Elsewhere I have argued that this would not always be the obvious rational choice of people so situated.[37] In some cases they might prefer to have goods distributed more evenly even if it did not maximize the position of the least well-off. (On other occasions they might choose to maximize total or average good.) Justice requires, according to this view, that policies be oriented to giving opportunities to bring people into positions that are more nearly equal, even if the result is not the same as it would be if the maximin formula were applied. From this perspective, the maximin formula is not an expression of a principle of justice, but a complex formula for resolving conflicts between efficiency and the requirements of justice. That guide, however, is nothing more than that. In some cases, the claims of equality might be seen even by the least well-off as weightier than the goal of improving their own lot.

If equal dollar amounts are to be expended on each person, some will use up their share quite early trying to make their contribution to the curve-squaring enterprise. Others who, as fate has it, are quite healthy during early life, will have resources to begin and continue life-span-increase treatments. The policy implication seems to be that life-extending technologies throughout the present life span and beyond will be important, although for different people.

If the objective is to provide health care opportunities sufficient to produce health equal, insofar as possible, with other people's health, variables such as future earnings, willingness-to-pay, sex, race, religion, and age are not directly morally relevant in policy formation, although they may be involved indirectly. The goal, we suggested, of a policy growing out of these considerations might be to relieve the suffering of those who are suffering most, or to increase the chances of survival for those most likely to die within a given period, without regard to whose suffering or life is involved. If, however, the goal is more opportunity for equality of health, choosing among life-extending technologies would depend on direct comparison of the weightiness of the claims of all people. Those who are suffering the most or who have the highest mortality risk would get the highest priority. Technologies that would achieve these objectives would be the policy choices. This seems to weight policy determination in favor of certain curve-squaring technologies, as well as technologies that may neither square the curve nor extend life span, that is, those that merely relieve suffering. To devote resources to life-span increase for those who are not suffering or are not in high mortality risk groups would be unjust in that it would divert resources from caring for the least well-off group.

THE "PRIME-OF-LIFE" POSITION

The first challenge to the all-lives-are-equal position might come from those who speak romantically of the "prime of life." To say there is a prime is like saying that some part (early to late middle-age) is more valuable, and therefore that the extremes—the beginning and the end—are less valued.

It stands behind the (often unexamined) intuition that it may be better to let a seriously and chronically ill infant die "before there has been much social learning and attachment." If infancy and childhood are preparation for the prime, and the prime is not likely to come, why bother at all? It also stands behind the "over-the-hill" attitude toward superannuated business executives, or the retired, waiting for their day to come. It may also be the foundation of Vaupel's argument for a greater priority for focusing on deaths in the 15 to 65 age group rather than the more general social utilitarian argument suggested above. The graph of this position would be a parabola, with the line beginning at the origin, rising to a peak at 35, 45, or 55 (depending in part on one's present age), and descending to a very low plateau at retirement.

Here it is important to distinguish between lives of value to society and lives of intrinsic value regardless of social usefulness. At this point, we are considering only the view that the prime of life is intrinsically valued because of its quality. If we were to shift and consider middle-aged life as instrumentally valued because of its usefulness to society, we would have shifted back to the aggregate utilitarian economic and social indicators position. Even those who focus solely on intrinsic value of individual life independent of its usefulness find it difficult to treat age as anything more than a high correlate of high quality life. There must be some for whom the "prime" is not approached gradually in middle years, then passed for a period of decline. To the extent that age is a critical variable in estimating the quality of life, it must be an approximation.

The policy implications of treating the prime of life as the most valued years are enormous. Rather than calculating the most valuable lives by willingness-to-pay or future lifetime earnings or giving each person an equal claim because each is equally valued, priority would go to diseases that cut people down in their prime. Diseases of infancy and childhood that, if treated, permit one to grow to the prime would be second in priority. Diseases of the elderly and of infants and children who will not reach their prime would have the lowest.

The prime-of-life position would provide unique patterns for distributing life-extending technologies. There may, in fact, be some correlation between the implications of this position and that of the economic formulas. The human capital approach produces dollar figures for the value of life, which increase gradually until they peak in the 25 to 34 age range and then decline, dropping rapidly in old age. (The present value of lifetime earnings discounted at 6 percent for all over 85 is $519, for white males $543, for nonwhite females, $128.)

If our policy objective is to maximize the additional years at the prime of life, disease interventions that extend the prime, or extend lives so they can be lived in what is considered the prime, will get priority. Life-span-increasing technologies would receive attention only if they also had an impact on life's prime—especially if they were to extend it.

THE "FUTURE-LIFE-IS-VALUED" OR "YOUNGER-IS-BETTER" POSITION

Still another challenge to the economic formulas and to the all-lives-are-equal positions is the view that the future is what is really valuable; the more future one has, the more one is to be valued. This position may be related to the human capital approach, since all future lifetime earnings are considered valuable, while any past experiences—even past earnings—count for naught. The human capital approach, however, discounts future earnings, making a young child "less valuable" than a 30-year-old employee. It may also stand behind the contemporary youth culture phenomenon and our social propensity to adopt the patterns of society's young. "A little child shall lead you," might be cited as the biblical text. If we were to graph the value of life against age in this case, the line would begin at its highest point and slope gradually down toward death.

There are really not one, but several closely related positions here. The differences can be seen by comparing two children of the same age who have differing life expectancies. If the critical element is the amount of future life remaining, then the one with the longer life expectancy would be more valued. If it is youthfulness that is valued, the two could be considered of equal value.

Comparing the value of lives in this context is very uncomfortable—even if the implications are tolerable in the end. Yet I do not think it necessary to retreat to the all-lives-are-equal position. There may be something sound in the perception that youth have a special claim on us. Maybe what we really sense is an argument from justice or fairness. The position would be that each person ought to have an equal claim to live to a particular age, insofar as possible, and that the claim to live to early ages is greater than the claim to live to older ages. The impact would be a descending priority for interventions against disease and death as a function of age, with the problems of the youngest having progressively less weight. In a forced choice between two critically injured people in an accident, it is not an implausible position to provide the single lifesaving device to the younger. The old lifeboat slogan "women and children first" is now seen as chauvinistic or discriminatory against adult males, depending on your point of view. The "children first" part, however, may make a great deal of moral sense.

The defense of this age-related priority principle must be an appeal to a sense of justice—a sense that each has an equal right to live to a particular age. Those who have reached that age, therefore, have less of a claim in any particular crisis than those who have not.

The future-life-is-valued and younger-is-better positions evaluate harshly death interventions that will extend the life span. There are two possible interpretations of this. One is that youth becomes only relatively valued. A formula might emerge so that priorities are assigned as a function of age, weighted by the factor 1/age. Thus a 25-year-old's life extension would count as 1/25, a 75-year-old, 1/75. This might be the policy implication of a value-of-life graph that slopes gradually and negatively as a function of age.

The other interpretation of this position is not so much a claim on the value of life as a claim of justice: that everyone has a right to a given minimal number of years. This argument from fairness might imply that 65 years or 21 years or 5 years is a just claim. It might also be interpreted as meaning that an absolute priority is given to the youngest age group before any is given to older people. This priority principle—sometimes called "lexicographical ordering"—if taken to its extreme would mean no life-extending research and treatment for older children and adults until the medical problems of 1-year-olds are solved. We would then move to 2-year-olds and so forth. Of course, the problem would be that we would probably never move beyond the intractable cases of 1-year-olds diseases. Life-span-increase technology would have the lowest priority.

In spite of the fact that, when pushed to its extremes, the implications of this proposal are counterintuitive, I find the basic insight a plausible working-out of a notion of justice or fairness. Possibly other ethically relevant factors would push us in some other direction so that a compromise formula would emerge, but something seems right about the notion of giving priority to the youngest, so that everyone has a chance at some minimal number of years.

The reasonable person in "the original position," or the hypothetical ideal observer, in my estimation would find it plausible to give substantial weight—if not absolute priority—to the life extension of the youngest on grounds of fairness. That relief of suffering and other concerns would also be relevant in deciding what is right is obvious. Thus, this is a fairness claim, *ceteris paribus*.

THE "OLDER-TENDS-TO-BE-BETTER" POSITION

This is a final position. The opposite of the future orientation and interpretation of justice just discussed, it is the view that "older-is-wiser" or at least that older tends to be better. Again there are several variants. One is that a person is to be valued to the extent he is wise. If wisdom comes with age, if experience is the best teacher, then increasing age may make life increasingly valuable. The age-grade cultures of the traditional East seem to venerate the elderly for reasons of this sort. This interpretation is compatible with the social usefulness as well as the individual perspectives on value.

A second variant is that what is really valuable in life is its memories. Again, this could be true from both social and individual value perspectives. The more memories, the more value; and the more age, the more memories. Emphasizing either wisdom or memories would lead one to value old age rather than youth—at least insofar as these correlate with age. The policy implications are great: priority ought to go to maximizing wise or memory-full old age. Diseases of the elderly might be a particular priority, especially those such as senile dementia, which have an impact on wisdom and memory. Diseases of younger people that will have an impact on old age would also get special attention. A holder of this view might believe it better to let natural selection take care of problems of childhood and the young adult period. Resources could be better spent elsewhere.

It might be fair, and possibly also utility-maximizing, to give greatest weight to extending the lives of some so that they can achieve highly valuable old age. Especially if one were selected into the pool of those who would get life-extending treatments by a lottery—by an actual drawing or by the natural lottery of genetics and body deterioration—a case could be made that this position is fair. Compared, however, to the claims of other groups, especially the young, the case is a difficult one to make.

JUSTIFICATION FOR A SET OF PRIORITY PRINCIPLES

These four alternatives to the determination of the value of life by the use of aggregating measures such as the willingness-to-pay and human capital approaches are themselves mutually exclusive, at least at certain points. What is needed is an integrated set of priority principles for evaluating public policy alternatives. Any such set will have to be derived from a basic normative ethical theory. The candidates for those theories cannot be fully outlined here much less a full defense given of one particular theory. I have throughout this chapter, however, provided the foundations for the normative ethical stance I find most plausible.

It rejects the validity of aggregate utility-maximizing as leading to conclusions that are unjust and liberty-constraining, violating basic rights held by our tradition to be inalienable. An ethical principle that ought to be put in its place is the principle that all have an equal claim to the health care needed to provide a level of health equal, insofar as possible, with other persons' health. As this is a ceteris paribus principle, it will necessarily have to give way to other claims upon occasion, but it should be the decisive starting point for evaluating alternative public policies. This being the case, several priority principles can be derived.

First, for reasons already argued, the relative social usefulness of individuals or members of a class, their willingness to pay for life-extending technologies, and the dollar value of their future production ought to be irrelevant to policy choices regarding alternative life-extending technologies.

Second, although use of broader social indicators and measures that take into account quality of life-year added, such as the measure of a QALY discussed by Zeckhauser and Shepard, correct some of the problems raised by the use of strictly economic measures, they are still aggregate measures and thus fall to any criticism of general social utility-maximizing formulas. In the end, I concede that aggregate measures of cost and benefit are relevant as well. I am willing to give some relevance to concentrating on diseases producing death in the prime of life simply because the social consequences will be good on balance if such deaths are reduced. But there are great dangers in the principle of producing good consequences; there are dangers that individual rights, liberty, and our sense of justice will be sacrificed. In a case of policy choice where these principles conflict, I am strongly inclined toward promoting justice, even if that means lower aggregate indicators of utility. Concern for individual rights and obligations—including claims of justice in distribution, self-determination, truthfulness, and other right-making characteristics—must be the central elements in the choice.

Third, the principle of justice requires that the younger the individual, the greater should be the priority his condition receives for life-extending technologies. An essential part of the egalitarian principle of justice is that there should be, insofar as possible, an equal opportunity to live to the same age as others. This means that high priority goes to those who have conditions that will end their lives at an early age.

Fourth, there should likewise be an equality of opportunity to live life without suffering. The objective of public policy should not be the maximum reduction in suffering. That would again be an aggregate measure that could lead to a policy of giving highest priority to a disease such as the common cold from which many people suffer, but each only a small amount. Rather, the priority should be on conditions that produce the greatest suffering in the individuals who have them, giving them an opportunity to lead a life with suffering more nearly that of other people's, even if it means that there is not a maximum reduction in the total suffering in the world and that we do not achieve the greatest possible additional number of life-years.

Fifth, unless the duties to prolong life and preserve health are absolute and take lexicographical precedence over all other duties and interests, in some cases the needs of the generally least well-off may have to be placed ahead of those who may die relatively early because of a medical problem. I reject the liberal economics view that Pareto optimality (the stable state reached when all parties have completed all exchanges that would maximize their welfare) ought to be obtained by distributing a generalized medium such as money so that individuals may buy what they most desire, whether it be health care or other goods. I reject this for a number of reasons.[38] The mere fact that someone desires something does not give it weight that is binding on society. If it is legitimate to distinguish between a need and a desire, and I am convinced that it is, we can also distinguish between more and less weighty claims against the society by individuals. Furthermore, goods such as research and development of interventions that add life-years are social goods. They cannot be easily individualized. One person's choice to use his resources has a direct effect on the ability of others to use their resources in ways they choose. The development of medical treatments and the facilities to deliver them depends on the collective cooperating to serve a common good, whether or not particular individuals find that good in their interest. Nevertheless, although the liberal commitment to individual preference cannot be fully defended, it is reasonable to recognize that some medical conditions, even ones that lead to earlier death, should not get as high a priority as other social goods.

Sixth, even in cases where individuals are of equal age and have conditions that, hypothetically, produce the same amount of suffering, not all conditions are equal. There is a moral difference in the claims of individuals with medical problems, even life-threatening ones, based on our understanding of the causal sequence leading to their condition. The principle that each should have an opportunity for health equal to that of other persons' does not require that everyone in the end must be equally healthy. It merely requires that each be given an opportunity, insofar as possible, to enjoy that degree of health. One of the inherent rights of individuals, which is morally relevant to policy making independent of its impact on aggregate social utility, is the principle of self-determination. We believe, I think rightly, that people should be free to engage in health-risky behavior even if that behavior cannot be justified in terms of the net increase in other good it produces.

Here are grounds for a major difference between my approach and that of James Vaupel.[39] For some reason, he wishes to give priority to deaths that result from life-style problems. I am convinced that we are becoming more and more aware of the correlations between life-styles and early death. I remain enough of a voluntarist to believe that one has both the right and the power to take such risks; if one does, however, the rest of us should not be responsible for the consequences. I, therefore, am dubious of an argument from paternalism. To the extent that one is not defending the attack on early death on the basis of costs to others, it is defended on explicitly paternalistic grounds. I agree that the government might adopt policies of education so that people would know they are voluntarily taking on increased risks of early death. Once that educational task is performed, however, I would place very low priority on preventing deaths that result from continuing the risky life-style. I have elsewhere proposed a health tax on tobacco—not to deter people from choosing to take a death risk from smoking, but specifically to reimburse the public treasury for the costs of health care related to smoking so that public funds could be spent on higher priority medical interventions.[40] Those deaths for which one is personally responsible ought to have low priority.

GUIDELINES FOR CHOOSING AMONG LIFE-EXTENDING TECHNOLOGIES

In summary, it is important to realize that there is a difference between what is valued and what is right or what the government or a society ought to do. There is also a difference between what is most valued in aggregate and what is valued by those least well-off or least healthy. While there are interesting differences among the cost-benefit analysis methods for determining the value of a human life or the value of a life-year added as a result of a particular intervention, all the presently discussed methods share the characteristic of being aggregating measures. I have argued that the ethical premises of these methods are untenable and that in their place several alternative approaches must be considered. The normative ethical theory I have presented leads to a set of six guidelines for choosing among life-extending technologies:

1. The relative social usefulness of individuals or members of a class, their willingness to pay for life-extending technologies, and the dollar value of their future production ought to be irrelevant to policy choices regarding alternative life-extending technologies.
2. Any other aggregating methods of determining which life-extending technologies deserve priority should be used cautiously, if at all.
3. The younger the individual, the greater should be the priority for life-extending technologies.
4. Medical conditions that produce the greatest suffering should be given priority.
5. The needs of the generally least well-off at times may have to be placed ahead of those who may die relatively early because of a medical problem.
6. A medical condition that is seen as involuntary, originating from causes outside the control of the individual, should get priority over conditions that have resulted from a voluntary choice of health-risky behavior and life-style.

NOTES

1. J. Mill, *Utilitarianism and Other Writings* (Cleveland: Meridian, 1962); J. Bentham, *An Introduction to the Principles of Morals and Legislation* (New York: Hafner Press, 1948); G. E. Moore, *Principia Ethica* (Cambridge: Cambridge University Press, 1903).
2. I. Kant, *Groundwork of the Metaphysic of Morals,* trans. H. J. Paton (New York: Harper & Row, 1964); W. Ross, "The Best Medical Care for the Hopeless Patient," *Medical Opinion* (February 1972): 51–55.
3. J. J. C. Smart and B. Williams, *Utilitarianism: For and Against* (Cambridge: Cambridge University Press, 1973); M. Bayles, ed., *Contemporary Utilitarianism* (Garden City, N.Y.: Doubleday/Anchor Books, 1968).
4. R. Zeckhauser and D. Shepard, "Where Now for Saving Lives?" *Law and Contemporary Problems* 40 (Autumn 1976): 5–45.
5. J. P. Acton, "Measuring the Monetary Value of Lifesaving Programs," *Law and Contemporary Problems* 40 (Autumn 1976): 46–72.
6. Ibid.

222   ROBERT M. VEATCH

7. See T. Schelling, "The Life You Save May Be Your Own," in *Problems in Public Expenditure Analysis,* ed. S. B. Chase, Jr., pp. 127–162. For a description of the methods see J. Acton, "Measuring the Monetary Value of Lifesaving Programs" (note 5); D. Rice, "Estimating the Cost of Illness," *Health Economics* 6 (1966). See also D. Rice and B. Cooper, "The Economic Value of Human Life," *American Journal of Public Health* 57 (November 1967): 1954–1956; B. Cooper and D. Rice, "The Economic Cost of Illness Revisited," *Social Security Bulletin,* Department of Health, Education, and Welfare Pub. no. (SSA) 76–11703 (February 1976): 21–36.
8. O. Eckstein, *A Survey of the Theory of Public Expenditure Criteria* (New York: National Bureau of Economic Research, 1959); A. Drake, R. Keeney, and P. Morse, eds., *Analysis of Public Systems* (Cambridge, Mass.: M.I.T. Press, 1972); A. R. Prest and R. Turvey, "Cost Benefit Analysis: A Survey," *The Economic Journal* (December 1965): 683–735; R. McKean, "The Use of Shadow Prices," in *Problems in Public Expenditure Analysis,* ed. S. Chase, Jr.; W. R. D. Sewell, J. Davis, A. Scott, and D. Ross, *Guide to Benefit Cost Analysis* (Ottawa, Can.: R. Duhamel, Queen's Printer, 1965); and R. Dorfman, ed., *Measuring Benefits of Government Investments* (Washington, D.C.: The Brookings Institution, 1965).
9. H. Klarman, "Application of Cost-Benefit Analysis to the Health Services and the Special Case of Technological Innovation," *International Journal of Health Services* 4 (1974): 325–352; "Application of Cost-Benefit Analysis to Health Systems Technology," in *Technology and Health Care Systems in the 1980s,* ed. Morris F. Collen (Washington, D.C.: U.S. Government Printing Office, 1973); "Present Status of Cost-Benefit Analysis in the Health Field," *American Journal of Public Health* 57 (November 1967): 1948–1953; and "Syphilis Control Programs," in *Measuring Benefits of Government Investments,* ed. Robert Dorfman (Washington, D.C.: The Brookings Institution, 1965). Also R. Bailey, "Economic and Social Costs of Death," in *The Dying Patient,* ed. Orville G. Brim, Jr., et al. (New York: The Russell Sage Foundation, 1970), pp. 275–302; V. Taylor, *How Much is Good Health Worth?* (Santa Monica, Cal.: The Rand Corporation, 1969), pp. 3945; R. Zeckhauser, "Procedures for Valuing Lives," *Public Policy* 23 (Fall 1975): 420–463; K. S. Bay, D. Flathman, and L. Nestman, "The Worth of a Screening Program: An Application of a Statistical Decision Model for the Benefit Evaluation of Screening Projects," *American Journal of Public Health* 66 (February 1966): 145 ff.; S. Pauker and J. Kassirer, "Therapeutic Decision Making: A Cost-Benefit Analysis," *New England Journal of Medicine* 293 (July 31, 1957): 229–234; A. Williams, "The Cost-Benefit Approach," *British Medical Bulletin* 30 (1974): 252–256, and "Measuring the Effectiveness of Health Care Systems," *British Journal of Preventive and Social Medicine* 28 (1974): 196–202; and J. Roberts, "Economic Evaluation of Health Care: A Survey," *British Journal of Preventive and Social Medicine* 28 (1974): 210–216.
10. V. Held, "PPBS Comes to Washington," *The Public Interest,* no. 4 (Summer 1966): 102–115; M. J. Buxton and R. R. West, "Cost-Benefit Analysis of Long-Term Hemodialysis for Chronic Renal Failure," *British Medical Journal* (May 17, 1975): 376–379; B. McNeil, P. Varady, B. Burrows, and S. Adelstein, "Cost

Effectiveness in Hypertensive Renovascular Disease," *New England Journal of Medicine* 293 (July 31, 1975): 216–220; B. McNeil and S. J. Adelstein, "Value of Case Finding in Hypertensive Renovascular Disease," *New England Journal of Medicine* 293 (July 31, 1975): 221–225; D. Neuhauser and A. Lewicki, "What Do We Gain from the Sixth Stool Guaiac?" *New England Journal of Medicine* 293 (July 31, 1975): 226–228; S. Schoenbaum, J. Hyde, L. Bartoshesky, and K. Crampton, "Benefit-Cost Analysis of Rubella Vaccination Policy," *New England Journal of Medicine* 294 (February 5, 1976): 306–310; D. B. Longmore and M. Rehahn, "The Cumulative Cost of Death," *Lancet* (May 3, 1975): 1023–1025; J. W. Bush, M. M. Chen, and D. L. Patrick, "Health Status Index in Cost Effectiveness: Analysis of PKU Program," in *Health Status Indexes,* ed. R. L. Berg (Chicago: Hospital Research and Educational Trust, 1973); G. M. Komrower, "The Philosophy and Practice of Screening for Inherited Diseases," *Pediatrics* 53 (February 1974): 182–188; S. Mushkin, "Health as an Investment," *Journal of Political Economy* 70, no. 5, part 2 (October 1962): 129–157; K. Steiner and H. Smith, "Application of Cost-Benefit Analysis to a PKU Screening Program," *Inquiry* 10 (December 1973): 34–40; The Advisory Committee on Inborn Errors of Metabolism to the Ministry of Health, "PKU Screening—Is It Worth It?" *Canadian Medical Association Journal* 108 (February 3, 1973): 328–329.

11. R. Zeckhauser and D. Shepard, "Where Now for Saving Lives?" p. 9.
12. R. Bauer, ed., *Social Indicators* (Cambridge, Mass.: M.I.T. Press, 1966), Stanford Research Institute, *Minimum Standards for Quality of Life*, PB 244808 (Springfield, Vir.: National Technical Information Service, 1975), and Statistical Policy Division, Office of Management and Budget, *Social Indicators 1973: Selected Statistics on Social Conditions and Trends in the United States* (Washington, D.C.: U.S. Government Printing Office, 1973).
13. R. Zeckhauser and D. Shepard, "Where Now for Saving Lives?" p. 11.
14. Ibid., pp. 14–15 (emphasis added).
15. Ibid., p. 24.
16. Ibid., pp. 44–45.
17. J. P. Acton, "Measuring the Monetary Value of Livesaving Programs," p. 71 (emphasis added).
18. J. Vaupel, "Early Death: An American Tragedy," *Law and Contemporary Problems* 40 (Autumn 1976): 73–121.
19. J. Vaupel, "Early Death: How Much Can and Should the United States Do About Death Between Ages 15 and 65?" (Paper presented at the Conference on Valuing Lives, Amelia Island, Florida, March 11, 1976, sponsored by the Institute of Policy Sciences and Public Affairs, Duke University), p. 20.
20. Ibid., p. 21
21. Ibid.
22. R. Fein, "On Measuring Economic Benefits of Health Programmes," in *Medical History and Medical Care,* ed. G. McLachlan and T. McKeown (London: Oxford University Press, 1971); L. Tribe, "Technology Assessment and the Fourth Discontinuity: The Limits of Instrumental Rationality," *Southern California Law Review* 46 (1973): 617–660; C. Fried, "Rights and Health Care—Beyond

Equity and Efficiency," *New England Journal of Medicine* 293 (July 31, 1975): 241–245, and *Medical Experimentation: Personal Integrity and Social Policy* (New York: American Elsevier, 1974), especially pp. 81–89.

23. J. Rawls, *A Theory of Justice* (Cambridge: Harvard University Press, 1971), p. 302.
24. B. Barry, *The Liberal Theory of Justice* (New York: Oxford University Press, 1974).
25. R. Veatch, "What Is a 'Just' Health Care Delivery?" in *Ethics and Health Policy,* ed. R. Veatch and R. Branson (Cambridge, Mass.: Ballinger Press, 1976).
26. B. Weisbrod, "Income Redistribution Effects and Benefit-Cost Analysis," in *Problems in Public Expenditure Analysis,* ed. S. Chase, Jr., pp. 177–209.
27. J. P. Acton, "Measuring the Monetary Value of Lifesaving Programs," p. 52.
28. Ibid., p. 60.
29. For a proposal that would have similar effect see V. Taylor, "How Much Is Good Health Worth," *Policy Sciences* 1 (1970): 49–72.
30. J. P. Acton, "Measuring the Monetary Value of Lifesaving Programs," p. 61.
31. Ibid., p. 70.
32. B. Williams, "The Idea of Equality," reprinted in *Justice and Equality,* ed. H. Bedau (Englewood Cliffs, N.J.: Prentice-Hall, 1971), p. 122.
33. J. Rawls, *A Theory of Justice,* p. 302.
34. The "National Health Insurance Partnership Act of 1971," introduced by Representative T. Railsback of Illinois, as H.R. 2618 (Washington, D.C.: U.S. Government Printing Office, 1971).
35. R. Veatch, "What is a 'Just' Health Care Delivery?"
36. J. Rawls, *A Theory of Justice,* p. 302.
37. R. Veatch, "What is a 'Just' Health Care Delivery?" pp. 133–136.

38. See Ibid., pp. 137–39, for a fuller discussion of this issue.
39. J. W. Vaupel, "Early Death: An American Tragedy."
40. R. Veatch, "Case Studies in Bioethics: Who Should Pay for Smokers' Medical Care?" *Hastings Center Report* 4, no. 5 (November 1974): 8–9.

11

Freedom, Uncertainty, and Life-Extending Technologies

We could, as a nation, initiate the research, development, and implementation of technologies and programs for achieving two separate goals: (1) the squaring of life-expectancy curves so that the majority of all segments of the population (male and female, white and nonwhite) live to a statistically equivalent age (perhaps 80 or 100 years); and (2) the significant lengthening of the life expectancy of some segment to a projected range of 150 to 200 years. These two goals are independent, since one could perhaps arrange this so that statistically anyone specified randomly at birth, whether male, female, black, white, Northerner, Southerner, rich or poor, would live an estimated seventy or eighty years, and at the same time refrain from increasing the life expectancy of any segment of the population to double or triple its present span. Likewise, one could aim to provide a technology to those who could afford it—upper-middle and high income classes, which would be largely white—so they could live 150 to 200 years while others would continue as they are. And perhaps a final goal could be to devise active techniques to make the entire squared life-expectancy curve that long.

This chapter considers the impact that pursuing and achieving these separate ends may have on freedom as we experience it in our daily lives as twentieth-century Americans.[1] I describe this as "lived freedom," to emphasize the experiential aspect.

One facet of freedom as we conceive it is the opportunity to work toward a vision or ideal for oneself (a career, for example), one's family (social mobility), and one's community (that is, local, state, religious). Another is the right to do flip, spontaneous, isolated, foolish, risky things; this allows us enjoyable activities outside of our roles or coherent life-styles.

Thus, several categories of freedom are important to consider: (1) *Autonomy* is freedom to discover the basic rules of a community of free and responsible rational agents and to will action only within those rules. It dictates mutual respect among individuals. (2) This is constituted by respecting the *self-determination* of each rational being, that is, (a) the freedom to try, within the limits of autonomy, to build the story of one's life or shape the contents of one's world and (b) the freedom to control one's own body. This second aspect of freedom depends in part on the degree of political independence one has for important or meaningful action as one defines that for oneself. (3) Connected with this is a third variety, that is, *self-indulgent freedom.* This is freedom (again within the bounds of autonomy) to travel, vacation, play sick to go fishing, sleep late, go for a ride, and so on. Autonomy has to do with free but responsible judgment, whereas the others have to do with free action.

All three are important, though the last two are our lived or experienced freedoms. It is not consistent with autonomy, the most basic and pervasive philosophic commitment to freedom (as the libertarians argue), to sacrifice or deprecate the place of self-indulgent freedom in favor of self-determination in any life other than one's own. This is true even though the latter is the primary locus of self-destiny or individuality. In our democratic philosophy it is clear that society is created for the individual, *and the individual's idiosyncrasies must be tolerated* (as long as he or she respects the freedoms of other persons). That is why spontaneous, self-indulgent freedom cannot be sacrificed. Because we cannot know and should not dictate what is meaningful to another person's life, and because persons should have the freedom to do meaningless things, we sustain apparently frivolous freedom.

I have listed some important aspects of freedom that provide the terms for assessing (1) the means to the end and (2) the effects of achieving them. These will be discussed separately but the second will be deprived of equal attention because of lack of space, and because such reflection would be highly speculative.

I make the assumption in the following discussion that many individuals will have to be forced to accept technologies. This assumption plays a major role throughout and so needs justification. To begin with, it is realistic; think how far beyond the grasp of the lower income or education groups biomedical technology is. More important are the observations made by Leonard Hayflick that "any method that might increase human longevity is unacceptable [that is, not accepted by the public] even if it [only] minimally affects the enjoyment of life. . . . The notion that any method guaranteed to reduce illness or extend life would not be used may at first seem to be naïve, but we are, nonetheless, surrounded by that reality."[2] Hayflick reviews the sharp decline in the use of poliomyelitis vaccine since its initial high use. He argues that such preventive technologies (in this case a simple, inexpensive, painless, and safe one) seem to be sought only when the disease's damage is recently apparent. Ill effects are soon forgotten, and knowledge of the need for the technology is increasingly repressed. In addition to neglecting available resources (such as vaccines), Hayflick reminds us, people often actively do what they know is risky for their health (such as smoking).

All this confirms that if we are to have a policy of achieving curve-squaring and/or life extension we might have to force it upon the public. Furthermore, it will not do to think that the official attitude will be tolerance of neglecting the resources. Antiabortion efforts and antieuthanasia attitudes are firmly entrenched. Philosophers, lawyers, and many others must wage an arduous campaign against other philosophers, and so forth, concerning rights in these areas. This situation shows that it is not a practiced tradition to let persons use the technology involving shortening life as they like. Thus, I must presume that the public will respond to the new technologies and knowledge as it has to smoking, driving, and vaccinations. It is unlikely that it will comply as the good diabetic complies with dietary and chemical controls. I thus understand "policy" in a strong sense, which includes enforced compliance and sanction. Opportunities will become obligations. Neglecting the technology may come to be a sign of irrationality or, regarding one's charges, of child abuse.

There is one further implication in Hayflick's essay as to why "policy" might best be understood in this strong sense. The cost-benefit ration of preventing polio versus supplying iron lungs and hospital beds is striking. For some economic and social reasons, then, we might want to force people to be sound until they collapse in a heap of dust on their one hundredth, one hundred fiftieth, or two hundredth birthdays (like the wonderful one-horse shay portrayed by Oliver Wendell Holmes in his poem "The Deacon's Masterpiece").

Given the clear difference between squaring the curve and elongating it, questions bearing on freedom may be asked about each separately. One methodological problem in doing so is that in either undertaking a great deal of thought and action would center around environmental considerations. Changes in the physical, social, and psychological environment might add many years to every citizen's life. This implies that a discussion of either curve-squaring or life extension alone may well have implications for the other. Nevertheless, squaring the curves as they are presently constituted will be considered first.

THE MEANS TO THE ENDS

As a heuristic device meant to display how we could and likely would go about squaring life-expectancy curves, I am going to use data on causes of death in subdivisions of the population based on age, race, and sex. These data are collected for a variety of sources and changes in time and are sometimes used in calculating a health hazard appraisal in samples of the population. They may then be used to calculate a given individual's specific risk of dying from any of those causes most likely to kill someone in his or her sex, age, and racial group. These calculations are done by assigning a weighted score to specific categories of behavior, family history, present health, and so on, as a means of estimating the personal risk or appraisal age of the individual.

The state of the art of preventive medicine in the typical doctor-patient relationship consists in knowing which factors make an individual's appraisal age lower than his or her chronological age and which therapies, behavioral changes, and so on may alter that discrepancy and improve the duration of the individual's life. These methods are used to sensitize prospective physicians to the virtues of practicing preventive care with their patients.[3]

As an example of how preventive medicine could be used and how this issue bears on freedom, consider that for white females in the 30 to 34 year range who will die within the next ten years,[4] breast cancer is the most frequent cause of death. The sixth most frequent cause of death for this group is cancer of the cervix. Together these account for a projected 13 percent of those who will die within the next ten years. Pap smears are currently being used to detect cervical cancer years ahead of its serious stages. Often breast examinations for signs of cancer are coordinated with taking the Pap smear. Were "white females" a population category that needed to have its life-expectancy curve squared, suppression of these two causes of death might command attention. If policy dictated suppressing them, requiring regular Pap smears and monthly breast examinations, and requiring treatment where tests were positive, would be tempting steps. Nonetheless, requiring examinations and treatment would infringe on bodily self-determination as we now construe it. Infringing upon freedom by requiring submission to a test for communicable disease has precedent, but even in these cases persons may refuse therapy, for tuberculosis as an example, and accept quarantine. The imposition of treatment for breast cancer might occur in ways we currently would not and should not approve. For example, chemical radiological and surgical procedures might vie for favor. If surgery is clearly the most efficacious treatment for breast cancer, it might also cause great trauma to an individual with a certain sense of identity and set of aspirations for the future. Such a woman might wish to take her chances with a less efficacious course of treatment or even with no treatment, in order to preserve her beauty. Some people may consider this a distorted priority and foolish risk-benefit gamble, but no one can dictate a person's identity. It is necessary (under respect for autonomy) to honor her self-concept, priorities, and freedom to act upon them. Were she coerced through a public policy into submitting to surgery (radical mastectomy or lumpectomy), an established freedom would be lost to a political mechanism. What her friends and relatives may do to manipulate her is not a political issue and is not relevant here.

Likewise, a white male, age 40, has as his single most likely cause of death (were it to occur by age 50) arteriosclerotic heart disease and chronic endocarditis. His second most likely cause is motor vehicle accidents. To suppress the latter, we would add air bags to the automobile, require seat belts, and lower speed limits, and so on. When the speed limits are lowered because of a fuel crisis, the public tolerates it. When they are lowered to save lives or when helmets are required of motorcyclists, freedom is felt to be impinged upon and resistance to the law rises furiously. To control the primary cause of death in this group, weight, exercise, diet, and smoking would have to be regulated. The losses of (self-indulgent) freedom might be staggering.

A general inference may now be drawn. If we are interested in squaring curves, we may have to find ways of controlling daily behavior that is ordinarily considered the realm of freedom and privacy. For example, we might search for weapons on all persons going into bars as we search at airports to control hijackings. Violent death is frequent among white males of most age groups. It is not until the age group starting at 55 to 59 is considered that violence is not in the top ten causes of death for white males. Among white females in the 15 to 19 age group, suicide is the second and homicide the tenth most frequent cause of death. When the fifty to fifty-four age group is considered, violent acts are not among the ten most frequent causes of death for them.

It is also true that black males die youngest. To make some unsystematic comparisons, there were 530 white infant male deaths per 100,000 in the 5 to 9 age group as compared to 750 deaths of blacks. There were 350 per 100,000 white female deaths in that age group and 530 black females in the same age group. To square the curves from the start would require controlling the familial context regarding swimming, firearms, driving and other transportation to address the accidents. But of the black male deaths, 159 per 100,000 are classified as homicides (the third most frequent cause) compared to 10 per 100,000 black female deaths. Just eliminating male homicides would tend to make the curves squarer. But how do we suppress murders? Freedom may require that we allow risk of murder to remain higher than levels we could achieve by adopting severe invasions of privacy and strict control of behavior.

The question of how to suppress murder could become nagging. In the 15 to 19 age group, of those black male deaths projected, almost a quarter (488 per 100,000) who die are victims of homicide. This is the most frequent cause of death in that group as it is for black females of the same age, where it accounts for 11 percent of the deaths (121 per 100,000). In white females of that age, homicide is the tenth ranked and accounts for 2.5 percent of the deaths (14 per 100,000). In the white male counterpart, homicide is the fourth ranked killer, accounting for 3.5 percent of the deaths (51 per 100,000).

Thus, in this age group (and in subsequent ones as well), if one tries to square the curve, one will want to suppress homicides, and the nagging question How? will provoke answers that may assault freedoms in ways reminiscent of Big Brother, as depicted in Orwell's *1984*.

Nor is homicide the only matter that might place freedom under threat. Many freedoms are bad for humans and many may be ugly and irrational, but tolerating those that do not significantly injure innocent bystanders is what democratic recognition and respect for idiosyncrasy is all about. It is a premier value in our society that someone may trade risk of harm or even actual harm for benefit, preference, or the hope of them. Justice may require helping those healthy, normal individuals who, from a mere knowledge of their sex and race, can be predicted to die early. Nevertheless, to weight freedom less than justice would be repugnant to much of American ideology.

It is important in regard to weighing freedom, justice, and cost-benefit analyses that, in going through the data tables, we can divide into two groups the causes of death that contribute to the slope of the curves. There are those that have to do with bodily health behavior, and those that have to do with psychological behavior. I have been attending to the latter because some freedoms are bad for human beings, including freedom of diet and exercise habits, freedom to smoke and work at hazardous jobs, and freedom regarding sleep habits. If this reads like a perverse bill of rights, its poignancy may still be recognized. Health is both an end and a means to ends; so, too, is life. If either is strictly an end, one cannot trade or risk it for other ends, but this is clearly done and sanctioned. One can risk one's life for the thrill of climbing a mountain or risk one's life by refraining from all exercise.

All this is pertinent to squaring life-expectancy curves because much epidemiological thinking deals with preventive interventions such as fluoridation of public water supplies, which seem to be intrusions on free choice. Consideration of these highlights the costs to freedom implied in the process of squaring the curve. But the cost to freedom in tampering with bodily health behavior could be equally great.

Eating behavior exemplifies the point and undermines the distinction between bodily health and psychological behavior. Eating is a health habit involving weight and nutrition, generally; it is also a social activity and can be a psychological expression of anxiety or aggression. It is a cultural phenomenon as well, in that, for example, Italians define themselves (or concretize their identity) partly through pasta, Germans through potatoes and beer, and Jews through chicken soup and lox. Tampering with or manipulating diets can be construed as an assault on the identity either of the individual as a group member or of the group itself.

To attend to a different cause of death, we know that smoking is probably a major contributing cause of death from heart disease and cancer. Pneumonia accounts for 2.3 percent of deaths among white males (ranked as the eighth most frequent cause of death), 4.4 percent among white females (ranked fourth), 3.3 percent among black males (ranked fifth), and 7.5 percent among black females (ranked third), in the projection for the 5- to 19-years-olds (that is, for those in that group who will die by age 19). Risk appraisals are high due to smoking and more so to alcohol habits. We try to inhibit smoking and drinking in this age group, but in older groups the risk factor (especially in predicting deaths due to accidents) remains very important. We legitimize controlling these (for example, through laws against drunk driving) because of the damage or threat they pose to others. Otherwise we would be violating the agent's autonomy (each person's competence for discovering the rules of a society that are necessary for it to be one of adult persons) and self-determination. Rules against risking injury through action that threatens no one else should not be tolerated if one takes seriously the rubric of autonomy.

A fatal disease of high frequency is arteriosclerotic heart disease. The likelihood of contracting it depends both on factors already mentioned (weight, smoking, exercise, cholesterol levels) as well as on other factors (family history, blood pressure, and whether one is a diabetic). The impact on freedom of treatment of these latter features is discussed later. It should, however, be pointed out that some technologies are at least temporarily accepted by many persons on an individual basis in spite of the resultant loss of freedom. This introduces a sense of "freedom" not specified in our earlier definition: free from inconveniences that are necessarily and naturally associated with certain courses of action.

That many treatments that are not free in this sense are accepted, even esteemed, cannot be doubted. Nonetheless, it is true that loss of freedom follows use of a technology such as kidney dialysis or something analogous that might be invented for arteriosclerosis. But this loss is ideally self-imposed and should not be a concern of political policy (except for its possible impact on costs to others), and it is not a requirement of government to protect or restore that sort of freedom. Loss of self-determination due to the vicissitudes of nature is perhaps a natural evil, but is not politically wrong unless due to unjust social conditions. It would be much worse if a patient were forced to use a technology; as patients often tire of therapy and refuse to continue it, their choice must be respected.

Five categories of procedures could be used to increase life expectancy: (1) life-span-increasing (antiaging) technologies, (2) specified disease treatments, (3) artificial prostheses, (4) tissue regeneration technologies, and (5) technologies controlling environment impacts on health (which we have already discussed).

LIFE-SPAN-INCREASING TECHNOLOGIES

One technique (hardly a technology) is the so-called McCay effect. By severely restricting and controlling caloric intake but providing adequate amino acids, vitamins, and minerals, the period prior to sexual maturity was lengthened (in rats) and life span increased. The question is how we can react to this freedom as our focus?

Currently, malnutrition and neglect of children are considered subject to social control. Governmental concern for the abused child also covers the neglected child. Parental behaviors that place a child at risk are also somewhat controlled—for example, parents may not encourage their children to handle snakes even as part of their exercise of freedom of religion.

Restrictions of this kind are few. Agencies do not as a rule consider most coordinated family activities, such as celebrations or meals, subject to control. If parents take what they think to be an active and well-motivated part in structuring diet and eating habits of offspring, and even if they encourage atypical and less than ideal behaviors, they are, within broad limits, free to do so. The same goes for behavioral discipline. Although very poor disciplinarians may endanger their children's social and psychological adaptation, rarely would such failures become the subject of formal complaints to which authorized intervention would be a legitimate response.

If the McCay effect were ever to be urged or required, it would surely be resisted until it had been established for generations. People accustomed to using food for rewards, treats, and statements of love, affection, or celebration would feel deprived of freedom under such a policy. Further, they might be prohibited from teaching their children aspects of their cultural legacy (such as those involving ethnic food like lox or pasta). They might feel legally obliged to deprive their offspring of good things to eat or to force hunger on them. If the dietary restrictions were removed at puberty (say age 25, now that this and other techniques are in effect), parents would no doubt either feel discomfort at eating well in the presence of their children or else not feel free to eat with them.

Perhaps technologies could be evolved to defeat some of these issues, but they in turn might put people at risk. For instance, an early surgical procedure or an ongoing pharmacological technique to make hunger unproblematic might put the infant at risk.

Implementing the McCay effect, then, would influence many of the daily freedoms and joys of children and childbearing. Monitoring and enforcement would no doubt compromise freedom further. The relationship between family and pediatrician would not be a happy one. Neighbors would have to report acute abuse. Grandparents and parents might fight about whether they could violate the rules once in a while and give the child a treat; parents might disagree about what was done in the home on a given day, or they may disagree about what is permitted, and begin to use associated sanctions as weapons. These reactions could have serious ramifications for freedom and family life.

We would also have to think carefully about enforced drug use as a policy and its implementation as a technology. Possibly the use of oral or injected hormones, or any other pharmacological technology, could be at the option of parents for their children or of adults for themselves. But would policy rely on elective use of the gift of the fountain of life? Would it tolerate nonacceptance?

This presupposes with Hayflick that governmental programs to publicize facts, educate the public, and orchestrate the preparation, packaging, and marketing of foods, and so on, would not achieve the goals or sustain them if they were achieved. Still they would, like fluoridation programs, compromise some freedom of action.

The technologies discussed thus far would likely be used after birth, if at all, and so affect the freedom of today's populace. Other technologies, aimed at genetic changes to alter the molecular biochemistry of aging, might have to be applied long before birth, possibly before conception. This would not constitute infringing on the freedom of individuals for no person would yet be involved,[5] but it might infringe on the person to come. The point is that a technology applied before the age of rational judgment would not compromise freedom at that time, but the experimental designs of getting (prenatal?) subjects and carefully tracking their health (and possibly their behavior) would cost them freedom when they ought to be respected as rational free agents. Screening and other activities undertaken in this regard would likely affect the freedom to mate as well as its aesthetics. Another injury to freedom might lurk in surgical procedures done at birth or early in childhood (for example, for birth control purposes) that might require further surgery for maintenance or reversals (for example, of vasectomy) when the citizen is later free of such requirements. This, too, assumes that the technologies go well; on the way to developing and refining them, the risk and injury to adults raised in the process might be severe.

DISEASE CONTROL

Arteriosclerotic heart disease and vascular defects on the one hand, and cancer and other neoplastic disorders on the other, are the primary fatal diseases today. The former group affects us in such a way that we can only prevent or retard the disease or treat particular insults after they occur. We cannot as yet predict closely the what, where, when, or how of an insult; we find one only retrospectively. Obviously, we cannot replace the entire arterial network, though we can replace a heart. Behavioral prevention remains the best currently available control of these diseases, for, even with increasingly reliable predictors, the uncertainty will likely continue. This applies even to neoplastic disorders; for instance, cervical cancer is unusual in that it starts in a narrowly localized place and is slow to grow. Pap smears, coupled with dilation and curettage are possible procedures for dealing with it. Lung cancer, by contrast, can start anywhere in the lung, so that routinely testing lung tissue for early discovery is unfeasible, and even the earliest detection by X ray comes too late to be of significant use given current therapies.[6] This is likely to be all the more true when it comes to predicting heart and circulatory trauma. Clearly, effective predictors and therapies would be welcome as would a knowledge of agents to help reduce factors in the body that detract from the healthy circulatory system (aspirin was mentioned as an anticlotting agent). Meanwhile, behavioral prevention offers the best hope.

Cancer, too, seems best defeated by prevention. Some threats to freedom in this connection were mentioned in the discussion on curve-squaring. Inhibiting a behavior such as smoking is an assault on the autonomy and self-indulgence, if not self-determination, of rational free agents. The ability to trade health and life for pleasures and triumphs is implied by the fundamental tenets of our society. Pursuit of happiness may be dangerous.

Part of behavior is routinely undergoing or failing to undergo physical examinations. If an annual proctoscopy were included from age 40 on, and cancer of the colon were thus detected early, many lives might be saved, and an unpleasant death avoided. This could be encouraged but not required. Bodily self-determination is so fundamental in our society that any procedure required of a normal rational adult solely for his or her own good would be repugnant to our values and ethical sense. Thus, any procedure would have to await the competent individual's concurrence, just as procedure today requires or presumes informed consent.

PROSTHESES

Development and use of prostheses should not have a different effect on freedom than use of any other technology. Artificial hearts, kidneys, and livers, which could be chosen or declined in adulthood, would be a great boon to those needing organ help. Public funding of the development of such devices, however, should mean they belong to the public and that all citizens have equal right of access.[7] The possession and control of prostheses, including their availability and upkeep, has great potential for political coerciveness and injustice. One could, for example, wonder who would own the developed drugs. Would rich and poor, urbanite and rural citizen, have equal access and right to them? Would availability be better than it is for health care generally? Would prejudiced physicians employ them equally among races? Would access to a test population be available? When would one be placed in a "control group" and could this action be abused?

Regarding prostheses, however, special threats arise: If harvested organs for transplanting are relatively scarce, a campaign to redefine "death" or "ownership of the corpse and its parts" might be waged. Religious values and freedoms might again be threatened (where, for example, a person's body is supposed to be buried with all of its parts). Especially frightening is the possibility that one's ultimate freedom—remaining alive—might be lost to a definition of "death" based on a public policy regarding harvesting. We would also be likely to legislate against an individual selling his or her organs, say one kidney or one heart, because such freedom is repugnant to us. Such restriction of behavior, if it does not truncate self-determination, at least indicates that we do not believe in the individual's ultimate control over his or her body (a claim often heard in defense of elective abortion).

TISSUE REGENERATION

The tissues most in need of regeneration technology are brain and nerve tissues. Cells of these sorts are lost daily and do not regenerate. One technique for regeneration is akin to seeding or salting (in the sense of priming the pump—adding water to a dry pump to get it started) with tissues harvested earlier. Perhaps it is akin to a transplantation. The source of fresh tissue is "possibly from samples removed from the individual during fetal life or infancy and then maintained either in tissue culture or cryonically" (see Chapter 1).

Admittedly, this is a remote possibility, but it has implications for freedom. Would parents not have to place their tissue at risk, including the risk of anesthetic, to obtain the supply? (If done to the fetus, the mother would also run that risk.) How would subjects of research be recruited and tracked? These two questions indicate possible impact on freedom. Ordinarily, we want to prevent parents from putting their offspring at risk; we would not normally allow them to submit their children to the experimental and research conditions likely to be required in developing this technology. On the other hand, this limits the freedom of parents to do what may be best for their children. And, as freedom is practiced currently, we would have no right to force the adult subject to receive the tissue taken when he or she was a neonate.

Other technologies have to do with preventing autoimmune diseases and discovering pharmacological means of enhancing the performance of cells that remain. Research and development here, and the use of the results, would have to conform to all the philosophical and/or legal requirements appropriate to any human research and treatment. Informed consent would be the principal requirement.

One remaining technology has to do with the external storing of neutral information and the possible use of computers synergized with brains. This is not foreseen for the near future, and questions about it are both troublesome and highly speculative. How would the information be gathered? How would confidentiality be secured? How would the individual's access to and control of information be guaranteed? How would it be protected from tampering? Turning to the experience of freedom, one might wonder how persons would feel about using such a technology—as though they were looking something up in their library or as though they were dangling by a lifeline?

ENVIRONMENTAL CONSIDERATIONS

The kinds of impact on freedom that might follow on control of the environment have been partially indicated in the discussion on curve-squaring. Given the space limitations, I will simply presume that sufficient discussion has been offered to cause caution in this regard.

In the remainder of the chapter, I want to reflect on the possible impact on freedom that achieving a life expectancy of 200 years with a squared curve might have.

QUESTIONS ABOUT THE END PRODUCT

It is excessively speculative to ponder what the world would be like if and when techniques for extending youth, life span, and life expectancy were to be successful. Because reflections of this sort have a naggingly abstract quality and uncertainties abound, one cannot help but be somewhat ironic in writing about them.

A manageable way to reflect on freedom or any value might be to focus on major stages of the life cycle and discover the most important rights and duties involved in each. Another heuristic device is to specify the importance of freedom in major events and activities at various ages. These methods will be used in a fragmentary fashion.

Making the speculative exercise concrete requires knowing whether all stages of the present cycle would be elongated or just one, for example, early adulthood. If all stages were lengthened, would we be committing parents to changing an offspring's diapers for ten years? Would we lengthen the anguish of puberty or ease adjustment to it? Further complications would arise if new stages of the cycle emerged. These could be the greatest boon to life. Achievements in wisdom or what Jung called "individuation" might become more frequent or reach levels never before enjoyed.

What, however, would be the worldwide effects of life-expectancy technology? Would all countries or only, for instance, the oil-rich ones, buy into the "immortalizing" process? How would many conscientious citizens of this nation or of India (with her starvation and other problems) accept this breakthrough—including, perhaps, bestowing the benefits of miracle pharmacology and tripled life on Americans' pet cats, dogs, and horses? Could those whimsical freedoms of pet owners be retained?

To respond to the general thrust of these questions, I should say more about freedom. Throughout this chapter, *freedom* has been considered a value, but one primarily characterized negatively as the absence of obstacles or restraints. This is one-sided, for freedom also has a positive sense that suggests that certain opportunities or goods are available. Accordingly, education and citizenship may make one free in a rich and traditional sense. Both to explain what is wrong with relying too extensively on the negative sense of freedom, and to suggest some of the aspects of its positive sense, I will move to the end of the life cycle and imagine a death scene.

Sometimes when someone has died, for example, when Spartacus was crucified, others tend to say, "Well, at least he's free now," meaning that suffering has ceased forever. This is a negative sense of "free," which suggests that someone is rid or unencumbered of something bad. But in the context of a postmortem remark the "one" referred to also has ceased. One is *not* most free when dead; so when *is* someone most free?

Vacations are interesting to reflect upon in juxtaposition to dying. On an ideal vacation, we put many cares aside, rest, recreate, and pursue things we are not ordinarily free to pursue. Similarly, if economic and other resources are adequate, we are free to enjoy ourselves, try to accomplish certain goals, and so forth. These are the positive freedoms that make life enjoyable.

It also appears—in light of established Freudian doctrine—that adult humans need meaningful work for satisfaction in life. Many rich people continue to work for money, some (like the Rockefellers) work for other reasons or motives.

This last reflection paves the way for consideration of the kind of freedom that applies uniquely to us as rational adults. When we are on vacation, many of us are more like animals (in an innocent sense) than rational adults. It is inappropriate to think of a puppy or a snake as on vacation, but when such creatures eat well, sun themselves contentedly, and romp with a playmate (I don't suppose snakes do that), theirs resembles prototypical vacation behavior. When we leave our animality for engagement in the social, productive order, or when we leave it for work or reflection, we have a sense of freedom that some authors (Plato, Hegel, Hannah Arendt) find especially important and declare uniquely human.

We might develop what freedom is in relation to the rational adult by considering what Plato wrote in his *Crito*. To explain to Crito why one should not flee, even from a mistaken sentence of punishment, Socrates constructs an imaginary dialogue between himself and a personification of the Laws of Athens. The Laws tell him that he cannot rightly damage them by fleeing because (1) they are his parents, (2) they are his guardians, and (3) he has not tried to change them from within. The last has little importance to this essay.[8] The other two are important because they summarize the fact that Socrates was born, raised, and educated in the context of the state and through its good offices.

Whether this applies more to Americans today than to ancient Greeks is not important. The point is that if an individual's identity has been made or allowed to develop in certain ways that foster the ability to act on opportunities, that ability is interesting and valuable only when public organizations and the administration of justice provide a workable context. Social and political contexts make possible a high level of freedom. It is part of both the Greek concept of freedom and our own that humans are most actualized by interaction; the hermit's freedom is only an escape, almost a death. This thesis helps give credence to the idea that freedom entails having the motivation, opportunity, and energy to pursue meaningful and planned, or flip and spontaneous, activities.

In this regard, I am inclined to recommend a point by Erik Erikson, which I interpret to fit with this consideration of freedom. Erikson suggests that when one's self-identity and the identity of the group by which one is primarily defined are mutually complementary, both profit from increases in energy, organization, direction, and so on.[9]

Identity relates in a most profound way to *whose* freedom is experienced and how and why it is important. One's rights and freedoms are constitutive of the individual's identity, at least as regards others' conceptions of him or her and to some extent his or her own conception of him- or herself. Erikson writes: "Each group identity cultivates its own sense of freedom which is the reason why one people rarely understands what makes another people feel free."[10] This has momentous implication for our discussion; were we to implement longer life spans and squarer curves, we might find living with losses of freedoms dreadful, but those who grew up under such conditions might not. That they might feel comfortable would not prove much, however, since *we* would make *their* world according to our own visions of freedom and other values.[11] To help in assessing these, I turn now to other stages of the life cycle.

It is strange to introduce notions of freedom into discussions of the fetus except perhaps as one also speaks of a physical object being free. This has already been alluded to. Inflicting biomedical technology on a fetus (for its own good, the eventual good of the person it will become, or even the eventual good of the society it will inhabit) does interfere with raw natural freedom but not with the moral ideal we cherish. I conclude that loss of freedom at this stage of the life cycle is not morally problematic.

Furthermore, we do biomedical things to our offspring upon their birth. We test for milk allergies that might cause brain damage and we bathe the neonate's eyes with silver nitrate as a prophylaxis against gonorrhea. In the past we were willing even in early months to inoculate infants against smallpox and other dread diseases. There are, then, precedents for medicating humans early in their lives. In some ways, however, as mentioned, society might be acting on an infant in such a way as to commit the adult to certain regular or sporadic interventions (vasectomy or pacemakers). Some actions might affect freedom to emigrate, or assume space travel, or whatever, because recipients would have to stay where the treatment was accessible.

Such continued dependency also introduces a potential for threat or possible coercion. If society has the goods, the technology, and the resources, it can, given that power, withhold, threaten to withhold, or manipulate. The potential misuse of the power is a genuine threat to adult freedom. Thus, though in no intelligibly realistic sense may the freedom of the infant be at risk, what we do to it may affect the freedom of the person it becomes.

The primary task of the human in early childhood involves generating bodily skills of coordination as well as a sense of independence. According to Erikson[12] these are means toward the end of providing the needs and fostering the talents that eventuate in emancipation from the parents. But the model we have of the emancipated child should be assessed; it seems consistent with the spirit of the machine age which "has provided the ideal of a mechanically trained, faultlessly functioning, and always clean, punctual, and deodorized body. In addition, it has been more or less superstitiously assumed that early and rigorous training is absolutely necessary for the kind of personality which will function efficiently in a mechanized world. . . . Thus a child becomes a machine which must be set and tuned even as before it was an animal which must be broken— while, in fact, will power can develop only by steps."[13]

To foster such will power, self-determination, or free will as Erikson here describes, one must encourage and allow a sense of successful risk-taking that should continue throughout life in thought, career, relating to others, and so on. How the knowledge of life span enters into the psychology of living is not firmly understood. Does a sense of urgency growing out of fear accelerate progress? If so, what will happen when we make longevity so important? Will fear increase or decrease?

And should we supervise child-rearing practices? Should we enforce rules against practices that foster shame and doubt in order to assure that no suicidal tendencies arise? Some of this we feel justified in doing now, for we require the reporting of child abuse, but we do not engage in general surveillance or violate other intelligible values. Yet some parents today would risk having doubting, shamefaced, suicidal children for the sake of their being godfearing. Currently we have to tolerate their patterns.

If poor self-esteem (which, many believe, shortens life even if not through suicide) is picked up from parents, and if longevity becomes an urgent rational priority, would we confiscate the child to protect his or her longevity? If, as the Freudians insist, the early years of life are formative of the personality, and if the models in the home are most influential, and if personality puts wear and tear on the body to shorten life, then the threats to freedom within child-rearing could be enormous, given that quantity of life becomes a top priority. How much more so is the threat if we attend to the quality of life as a policy! Erikson's description of the problem is powerful and bears on questions of how to control morbidity or mortality.

> Many adults feel that their worth as people consists entirely in what they are "going at" in the future and not in what they are in the present. The strain consequently developed in their bodies, which are always "on the go," with the engine racing even at moments of rest, is a powerful contribution to the much-discussed psychosomatic diseases of our time. It is as if the culture had made a man overadvertise himself and so identify with his own advertisement that only disease can designate the limit.[14]

What we should do to or with such people (that is, to or with ourselves) is a nagging question. I suspect that a workable answer would restrict freedom as currently construed—at least in its large economic sense. We would have to educate or indoctrinate the population in order to reduce this apparent economically constituted ego-drive. Restructuring the economy would be bound to impinge on the lives and lived freedom of advertising executives, automobile manufacturers, fashion designers, travel agents, builders, and architects, to mention a few.

This is only one aspect of how our economic freedoms and investments might be compromised. We know well enough, from the popular press, how retirement plans and programs, especially the federal social security programs, are endangered. How much more upset would they be if recipients lived for a century beyond retirement? Inheritance of capital, power, and position would alter national and individual access to resources, so economics would have to be drastically changed. Those living during the process of changing economics, one of the most esteemed areas of activity, would feel and be very unfree.

Since our philosophic commitment is to freedom of rational adults, it is important to consider how adult life would be lived in the event of much longer life expectancy. We must think about the loss of parental freedom and the loss of religious expression that that implies. We might think of the strangeness of alimony lasting for 150 years, and of population distribution that was almost uniform rather than pyramidlike. This would make promotion in any hierarchy a long waiting game, and have ramifications in terms of who was economically supporting whom (for example, people aged 30 to 100 supporting all those from birth to 29 and 100 to 200).

Even if economic changes were handled smoothly, entertainment, hobbies, recreation, and so forth for people who had been alive so long and seen so much, would likely be quite different. Training and career definitions, as well as self-definition in terms of career, would change dramatically.

When reaching school age, the child's primary undertaking, according to Erikson, is learning to define vocations and tasks and acquiring general skills that open the greatest number of career opportunities or routes. With increasing social complexity and specialization of tasks, the parent's role, Erikson tells us, becomes increasingly vague. (I'm not sure whether that is true.) Certainly it will become more difficult for a child to know what his or her parents do for a living, what they were, what they will become. Especially if parenting begins at the ages we now call mid- and late middle-age, the distance and estrangement between parent and offspring might be enormous. Alternatively, if the age of parenting is kept approximately where it is—late teens through the mid-thirties—and the parent and child mature as contemporaries for well over a century, inevitable estrangement might continue to occur just where it occurs now in life. Parents and children might lose touch gradually; if each is an adult they may have little more than a ritualized relationship. This is true today, but what it would mean over a longer life is unclear. All this could affect the parent-child relationship and perhaps intimacy and friendship in general.

The uncertainties of relationships and projected relationships may then be a bit disturbing, and the protraction of responsibility may give us pause. Surely to think of anyone being legally or financially responsible for another for over a century is staggering. For example, if parents have a legal obligation to see their children through school (college and beyond, if longer life spans warrant), or if a spouse must pay child support until majority (when will childhood end in a 150-year life span?), then the sacrifice of freedoms to responsibilities seems formidable.

Erikson tells us that education currently seems aimed at two goals: (1) converting the child into a miniature adult by emphasizing self-restraint and (2) providing a strict sense of duty to obedience.[15] He claims that children enjoy being coerced into making progress, in growing into adulthood. It is important, however, that this desire be outgrown when, in adolescence, learning to will freely is the second key stage in the identity crisis. The prior stage in the crisis turns on issues of faith in ideas and models, or heroes.

Both stages have to do with choosing futures—which this chapter is all about. Choosing concerns a very important aspect of freedom, in that choosing a vocation is construed as tantamount to choosing a life. There is an embarrassment of riches from which to choose; the future to which one must apparently commit oneself is a source of fright, even paralysis. To have to choose for a lifetime can be a crushing task. It has occasioned (by Erikson's reckoning, and I agree) the so-called dropping out, at least temporarily, of flower children, and others. Erikson quotes Biff from Miller's *Death of a Salesman*: "I just can't take hold, Mom, I can't take hold of some kind of a life."

As things are now, most middle-class individuals need or take a moratorium, to fall back and regroup, in their late teens. New stages in the cycle may require similar pause and preparation for growth. Tolerance of these pauses will have to be won. But more urgent than that is the consideration of other socioeconomic classes in the present.

We still send workers into the mines. Malnutrition and starvation are present in every depressed neighborhood in America. Our energy problems are, like the impossible, going to take a little longer to solve. So, in addition to the identity crisis of the all-American teenager, there is frustration and shame for the poor, the minorities, and other groups. I suspect that during the transitional years frustration, anger, guilt, and shame will be more widespread, but they haunt many today—often, according to Erikson, because of the failure of individuals to reach infantile or adolescent ideals. Longevity would obviously afford a longer opportunity to realize ideals; this could reduce some pressures and make life more promising, if not more carefree. Still, I can't help but believe that if life spans were doubled, those desires—economic and otherwise—would double or become proportionately inflated, and longevity alone would not supply the other ingredients necessary for satisfying development. I wonder whether anything would really be gained along these lines.

Perhaps the greatest cause for celebration of increase in life span is that it may allow for a final integration of identity, a resolution, sense of completion, and fulfillment that old age is supposed to produce but that so few people seem to achieve. Perhaps the shortest resource toward that end is time. If we agree with Erikson that "a civilization can be measured by the meaning which it gives to the full cycle of life,"[16] we might view opportunity to achieve wisdom and integration as a high mark, and thus construe the increasing life span as a necessary condition for achieving the fullest measure of our civilization. I tend, however, to think that most of us would still need lessons in integrating. Time alone would not suffice.[17]

NOTES

1. My primary purpose is to consider the impact this would have on freedom, but it is also part of my purpose to raise questions about truth-telling, knowledge, and uncertainty—for example, requiring truthfulness of insurance companies that could use one set of actuarial tables for life insurance and a different table for health insurance for windfall profits; or speculating about how family relationships might hold up. This aspect receives only secondary attention throughout the chapter.
2. L. Hayflick, "Perspectives in Human Longevity," in *Extending the Human Life Span: Social Policy and Social Ethics,* Report for the National Science Foundation (Chicago: University of Chicago Press, 1976), p. 4.
3. The primary resource for the data and manipulation of data is L. Robbins and J. Hall, *How to Practice Prospective Medicine* (Indianapolis: Methodist Hospital of Indiana, 1970). Their categorizations (white-negro, male-female, age groups

5-9, 10-14, 15-19, 20-24, and so on) and their data are used in this chapter. But all this is heuristic. Variance with more up-to-date data is not especially significant for reflection on freedom.

4. These tables predict what will cause death within the next ten years of a person's life, not necessarily *at* the age of the group being assessed.

5. H. T. Engelhardt, Jr., "The Ontology of Abortion," *Ethics* 84, no. 3 (April 1974): 217.

6. K. Boucot, D. Cooper, and W. Weiss, "The Role of Surgery in the Cure of Lung Cancer," *Archives of Internal Medicine* 120 (August 1967): 168.

7. This argument was used years ago regarding dialysis.

8. Except that it would be freedom's requirement that the public participate fully in deciding whether to forge ahead on a policy lengthening life span or funding research.

9. E. Erikson, *Identity: Youth and Crisis* (New York: W. W. Norton, 1968), p. 50.

10. Ibid., p. 89.

11. This is one of the reasons I personally fear that the losses to lived freedom will be suffered most severely by people whose lives are spent during the transition to the age of longevity—as most factory workers were exploited during the transitional years into the Industrial Age.

12. E. Erikson, *Identity: Youth and Crisis*, p. 107.

13. Ibid., p. 108. This (to make a relevant aside) seems to be the sort of distortion of the nature of man and nature of value and even the nature of nature that occasions some of the passion for research. An antidote to some of this may be found in E. Becker, *The Denial of Death* (New York: The Free Press, 1973).

14. Ibid., p. 120.

15. Ibid., p. 126.

16. Ibid., pp. 140–141.

17. I wish to thank John Moskop and H. Tristram Engelhardt, Jr., for important help on earlier drafts.

12

Law, Technology, and Public Policy: Suicide and Euthanasia

MARSHALL BREGER

It is a difficult assignment for a lawyer to assess the effect of technological change on legal norms and institutions. To the attorney, legal relations possess their own logic of development. Even among commentators who agree that law is molded by social and economic pressures, few have considered the direct effect of technology on legal processes. Scientific breakthroughs and technological development may indeed pose problems for the law; their effect is mediated, however, by a society's cultural norms. Hence, what begins as a study of legal developments rapidly becomes an inquiry into social and ethical values in the light of biomedical technology.

This chapter considers legal and ethical aspects of one facet of gerontology—the likelihood that science will develop mechanisms to substantially extend the normal life span or life expectancy.[1] It will focus on the effect of such new technologies on social policy associated with euthanasia and suicide.

As more people live extended lives thanks to some form of artificial support system, psychological if not philosophical, concerns about prolonged existence will become acute. The option of ending life on one's own terms will be explored by many people and will force us, as individuals and as a society, to consider what should be the *natural*[2] or *reasonable* term of human existence on earth.

There are two ways in which we can envision societies whose

members live prolonged life, as we presently understand it. In one model, life-extending technology merely lengthens life's declining years. Death is staved off, while bodily infirmity is not. This was the lot of the *struldbrugs*, those unfortunate creatures whom Gulliver met in his visit to Luggnagg.[3] The "most mortifying sight" he beheld on his travels, they lived forever in a condition of continuous mental and physical decline. In the other model, life-extending technology adds years of vigorous and healthy life. While the latter scenario is the goal of those scientists presently working to retard the aging process, one cannot rule out success with more limited modes of life extension. Clearly, the attitude toward suicide and euthanasia in a society will be affected by the character of the available technology.

PRESENT LAWS RELATING TO SUICIDE AND EUTHANASIA

Attitudes toward suicide and euthanasia are changing at a rapid rate, and to both physicians and the general public euthanasia has become a subject of serious concern. Legislatures in eight states have passed "right to die" laws.[5] Similar bills were introduced in the legislatures of at least twenty-seven other states during the 1978 legislative session.[6] A recent Harris poll suggests that forty-nine percent of the American public believes that a terminally ill patient has the right "to tell his doctor to put him out of his misery."[7] At the time, courts are increasingly disposed to allow severely ill patients to refuse treatment although death may result. In the celebrated cases of *In re Quinlan*[8] and *Superintendent of Belchertown State School v. Saikewicz*,[9] guardians were permitted to withdraw treatment on behalf of imcompetent patients.

At present, no state makes suicide or attempted suicide a statutory crime, although the common law so regarded it.[10] Twenty-five states do have statutes which make aiding and abetting a suicide a crime[11]—usually a felony, and in some instances a misdemeanor. In states without specific criminal statutes governing aiding and abetting a suicide, there is little doubt that such aid would be dealt with under the general law of homicide. The penal codes of a number of European and Latin American jurisdictions specifically provide for lesser penalties either for "aiding a suicide" or for "killing on request."[12]

While not illegal, suicide is frowned on by both society and the state. Suicidal tendencies are often a ground for civil commitment in those jurisdictions in which "dangerousness to others" is not the sole criterion.[18] While the suicide's body may not, as in days of yore, be buried "in the highway with a stake driven through his body,"[14] one who commits suicide is still *prima facie* thought to be psychologically ill. Most suicides are perceived as a "cry for help" on the part of an anguished soul, and the burden is on the individual choosing suicide to convince us that the contrary is true.[15]

The rationale justifying the removal of suicide from the law's reach is unclear. For some, the decision to take one's own life is viewed as a purely personal one, which need not (excepting obligations to family or friends) concern other persons. It lies in the realm of private morality and is thus deemed immune to legal encroachment. The choice of suicide is understood as an assertion of an individual's personal autonomy. An opposing view treats suicide with less magnanimity, characterizing it as immoral or sinful. The absence of legal sanctions against suicide is justified by prudence rather than principle; it is impossible in the modern world to punish a successful suicide, and it is unseemly to punish an unsuccessful attempt. These distinct approaches are more than academic; they relate directly to the moral and legal view a society will take toward the aiding and abetting of suicide or euthanasia.

Commentators have distinguished between several types of euthanasia, ascribing varying degrees of disapproval to each. Thus, distinctions are commonly made between voluntary and involuntary, active and passive, euthanasia. They reflect polar perspectives on the act of euthanasia—the perspective of the patient and the perspective of some other agent, such as the physician who is treating the patient.

Voluntary euthanasia is a special case of suicide, or more precisely, of assisted suicide.[16] It reflects the individual patients claim to personal autonomy over the time and character of his death. Involuntary euthanasia involves a determination by another that an individual should not continue to live for reasons (either noble or ignoble) often premised on the patient's "best interests."

The active/passive distinction turns on the means used by the physician or other agent to bring about the patient's death. In some interpretations of law or ethics, passive euthanasia, i.e., allowing a patient to die, is acceptable, while more active modes of intervention are not. This distinction may well affect the legality, if not the morality, of a physician's decision about the treatment. The validity of these distinctions will be discussed later in this chapter.

RECENT STATUTORY AND JUDICIAL DEVELOPMENTS

As mentioned above, eight states have already passed natural death acts which insure patients with terminal illness control over decisions regarding life-sustaining treatment in specific contexts.[17] The California legislation, effective January 1, 1977, was the first to be enacted.[18] It has served as a model for legislation in other states.

The act creates a procedure whereby a competent adult may execute a "directive," instructing his physician to withhold or withdraw medical treatment which "would serve to artificially prolong the moment" of death should he suffer a terminal illness or injury. If a patient executes the prescribed directive in the form of a "living will," a physician or health care professional following the patient's instructions is immunized from both civil and criminal liability.[19]

The California legislation has a decidedly limited scope. The "right to die" is restricted to people afflicted with a terminal disease where death is imminent. It does not cover situations, like that of Karen Quinlan, in which death is not necessarily imminent, but where the patient survives in an incompetent, painful, or severely debilitated state. Further, for the patient's directive to be legally binding, the patient must reaffirm it after learning of his terminal condition.[20] Thus, the patient must be clearly in full possession of his faculties when the directive is executed. No one can give permission to withdraw or withhold life support on his behalf—even in his best interests.

One cannot definitely state that a right to refuse treatment has been established in case law when the refusal would lead to death, but the trend is clearly towards legitimating such a right of refusal. While many of the cases have concerned the refusal of treatment on religious grounds, an increasing number have faced the issue squarely. They have viewed the refusal of treatment as part of an inchoate constitutional right of privacy.[21]

The extent to which this right may be extended to incompetent patients is considered in the cases of *In re Quinlan* and *Superintendent of Belchertown State School v. Saikewicz*. As is now well known, on the night of April 15, 1975, for reasons still unclear, Karen Quinlan "ceased breathing for at least two 15–minute periods."[22] She was placed on a respirator to assist her breathing, but was found to be in a "chronic or 'persistent vegetative state.' "[23] While it did not appear that she could be "restored to cognitive or sapient life," she still did not meet any of the standard criteria for "brain death."[24] Her father applied to the New Jersey courts for guardianship in order to seek the termination of life-support measures sustaining her.[25]

The State of New Jersey argued that removal of Ms. Quinlan's respirator must be considered homicide. The Supreme Court of New Jersey, however, observed that

> [t]he termination of treatment pursuant to the right to privacy is, within the limitations of this case, *ipso facto* lawful. Thus, a death resulting from such an act would not come within the scope of the homicide statutes proscribing only the unlawful killing of another. There is a real and in this case determinative distinction between the unlawful taking of the life of another and the ending of artificial life-support systems as a matter of self-determination.[26]

The court concluded that the constitutional protection afforded one who chooses to refuse treatment extends to a guardian who decides on the patient's behalf, when a guardian is needed for the successful exercise of the patient's right of privacy.

The *Quinlan* court specifically concluded that when a doctor's fiduciary duty does not extend to the use of life-support apparatus, he is insulated from criminal liability if he discontinues that treatment upon the guardian's instruction. This is a narrow holding, yet the national attention paid to the case suggests that its implications are extensive, as the parties to the lawsuit clearly recognized.

Does the rationale advanced for insulating a physician from criminal sanction when a competent patient refuses treatment, as under the California statute, apply equally to a refusal expressed vicariously by a guardian, as in the *Quinlan* case? Under the California statute, an individual must knowingly sign a "living will" in front of witnesses. After five years, if the will is not renewed, it ceases to be valid and the role of the potential decision-maker is once again unspecified.[27] In *Quinlan* the patient could not articulate her desires. She lacked both cognition and volition, the traditional criteria of autonomy. Her family's vicarious consent to the removal of life-sustaining procedures may only be defended on autonomy grounds if it can be shown that they were, in fact, asserting rights which Karen would have asserted, were she competent. Alternatively, one might urge the primacy of competing social values, be they paternalism, familial autonomy, or consideration of social cost, when evaluating her family's actions.

A comparison of *Quinlan* with a recent Massachusetts case, *Superintendent of Belchertown State School v. Saikewicz*, may clarify the problem of making decisions about euthanasia on behalf of imcompetents. Saikewicz was a 67-year-old severely retarded leukemia patient who had resided in a mental institution all his life. A disciplined course of chemotherapy would arrest his leukemia, but there was little hope of more than a few months remission. Without such therapy, Saikewicz would die "within a matter of weeks or months." While most persons would likely choose chemotherapy, the superintendent of the mental hospital where Saikewicz resided sought judicial permission, on Saikewicz's behalf, to forego such treatment. In response, the trial court appointed a guardian *ad litem* who determined that "Saikewicz's illness was an incurable one, and that although chemotherapy was the medically indicated course of treatment it would cause Saikewicz significant adverse side effects and discomfort."[28] The guardian concluded that the adverse side effects

> as well as the inability of the ward to understand the treatment to which he would be subjected and the fear and pain he would suffer as a result, outweighed the limited prospect of any benefit from such treatment, namely, the possibility of some uncertain but limited extension of life. He therefore recommended "that not treating Mr. Saikewicz would be in his best interests."[29]

These recommendations were approved both by the trial court and the Supreme Judicial Court of Massachusetts.

Both of these cases suggest that in attempting to assimilate the termination of life-sustaining procedures for incompetents into the principle of personal autonomy espoused by partisans of a natural death act, the basic problem is an evidentiary one. How are we to know the desires of those who are incompetent regarding ultimate issues of life or death? The plain fact is that in numerous cases we cannot do this. The approach taken by the *Quinlan* court was to "permit the guardian and family of Karen to render their best judgment . . . as to whether she would exercise" her right to decide upon discontinuance of the life-support apparatus.[30] The court approved a family decision to suspend life support because it concluded that "the overwhelming majority" of persons in Karen's situation would choose this form of voluntary euthanasia.

The *Saikewicz* court took a different tack. It determined that the guardian must make that choice which the patient, if competent, would make—"the primary test is subjective in nature—that is, the goal is to determine with as much accuracy as possible the wants and needs of the individual involved."[31] Thus, in contrast to the *Quinlan* court, the Supreme Judicial Court of Massachusetts did not accept an objective or consensus standard for vicarious decision-making. It recognized that the majority would be likely to choose chemotherapy if faced with Saikewicz's choice, but required the guardian to attempt to divine Saikewicz's own desires regarding chemotherapy, as distinct from what the majority or consensus opinion might be. The Massachusetts court thus paralleled John Rawls's view that the integrity of a person can only be maintained in surrogate decision-maker contexts if we act for incompetents "as we have reason to believe they would choose for themselves if they were at the age of reason and deciding rationally."[32]

While some commentators have applauded use of this methodology of "substitute judgment," one may question whether the surrogate decision-maker can really know the preferences of an incompetent. This is especially true when one deals, as in the *Saikewicz* case, with persons who never were competent. Attempts to make determinations of this sort will, of necessity, result in the surrogate's intermingling his own views on death and dying with the putative views of the incompetent. The attempt by the *Saikewicz* court to rescue the autonomy principle in the context of vicarious decisions for the termination of life-sustaining treatment may be little more than a legal fiction.

The *Saikewicz* court touched on a further issue of relevance to our concerns. In reviewing the arguments for withholding treatment marshalled by Saikewicz's guardian, the trial judge considered the "quality of life possible for [Saikewicz] even if the treatment does bring about remission."[33] This was a clear reference to considerations of the "quality of life" disapproved by the Massachusetts Supreme Court, which observed that to the extent that this formulation equates the value of life with any measure of quality of life, we firmly reject it."[34] The Massachusetts court further limited its approval of a court decision not to provide life-prolonging treatment to those patients whom we can conventionally consider to be on the threshold of death. Like the California Natural Death Act it did not speak to the situation of incurables or persons who have debilitating conditions but are not yet about to die.

Attempts are already underway to liberalize the California Natural Death Act so as to make it easier to insure patients the "right" to die.[35] The gravamen of these efforts is to allow unconscious or incompetent persons (including children and persons in a permanent noncognitive state)[36] to exercise, albeit through a substitute, their putative right to decline further medical treatment. In this respect, a revised act would take into account considerations involving "quality of life."

The effect of these changes, if adopted into law, would be first of all to shift the focus of the act away from insuring personal autonomy, i.e., the "right" of an individual to reject life-continuing therapy. By allowing third parties, be they relatives, courts, or doctors, to make decisions about life continuance *on behalf* of incompetent, noncognitive, or minor patients, the act will, in fact, emphasize paternalism in the guise of maximizing autonomy.

The second shift discernible in attempts to revise the California act is the movement towards expanding the conditions under which a patient (or his proxy) can choose to reject life support and require doctors to follow his request. The original Act states that persons must be in a terminal condition before physicians may withhold or withdraw life-sustaining procedures. The act defines "terminal condition" to mean

> an incurable condition caused by injury, disease, or illness, which, regardless of the application of life-sustaining procedures, would, within reasonable medical judgment, produce death, and where the application of life-sustaining procedures serve only to postpone the moment of death of the patient.[37]

This simply means that for the directive to take effect, the patient must suffer from a condition which will result almost immediately in death. Further, that condition must have existed for at least two weeks.

The act provides a technical definition of "life-sustaining procedure," limiting that term to encompass

> any medical procedure or intervention which utilizes mechanical or other artificial means to sustain, restore or supplant a vital function, which, when applied to a qualified patient, would serve only to artificially prolong the moment of death and where, in the judgment of the attending physician, death is imminent whether or not such procedures are utilized.[38]

The definition of "imminence" is deliberately ambiguous. Our ordinary understanding of imminence is that life will end in a very short period of time. Assemblyman Barry Keene, author of the present California act, has suggested that periods of up to ninety days would be consistent with that term.[39] He suggests, however, that we should move radically away from the concept of imminence to a concept of "perceptible and predictable physical decline."[40] This "cancer model," as he terms it, would allow patients to issue an enforceable directive at the beginning of a prolonged malignancy. Keene also urges that the directive be triggered when a patient is in a "permanent noncognitive" state and has been in that condition for over 180 days. Other commentators have urged that the presence or absence of cognition is too limiting a criterion.[41] They would allow that all persons suffering from a debilitating and incurable, albeit nonterminal, illness should be allowed to make use of a natural death act.

While in theory the result of the shift away from the criterion of imminent death may be to enlarge autonomy, this is not likely, in practice, to be the case. At present, a competent patient can often refuse life-extending treatment. He can check himself out of the hospital at will, or he can refuse medication or therapy in the hospital if he appears competent to make his own decisions. A patient told that he has cancer may drink the proverbial cup of hemlock within or without the hospital walls.

The incompetent, however, by definition, cannot make such a decision. Thus, the surrogate doctor, family member, or guardian must act for him. Expanding the class of persons for whom a directive can be made will mean that the surrogate will no longer be merely engaged in preventing the dying process of a patient from being unnecessarily lengthened. Instead, he will decide when an incurable incompetent should die. This decision will, of necessity, involve judgments about quality of life and about the social cost and social value of keeping incurables alive.

THE EFFECT OF NEW LIFE-SUPPORT TECHNOLOGIES ON LAWS RELATING TO EUTHANASIA AND SUICIDE

Legal institutions respond to cultural change, not to technological advance. Thus, any effects of new life-saving technologies on laws regarding euthanasia or suicide will be mediated through broadly shared cultural values. Technological developments, however, may increase the strains resulting from a disjunction of technology and culture and exacerbate legal anachronisms resulting from these developments.

Changes in autopsy laws in both the nineteenth and twentieth centuries were brought about largely by the opportunities created by new medical technologies. Some commentators have suggested that recent legislation to rework the definition (and by implication the time) of death was fueled by a recognition of the possibilities inherent in transplant technology. Still, the controversy over autopsy laws in Israel—which are anathema to many religious groups which reject secular attitudes toward the human body—suggests that culture, not technology, is the ultimate arbiter of legal relations.[42]

New life-extension technologies will change the factual predicates on which many of our laws are based.[43] For example, the continuing refinement of biomedical technology for prolonging life will make it increasingly difficult to distinguish between active and passive forms of euthanasia, between "killing" someone and "allowing" him to die. The purpose of these distinctions was to separate cases of affirmative action from cases of "mere" omission or inaction in causing euthanasia, and to hold the latter, in some instances at least, not to be legally or morally culpable. Many commentators have long supported the distinction as a bedrock for moral discussion of this subject, although contemporary legal thinking, as we will show, has questioned the distinction's validity in many areas.

Thus, if we use antisenescence drugs from birth, are provided with long-life cardiac pacemakers while still fairly healthy, or change our diets when young, the concept of an "act of omission" will be of little use. In that event, it will be difficult to argue that halting the drug regimen or removing the implant would merely restore the *status quo ante* of our health. If we undergo treatment to prevent aging, all of us will be kept alive—in our dotage at least—by a variety of techniques; no longer will there be a "state of nature" regarding health practice. Can it then be seriously argued that refusals to treat are merely acts of omission?

To be sure, some moral philosophers and theologians hold that stopping a life-support treatment such as a respirator is more akin to an omission than an action. But this is not necessarily the view of health care professionals who face the psychological and practical problems of "pulling the plug." A respirator is a device that needs repeated servicing—tubes must be cleaned and controls regulated—and patients may be temporarily removed from the respirator so as to ascertain their progress, if any. Similar problems occur when attempting to describe in conventional active/passive terms technological triumphs such as the servicing of pacemakers or the future possibility of an implanted artificial heart. With new technological advances, a majority of the elderly population may live with the aid of artificial devices. In such a context, it is unrealistic to draw hard lines between starting, stopping, or continuing treatment. The problem of active versus passive euthanasia will not be solved by reference to the distinction between actions and omissions. Ordinary language may once have paired these two distinctions, but rapid technological change has made the pairing more difficult to sustain and will increasingly blur notions of natural and artificial care and conduct. One would not, for example, consider the failure to provide insulin shots to a diabetic as a simple case of "allowing to die."

What are the legal implications of these developments? There is an old common law monster (oft summoned for first-year law classes) who watches gleefully while a young child drowns in a pool.[44] This paradigmatic wrongdoer, so the tyros are taught, will escape liability. He cannot be held liable for an omission—a failure to act so as to save the child—unless he can be shown to be under a specific duty to act affirmatively. Thus sayeth the common law. However accurate this articulation of common law principles may be, the distinction between acts and omissions for purposes of legal culpability has been increasingly narrowed in contemporary case law. If one can establish a special relationship between both parties, a duty to act may be created; this duty vitiates any claim that one merely failed to act.

Advances in life-extension technology will make the distinction between ordinary and extraordinary care more difficult to maintain. Both physicians and patients will be increasingly uncertain as to what constitutes essential care at any given place or time. This uncertainty may stir disputes among physicians and result in frustration and litigation for patients and their families.

In the past, the diffusion of knowledge from centers of medical learning to the hinterland often took a great deal of time. New equipment available at large medical complexes was often too expensive for hospitals in smaller cities. For these reasons, the traditional standard of liability for doctors in malpractice litigation has followed the "locality rule,"[45] requiring that doctors be familiar only with the standards of care current in their own or similar localities. Ordinary medical care for New York City, it was recognized, would differ from ordinary medical care for Oswego. However, modern education and communications technology have narrowed the geographical gap between ordinary and extraordinary. What is customary in the operating rooms of New York's Mount Sinai Hospital is increasingly deemed to be standard surgical practice in distant localities as well.[46]

There is clearly, of course, a difference between "experimental" treatment, which seeks to determine the success rate of a particular medical intervention, and customary treatment. At least hypothetically, canons of analysis could be developed to allow an objective assessment of the moment when a treatment was no longer experimental. The Food and Drug Administration, after all, makes such determinations in the drug field when passing on New Drug Applications.[47] Extraordinary care suggests something other than esoteric or "experimental" intervention. It is a cultural and not a technical phenomenon. This appears clearly from a statement by Pope Pius XII in his effort to state the physician's duty to care. "Normally, one is held to use only ordinary means—according to circumstances of persons, places, times and culture. . . ."[48] To some extent, technological advances will make the use of certain medical devices (such as dialysis machines) cheaper and therefore more likely to be socially acceptable, hence "ordinary." The extent and frequency with which a particular therapy is practiced is also likely to change the ways in which society perceives it (e.g., the acceptance of insulin and kidney dialysis). For a therapy to be extraordinary it need not be esoteric. At the same time, an intervention which is deemed necessary need not be simple or swift. A variety of factors must be considered before a medical innovation is considered part of ordinary care and therefore not to be rejected by those with the authority to refuse extraordinary treatment.

Further, we must recognize that the distinction between ordinary and extraordinary care is, in many ways, one of art. It need have nothing to do with customary medical practice, but instead may cloak "quality of life" or cost-benefit assessments by the physician. In some contexts, it may focus on the relationship between the technique used and its effect on the patient or his family. Extraordinary means, from this perspective, might be ones that involve great pain, hardship, or expense either to a patient or his family. According to this view the physician would surrender the decision as to what is ordinary or extraordinary medical treatment to the patient's family. This attempt at distinction involves various significant dangers. Patients with similar conditions might be treated differently as a result of family attitudes. It would seem better to limit treatment classification to criteria which involve a review of medical indications, allocation of resources, and the current availability of a proposed treatment, so that the preferences and values of the family, or even the patient, do not bear on this question.

Some commentators have suggested that there is a a heuristic value in completely jettisoning the "ordinary/extraordinary" care distinction. According to them, the terms have become entangled in rhetoric and generate more heat than light. Instead, one might make use of the standard of duty used in tort law generally—the duty of the reasonable man. Use of this abstraction often leads, however, to seemingly capricious decisions. To the extent that certainty and stability are goals in these matters (and it is clear to me that they should be), some more concrete method of structuring our decision-making in this area is vital. Otherwise, the decision as to when care is extraordinary will vary according to the idiosyncrasies of doctor, patient, or family.

DEMOGRAPHY, LIFE-EXTENSION, AND EUTHANASIA

An increase in the proportion of the aged in the population will accentuate the problems of suicide and euthanasia for doctors, lawyers, policy planners, and the public. Since we know little about how one would live one's old age in a context of life-extending technologies, it is futile to speculate about the quality of life or its status within future cultural values. After all, a society of senior citizens may well lose the youth orientation which is characteristic of contemporary society.

The effect of life-extending technology on public policy will turn on the social consequences of that technology. Many of our past ideals of extreme longevity have envisioned immortal man continually in his prime. As teachers, scientists, or day laborers, such a group would add immeasurably to the productive character of our society. As we have seen, however, longevity may also mean a stretching out of one's declining years—a staving off of death by extending the period of debility. Such a situation would drain society's resources. This drain, if serious enough, could invite debate about encouraging euthanasia or suicide after the completion of one's "natural" life span.

If life-extending technologies greatly lengthen either the period of senility or other unacceptable conditions of health, we may see an increasing readiness in patients to refuse life-extending treatment. We should even anticipate increasing pressures for stopping treatment against the patient's will, and indeed for mercy killing. These pressures may take direct form, such as efforts to legalize compulsory euthanasia, but more probably they will surface in the subtler form of vague social pressures to "step aside" so that life-prolonging resources can be used more equitably or more efficiently. Similarly, an informal consensus may emerge to expand the categories of patients to be "legitimately" denied life-extending treatment. These potential influences on our legal and ethical evaluations of suicide, euthanasia, and refusals of further treatment are likely to extend far beyond instances of relatively rare and exotic life-extending technologies. They may, in fact, transform our fundamental attitudes about life and death and their protection under our present system of law.

The principle of human autonomy has stressed the notion that euthanasia and suicide are to be understood as private privileges, in accordance with the desirability of allowing people control over their own lives. From this view of suicide or euthanasia, whether decisions to terminate life are foolish or wise, they remain the province of the individual concerned.

Advances in life-extending technology may well affect our social attitudes toward euthanasia and suicide. The "right to die" may be transformed from a private right, founded on considerations of private autonomy, to a public duty, necessary for the survival of society. The realization that the earth's resources are limited may lead to a recognition that they can be provided to the aged only at the expense of the productive segments of the community. In a variety of ancient and primitive cultures, the social duty of the elderly is to die gracefully so that younger members of the community might flourish. As one Netsilik Eskimo relates, the elderly "who can do no more and whom death will not take, help death to take them. And they do this not merely to get rid of a life that is no longer a pleasure, but also to relieve their nearest relatives of the trouble that they give them."[49] Such sentiments are not restricted to primitive cultures. Classical tradition speaks of those "very old men [who] came together, garlanded as if to a banquet, and drank hemlock when they realized that they were incapable of doing anything useful for their fatherland."[50]

Western society, with its individualistic orientation, has flatly rejected this position. It has held fast to the notion that each individual life is equal to any other, no matter what benefit that individual can bring to the community. Should pervasive use of life-extending technology dramatically change the demographic character of society, pressure may develop to change this attitude. Rather than rage against the dying of the light, we may well take the view of Germaine Greer, who has suggested that "dying is, after all, a service to the community, and ought to be honored as such."[51] Whether a shift of values will ultimately result in laws compelling euthanasia is a matter best left in the realm of speculation.[52] Such compulsion, if it comes, would do violence to one of our most cherished values—the autonomy of the individual. Much will obviously depend on the scenario for life extension that science will present us.

IS THERE A RIGHT TO REJECT LIFE EXTENSION?

As indicated above, one ultimate question concerns the extent to which the extension of life will reflect personal choice or a mandated state policy. While at first blush, one would assume that all reasonable persons would opt for longevity, this need not be the case. Certainly some may prefer a "natural death" over an artificially prolonged existence.

To some extent these choices, too, will turn on the character of the prevalent technology for life extension.[53] If the conventional "therapy" for life extension is adopted by the individual concerned, a personal choice may be possible. Should the indicated "therapy" require collective decision-making, the possibility of individual choice may prove less real.

Some life-extension scenarios may encompass interventions with children at an early stage. In that event, one would be unable either to choose or reject life extension; the decision would be made by a child's parents. New issues of parental autonomy and children's rights might develop. A number of models can be envisioned. In the "passive acceptance" case, life-extending technologies might be applied in a generally pervasive fashion comparable to fluoridation of water. It might be discovered that some chemical or biological agent will trigger retardation of aging only when ingested by young children. If that were the case, a societal decision would be made to extend life and the means used for that purpose would extend life for all, unless provisions of opting out were provided.

One might also envisage an "opting in" model by which life-extending agents would not be universally available. Instead, a child or his parents would be free to choose an individual treatment. In such an "active choice" situation, questions of parental control would arise.[54]

Traditional doctrine has given parents an extraordinary range of power over medical and social decisions concerning a child's upbringing, at least when his life is not in imminent danger.[55] In the main, parents can make decisions to rear children in their own image. They may refuse medical treatment that would clearly benefit the child.[56] Thus, parents opposed to surgical intervention on religious grounds can deny their child cosmetic surgery in instances where this surgery would be of medical or psychological benefit.[57]

Recently, some courts have begun to introduce a new element—the desires of the child—into the decision-making. Where children are *in fact* capable of making decisions, courts are considering the wishes of children as well as those of parents and the state. Intrafamily conflicts have not often been involved, yet the *ratio decidendi* of an increasing number of cases is the wishes of the child.[58] At the same time, many legislatures have reduced the age of consent both generally[59] and for special medical intervention.[60]

Again, the effect of legal developments depends largely on community perceptions regarding life extension. If it is perceived as an unmixed blessing, like the prevention of tooth decay, society may consider cost-efficient mechanisms to provide this "good" without reference to parental beliefs. Whether society would allow those whose religious beliefs reject life extension to opt out is a separate question. Solicitude for individual choices would depend on the weight given to societal judgments about the rights of the child, as opposed to parental preference. It would further turn on the extent to which society (as represented by our law-makers) would deem arguments against life extension to be irrational or frivolous.

To return to the fluoride analogy, the government might add a life-extending elixir to children's diets in ways from which they could not opt out. Such a policy would abandon the traditional concept of parental autonomy. Life extension, unlike inoculation, is not directly and obviously intended for the benefit of third parties. While it is likely to be seen generally as a "good," a parent's right to refuse it for his child would probably be given substantial weight, at least in a situation where the child's attitude were one of indifference. On the other hand, life-extending treatment could be considered, like blood transfusions, as necessary to maintain or restore "normal" health, in which case parental freedom of choice might be constricted.

As the concept of personal autonomy is extended to children, tensions will develop between the child's right to control his body and parental rights to control his upbringing. This dispute has already surfaced in the area of abortion, where the teenager's right to choose an abortion has generally prevailed. In regard to the extension of life, this conflict of "rights" will probably be fought out once again, as another example of the strains in our traditional legal system flowing from advances in biomedical technology. If we wish to minimize the need to reformulate the legal definition of the parent-child relationship, it will be necessary to develop life-extending devices that can be chosen by adults but not forced upon children.

SANCTITY OF LIFE AND QUALITY OF LIFE: SOCIAL VALUES AND THE LAW

It should be clear from the foregoing that present legal approaches towards euthanasia and suicide continue to reflect, in large part, our cultural and religious attitudes toward the sanctity of life. Despite the current emphasis on reinterpretation, we must recognize that traditional conceptions of the sanctity of life (grounded historically in Judeo-Christian theology) still hold considerable force. These conceptions underscore the infinite value of life *per se* (presumptively as a gift from God) and oppose all efforts to abandon principled commitment to the sanctity of life. Thus, the Chief Rabbi of England, Immanuel Jakobovits, in stating the traditional Jewish view, also reflects the conventional legal and religious position concerning the preservation of a particular life: "The value of human life is infinite and beyond measure, so that any part of life—even if only an hour or second—is of precisely the same worth as seventy years of it."[61] "Any fraction of life, however limited its expectancy or health, remains equally infinite in value."[62]

At present, there are indications of some shift away from the unqualified commitment to "sanctity of life" values toward the recognition of qualifying values such as the "quality of life," "social worth," or "social cost." Considerations, both subjective—regarding individual perceptions as to quality of life—and objective—involving social cost and social worth—are being increasingly used to justify the failure to provide life-support devices to infants with congenital birth defects as well as to adults suffering from incurable (albeit not terminal) illnesses. These trends are reflected, in part, in the recent *Quinlan* and *Saikewicz* cases and the spate of natural death acts passed by various state legislatures which were discussed above.

As the law now stands, consensual euthanasia is supported by concepts of personal autonomy, and indirect or third-party euthanasia (either active or passive) is justified by considerations emphasizing social conceptions of the quality of life. The future strength of these cultural concerns is impossible to gauge. Like Minerva's owl, we best understand cultural epochs in their concluding phase. What is clear at the present time is that the development of successful life-extending technologies will further highlight these issues and *weaken* our traditional commitment to the sanctity of life.

Technology has often carried its own imperatives in Western society and has developed independently of existing values, frequently with a great deal of consequent strain upon value structures and institutions. Although society eventually does adapt to technologically induced change, there is always a degree of cultural lag which has to be overcome. In many respects, American society has not learned to cope effectively with the increasing number of people living beyond the span of three score and ten as the result of existing medical techniques. How values and institutions would, or could, adapt to life extensions for a majority of the population must remain a matter for conjecture, but based on previous experience the outlook is not promising. As Byron Gold, a former Acting Director of the Administration on Aging has argued:

> While I am willing to accept the virtual certainty of the extension of life by science during the next 50 years, I am not at all sanguine that American society during that same period of time will be willing, or even able, to deal with the rather profound social changes which will inevitably accompany the extension of life. . . . The history of American public policy concerning the elderly does not give much cause for confidence that, once life is extended, the resources necessary to make life something more than a struggle to stay alive will be devoted to those citizens whose lives have been extended.[64]

Scientists are only now becoming fully aware of the value implications of supposedly value-free knowledge and techniques. Society is again beginning to question the view that man is, like nature, to be seen as raw material for manipulation. Man need not be a slave to technology—indeed much of traditional Western morality is based on that premise—but one does not have to be a technological determinist to recognize that the development of life-extension technologies may radically influence our moral, and by derivation, our legal, superstructure. A technology need only be implemented if society decides that the relevant scientific knowledge should be so used.

The appropriate time to review the propriety of adopting such a technological innovation as life extension is surely now, when we may make some evaluation of possible effects upon existing value structures and choose between alternative policies.

NOTES

1. This chapter retains the distinction, clarified in Chapter 1, between *life span* and *life expectancy*. It seems unlikely that abstract life-span variation will have a major impact on public policy toward euthanasia and suicide, and quite likely that changes in life expectancy will do so. Because people respond less to abstract hopes and fears and more to immediate travail—how long they, in fact, are likely to live—we shall focus on life-expectancy considerations.

   By increased life expectancy we do not mean the creation of innovative life-saving technologies which extend life by a few days or months, but that range of social speculation and scientific research which contemplates man restored to biblical longevity. In at least one speculative rendering of these events, they would not merely extend the period in which one exists in a continually degenerating state, but would delay the degenerative process and expand the active and productive period. Some scientific evidence suggests that such a breakthrough is no longer in the realm of science fiction.
2. Daniel Callahan, "On Defining Natural Death," *The Hastings Center Report* 7 (June 1977): 32.
3. Jonathan Swift, *Gulliver's Travels,* ed. R. Greenberg (New York: W. W. Norton, 1970).
4. Ibid., p. 183.
5. *Ark. Stat. Ann.* §82-3801 to 3804 (1977); *Cal. Health and Safety Code* §7185-7195 (West Supp. 1978); *Idaho Code* tit. 39 §4501-4508 (1977); *Nev. Rev. Stat.* §449.540-690 (1977); *N.M. Stat. Ann.* §12-35-1 to 11 (1977); *N.C. Gen. Stat.* §90-320 to 322 (1977); *Or. Rev. Stat.* §97-050 to 090 (1977); *Tex. Rev. Civ. Stat. Ann.* art. 4590h (Vernon Supp. 1978).
6. Society for the Right to Die, *Legislative Newsletter* (Summer 1978): 1.
7. See L. Harris, The Harris Survey, *The Ill Have the Right to Die* (March 24, 1977); the survey also found that 71% of Americans believe that "a patient with a terminal disease ought to be able to tell his doctor to let him die rather than to extend his life when no cure is in sight."
8. In re Quinlan, 137 N.J. Super. 227, 348 A.2d 801 (1975), *mod. and remanded* 70 N.J. 10, 355 A.2d 647, *cert. denied,* 429 U.S. 922 (1976).
9. Superintendent of Belchertown State School v. Saikewicz, Mass. Adv. Sh. (1977) 2461, 370 N.E.2d 417 (1977).
10. Six states which until recently had statutes making attempted suicide a crime have since repealed them: Nevada, New Jersey, North Dakota, Oklahoma, South Dakota, and Washington. *Nev. Rev. Stat.* §202.495 (1957), repealed 1961; *N.J.*

Stat. Ann. §2A:170-25.6 (Supp. 1968), repealed 1972; *N.D. Cent. Code* §12-33-02 (1877), repealed 1972; *Okla. Stat. Ann.* tit. 21 §812 (1958), repealed 1976; *S.D. Code Codified Laws Ann.* §13.1903 (1939), discarded with adoption of *S.D. Code Compiled Laws* (1967); *Wash. Rev. Code Ann.* §9.80.020 (1961), repealed 1975.

In 1961, North Carolina, which retains common law crimes, passed a statute abolishing suicide as an offense, thus overruling the holding of State v. Willis, 255 N.C. 473, 121 S.E.2d 854 (1961), making attempted suicide an indictable offense (misdemeanor). *N.C. Gen. Stat.* §14-17.0 (1975).

11. *Alaska Stat.* §11.15.050 (1949); *Cal. Penal Code* §401 (West 1970); *Conn. Gen. Stat. Ann.* §53a-56 (West 1972); *Del. Code Ann.* tit. 11 §645 (1975); *Fla. Stat. Ann.* §782.08 (1976); *Haw. Rev. Stat.* §707-702 (1976); *Ind. Code Ann.* §35-42-1-2 (1977); *Kan. Stat. Ann.* §21-3406 (1974); *Minn. Stat. Ann.* §609.215 (West 1964); *Miss. Code Ann.* §97-3-49 (1972); *Mo. Ann. Stat.* §559.080 (Vernon 1953); *Mont. Rev. Codes Ann.* §94-5-106 (1973); *Nev. Rev. Stat.* §202.490 (1965); *N.H. Rev. Stat. Ann.* §630:4 (1974); *N.M. Stat. Ann.* §40A-2-5 (1953); *N.Y. Penal Law* §120.30, 120.35, 125.15 (3) (McKinney 1975); *N.D. Cent. Code* §12-33-03 to 06 (1960); *Okla. Stat. Ann.* tit. 21 §813-818 (1958); *Or. Rev. Stat.* §163.125 (b) (1977); *Pa. Stat. Ann.* tit. 18 §2505 (Purdon 1973); *S.D. Compiled Laws Ann.* §22-16-37, 22-16-39, (Supp. 1977); *Tex. Penal Code Ann.* §22.08 (Vernon 1974); *Wash. Rev. Code Ann.* §9A.36.060 (1976); *Wis. Stat. Ann.* §940.12 (West 1958).

12. *Austrian Penal Act* §139a-b (*American Series of Foreign Penal Codes* 1966); *Codice Penale art.* 579 (Italy 1964); *Norwegian Penal Code* §235 (*American Series of Foreign Penal Codes* 1961); *Polish Penal Code* arts. 150, 151 (*American Series of Foreign Penal Codes* 1973); *Code Penal Suisse* (1962); *Penal Code of West Germany* §211, 216 (*American Series of Foreign Penal Codes 1961*). In Uruguay, "homicide upon request" which is motivated by compassion can exculpate the defendant. *Penal Code of Uruguay* art. 37 (1933).

13. Greenberg, "Involuntary Psychiatric Commitments to Prevent Suicide," 49 *N.Y.U.L. Rev.* 227 (1974).

14. William Blackstone, *Blackstone's Commentaries on the Laws of England,* Chase 3rd ed. (New York: Banks and Brothers, 1898), p. 938.

15. Norman Farberow and Edwin S. Schneidman, eds., *The Cry for Help* (New York: McGraw-Hill, 1961). See also Erwin Stengel, *Suicide and Attempted Suicide* (New York: Jason Aronson, 1975), pp. 137-49.

16. It could be argued that voluntary euthanasia differs from suicide in that the suicide commits the deed himself and actively wishes to die. In contrast, the individual who requests voluntary euthanasia wishes another to kill him or to allow him to die, as, for example, when he refuses further medical treatment; his direct motive may be to reduce pain or protect certain religious values, and death may be a foreseeable by-product of that goal. These distinctions need not concern us here, however.

17. See statutes cited in note 5, above.

18. *Natural Death Act,* ch. 1439, §1, 1976 *Cal. Stats.* (codified at *Cal. Health & Safety Code* §7185-7195 [West Supp. 1978]).

19. *Cal. Health & Safety Code* §7190 (West Supp. 1978).

20. Ibid., §7188.

21. Cases supporting a right to refuse treatment on grounds of personal autonomy include Perlmutter v. Florida Medical Center, 47 L.W. 2069 (Broward County, Fla. Cir. Ct., July 11, 1978); Palm Springs General Hospital v. Martinez, Civil No. 12687 (Dade County Cir. Ct., July 2, 1971), cited in R. Veatch, *Death, Dying, and the Biological Revolution* (New Haven, Conn.: Yale University Press, 1976), pp. 116 117; Erickson v. Dilgard, 44 Misc.2d 27, 252 N.Y.S.2d 705 (Nassau County Sup. Ct. 1962); In re Yetter, 62 Pa.D. & C.2d 619 (Northampton County Cir. 1973). See "Woman, 77, Who Refused Surgery, Dies in Milwaukee." *The New York Times,* March 7, 1972, p. 27. A string of cases protect an individual's right to refuse life-prolonging treatment on religious grounds. See, e.g., In re Osborne, 294 A.2d 372 (D.C. Ct. App. 1972); In re Estate of Brooks, 32 Ill.2d 361, 205 N.E.2d 435 (1965); *contra,* Application of the President and Directors of Georgetown College, Inc., 331 F.2d 1000 (D.C. Cir.), *cert. denied,* 377 U.S. 978 (1964).

22. In re Quinlan, 137 N.J. Super. 227, 237; 348 A.2d 801, 806 (1975), *mod. and remanded,* 70 N.J. 10, 355 A.2d 647, *cert. denied,* 429 U.S. 922 (1976).

23. 137 N.J. Super. 244, 348 A.2d, 810.

24. 137 N.J. Super. 243, 348 A.2d, 810.

25. As of this date, Karen Quinlan is still alive; See "Miss Quinlan Entering 3rd Year in Coma Unaffected by Court Ruling of Her Case," *The New York Times,* April 10, 1978, p. B3.

26. In re Quinlan, 70 N.J. 10, 51; 355 A.2d 647, 670, *cert. denied,* 429 U.S. 922 (1976).

27. *Cal. Health & Safety Code* §7189.5 (West 1976).

28. Superintendent of Belchertown State School v. Saikewicz, Mass. Adv. Sh. 2461, 2462 (1977), 370 N.E.2d 417, 419 (1977).

29. Ibid.

30. In re Quinlan, 70 N.J. 10, 41; 355 A.2d 647, 664, *cert. denied,* 429 U.S. 922 (1976).

31. Superintendent of Belchertown State School v. Saikewicz, Mass. Adv. Sh. 2461, 2489-90 (1977), 370 N.E.2d 417, 430 (1977). Note that the most systematic analyst of this problem, John Robertson, concludes his discussion by pointing out that "the [substituted judgment] doctrine is unlikely to support decisions in favor of passive euthanasia of defective newborns or the chronically vegetative." John Robertson, "Organ Donations by Incompetents and the Substituted Judgment Doctrine," 76 *Colum. L. Rev.* 48, 77 (1976), footnotes omitted.

32. J. Rawls, *A Theory of Justice* (Cambridge, Mass.: Harvard University Press, 1971), p. 209.

33. Superintendent of Belchertown State School v. Saikewicz, Mass. Adv. Sh. 2461 (1977), 370 N.E.2d 417, 432 (1977).

34. Ibid.

35. One year after passage of the California Natural Death Act, California doctors reported only a few patients had signed written directives. See "Doctors Report Minimal Response to 'Right to Die' Law in California," *The New York Times,*

March 17, 1978, p. 8. Committee on Evolving Trends in Society Affecting Life, *Survey, Results Following One Year's Experience with the Natural Death Act, Sept. 1, 1976–August 31, 1977* (Oct. 31, 1977).

36. Barry Keene, Assemblyman, "Toward Development of a Policy on Life Support Systems" (presented to the Health, Science & Society Conference, University of California, April 21, 1978), pp. 7-9. See also *Ark. Stat. Ann.* §82-3803 (1977); *N.M. Stat. Ann.* §12-35-4 (1977); both statutes allow families to substitute their judgment in the case of minors or incompetents who are terminally ill.

37. *Cal. Health & Safety Code* §7187 (f) (West 1977).

38. Ibid., §7187(c).

39. Barry Keene, Assemblyman, "Can We Make the Natural Death Act a Better Law?" (presented to the 1978 California Medical Association Annual Scientific Assembly, San Francisco, Cal., March 19, 1978), pp. 10–11.

40. Ibid., p. 11.

41. Gerald A. Larue, "Ways of Looking at Death: Bioethics and Public Policy: A Discussion of Alternatives to the Natural Death Act" (report of the Conference sponsored by the National Conference of Christians and Jews, Los Angeles, Cal., January 17, 1978); see also the comments of William W. May in "Summary of Presentations," p. 11. Note the prescient discussion in Jonsen, "Dying Right in California: The Natural Death Act." *Clinical Research* 26, no. 2 (1978): 55, 57–58.

42. Rosner, "Autopsy in Jewish Law and the Israel Autopsy Controversy," *Tradition* 11, no. 4 (Spring 1971): 43. See also Jacobovits, "The Dissection of the Dead in Jewish Law," *Tradition* 1, no. 1 (1958): 77.

43. Indeed, Laurence Tribe, among other public policy theorists, has argued the case for "legal intervention deliberately aimed at shaping the earliest stages of technological development"; L. Tribe, "Channeling Technology Through Law" (1973); See also Tribe, "Legal Framework for the Assessment and Control of Technology," *Minerva* 9 (1971): 243.

44. Gregory, "The Good Samaritan and the Bad: The Anglo-American Law," in James M. Ratcliffe, ed., *The Good Samaritan and the Law* (Magnolia, Mass.: Peter Smith, 1966), p. 23. See text and authorities cited in Fowler v. Harper & Fleming James, Jr., *The Law of Torts* 2 (Waltham, Mass.: Little, Brown, 1956), §18.6, p. 1044 *et seq.* This is decidedly not the position in continental jurisprudence: see Rudzinski, "The Duty to Rescue: A Comparative Analysis," in *The Good Samaritan and the Law*, p. 91.

45. Michael v. Roberts, 91 N.H. 499, 23 A.2d 361 (1941); Wiggins v. Piver, 276 N.C. 134, 171 S.E.2d 393 (1970); Nation v. Gueffroy, 172 Or. 673, 142 P.2d 688 (1943); Hoover v. Goss, 2 Wash. 2d 237, 97 P.2d 689 (1940).

46. Shilkret v. Annapolis Emergency Hosp. Ass'n., 176 Md. 187, 349 A.2d 245 (1975); Brune v. Belinkoff, 354 Mass. 102, 235 N.E.2d 793 (1968); Pederson v. Dumouchel, 72 Wash. 2d 73, 431 P.2d 973 (1967).

47. *F.D.A. New Drug Applications,* 21 C.F.R. §314 (1977).

48. Pius XII, "Prolongation of Life," *The Pope Speaks* (1958): 393, 395-396.

49. K. Rasmussen, *The Netsilik Eskimos* (Report of the Fifth Thule Expedition), vol. 8 (Copenhagen: 1931), p. 144; but see Asen Balikci, *The Netsilik Eskimo* (Garden City, N.Y.: Natural History Press, 1970), pp. 162-172. Other discus-

sion of Eskimo suicide or voluntary euthanasia may be found in Peter Freuchen, *Book of the Eskimos* (New York: Fawcett World Library, 1961), pp. 194-206; E. Weyer, *The Eskimos: Their Environment and Folkways,* (Hamden, Conn.: Anchor Books, 1962), pp. 136-139, 248-249; Franz Boas, *The Central Eskimos* (Toronto: Coles, 1974), p. 615 ff.; Leighton and Hughes, "Notes on Eskimo Patterns of Suicide," *Southwestern Journal of Anthropology* 11 (1955): 327.

50. Aelian (Claudius Aelianus), *Varia Historia,* vol. 3, p. 37, in J. Choron, *Suicide* 105 (1972). Such acts would be classified as examples of 'altruistic suicide' in Durkheim's typology. Emile Durkheim, *Suicide: A Study in Sociology,* trans. John Spaulding and George Simpson, ed. George Simpson (Glencoe, N.Y.: The Free Press, 1963), pp 217-240.

51. *Sunday Times* [London], December 3, 1972, cited in Slater, "Assisted Suicide: Some Ethical Considerations," *International Journal of Health Services* 6 (1976): 321, 323.

52. In this regard, one might consider the indifferent success of compulsory sterilization legislation in parts of India and other third world countries. See the discussion in Novak, "Fear, Force and Sterilization in India," *America* 135 (1976): 362; Warwick, "Compulsory Sterilization in India," *Commonweal* 103 (1976): 582.

53. See J. Kurtzman & P. Gordon, *No More Dying: The Conquest of Aging and the Extension of Human Life* (Los Angeles: J. P. Tarcher, 1976); Osborn Segerberg, Jr., *The Immortality Factor* (New York: E. P. Dutton, 1974); Albert Rosenfeld, *Prolongevity* (New York: Alfred A. Knopf, 1976).

54. It is unclear whether the decision to ingest a life-sustaining agent should be seen as a medical or social decision. It depends on cultural perceptions of the risks involved; as to the issue of parental control when there is no danger, *see* In re Frank, 41 Wash. 2d 194, 248 P.2d 553 (1952).

55. Wisconsin v. Yoder, 406 U.S. 205 (1972); see also, Goldstein, "Medical Care for the Child at Risk: On State Supervention of Parental Autonomy," 86 *Yale L.J.* 645 (1977).

56. In re Green, 448 Pa. 338, 292 A.2d 387 (1972); In re Frank, 42 Wash. 2d 294, 248 P.2d 553 (1952).

57. In re Seiferth, 309 N.Y. 80, 127 N.E.2d 820 (1955); *contra,* In re Sampson, 65 Misc. 2d 658, 317 N.Y.S. 2d 641 (Fam. Ct. 1970), *aff'd,* 37 App. Div. 668, 323 N.Y.S. 2d 253 (1971), *aff'd,* 29 N.Y. 2d 900, 278 N.E.2d 918, 328 N.Y.S.2d 686 (1972).

58. In re Green, 448 Pa. 338, 292 A.2d 387 (1972).

59. See, e.g., *Ala. Code* tit. 22 §104(15) (Cum. Supp. 1973); *Miss. Code Ann.* §41-41-3(h) (1972).

60. *Mich. Comp. Laws* §701.19b (Supp. 1970), (age of consent for kidney transplant lowered to 14).

61. I. Jakobovits, "Medical Experimentation on Humans in Jewish Law," in *Challenge: Torah Views on Science and Its Problems,* ed. A. Carmell and C. Domb (New York: Philip Feldheim, 1976), pp. 472-475.

62. I. Jakobovits, *Jewish Medical Ethics* (New York: Bloch, 1975), p. 276. The Chief Rabbi's view follows the talmudic exegesis on the creation of Adam which notes:

Therefore but a single man was created in the world, to teach that if any man has caused a single soul to perish from Israel Scripture imputes it to him as though he had caused a whole world to perish; and if any man saves alive a single soul from Israel Scripture imputes it to him as though he had saved alive a whole world.

Sanhedrin 4:5, the Mishnah 388, trans. H. Danby (1933). See also Semahoth, 1:1, 4; *The Minor Tractates of the Talmud,* vol. 1 (London: The Soncino Press, 1965), pp. 326-27.

63. See statutes cited in note 5. But see Maine Medical Center v. Houle, no. 74-145 (Me. Super. Ct., Feb. 14, 1974), which held that parents of an infant with congenital birth defects could not refuse surgery for the child on the basis of a doctor's opinion that the life was "not worth preserving."

64. Byron Gold, "A Few Questions Concerning the Implications For Public Policy of Longevity and Aging Research." Paper presented to the Conference of the Center for the Study of Democratic Institutions (on Human Life Extension), Santa Barbara, Cal., April 1976, pp. 1-2.

65. Some commentators would view this suggestion as naively fanciful. For example, Harvey Brooks (Dean of Engineering and Applied Science, Harvard University) has argued that "man in fact has no choice but to push forward with his technology. The world is already irrevocably committed to a technological culture," in "Technology Assessment: Hearings Before the Subcommittee on Science, Research and Development of the House Committee on Science and Astronautics," 91st Congress, 1st Session 331 (1969). The general question of the political theory of technological determinism is discussed in Langdon Winner, *Autonomous Technology* (Cambridge, Mass.: The M.I.T. Press, 1977).

V
EPILOGUE

13

Life-Extending Technologies

ROBERT S. MORISON

Life-extending technologies may be divided into two broad categories: those directed at eliminating conditions that keep an individual from reaching what may be regarded as the normal life span, and those directed at understanding the aging process itself with a view to controlling it and extending the life span beyond that considered normal for the human species. This distinction implies a significant, even fundamental, difference between (normal) aging and the diseases and traumas that ordinarily shorten life; two lines of evidence suggest that it is valid. The development of modern technologies, not only in medicine and public health, but in agriculture, housing, and communication, have resulted in a marked reduction in deaths in early life, some modest improvement in middle-age (especially for women), but virtually no change in life expectancy over age 75 or 80. These results can be graphically illustrated by plotting the percentage of a given cohort of individuals still alive at various ages. Until the middle of the nineteenth century in all countries, many deaths occurred during the first few years of life, as they still do in many underdeveloped countries. A curve that reflects such an early death rate drops sharply at the very beginning, indicating that perhaps only 50 percent of children born are still alive at adolescence. Thereafter, the typical curve proceeds more or less lineally downward until the slope flattens a bit to approach zero between 80 and 100. At the present time, in advanced countries the curve has only a slight notch in the first year, falling just perceptibly to about 98.5 percent from the previously typical 75 to 80. It then moves very gradually downward to about age 70, where in some populations as many as 75 percent of the cohort may still be alive. It then turns down and descends quite rapidly to join the earlier, historically typical curve between 85 and 100.

The more one looks at this curve, the more it seems that the psalmist was right and that the days of our years are three score and ten. Perhaps he underestimated the average a bit, and he might have left more room for "normal variation," but overall the conclusion is inescapable—we are meant to die somewhere between ages 70 and 100 if something untoward does not happen before that. In this sense, death can be regarded as a "natural" event, although there is a continuing debate about the propriety of the phrase "natural death."

Recent biological studies reinforce the conclusion that aging is scheduled rather than accidental, by revealing the existence of genetically determined chemical mechanisms at both the cellular and whole animal level that seem designed to ensure the death of all multicellular organisms. Furthermore, the notion of design is strengthened by the observation that a given age range at death is species specific. From the biological standpoint, therefore, the ethical and value implications of technology directed at enabling as many people as possible to reach the normal life expectancy are quite different from the implications of research designed to lengthen the life span itself.

In general, the value implications of helping more people to reach normal life expectancy are already with us. Indeed, we know the general dimensions of most of them, and solutions are under active discussion. There is virtually no disagreement that the extension of life expectancy achieved in the last hundred years has been a good thing. In the bad old days, it was almost universally regarded as sad when a newborn baby died of pneumonia or diarrhea, or a beautiful young wife wasted away from tuberculosis. Most of the life extension achieved during the past century has been due to the virtual elimination of such infectious diseases. In general, their elimination has simultaneously improved the quality of life, since many of them, when they did not kill, left visible and invisible scars that interfered with the pleasure and effectiveness of living.

Recent events, however, have raised the public consciousness that every technological advance is accompanied by unexpected costs and undesirable side effects. These may involve society as a whole or primarily selected individuals. Perhaps the most serious societal side effect of the reduction of infectious disease has been the rapid rise in total population in the last two centuries. This, however, is coming under control in most advanced countries; it is controllable, at least in principle, in less advanced areas as well. The ethical and value questions raised by campaigns for population control have already commanded the attention of philosophers and sociologists, and need not be pursued here.

Not only has the overall number of people increased; there are marked changes in the demographic patterns at various ages as well. They are complicated and irregular because death and birth rates do not change in an immediately related way. Nevertheless, the ultimate result of life-extending technologies is clearly an increase in the proportion of older people. The so-called age pyramid comes to look more and more like a cylinder. These changes and the concomitant economic and social adjustments have been extensively studied and are well reviewed elsewhere in this volume. Society is still in the process of adjusting to them, but it seems unlikely that any really new value problems will be uncovered by further changes in demographic patterning within the normal life span. Indeed, the progress already made has brought us more than two-thirds of the way from the primitive survival curve to a "square wave" with almost everyone living into their seventies.

The most serious individual ethical questions raised by the control of infectious disease concern the problems involved in maintaining the lives of severely deformed or deteriorated persons. The number is not large in comparison with the number of cases in which prolongation of life may be regarded as unquestionably good, but it is significant and has attracted a great deal of comment, debate, and soul-searching. Most of the problem cases occur at either end of the life span, but they are not unknown in middle life. In the past, individuals severely handicapped by failures of normal development or gravely deteriorated from intercurrent disease or trauma, normally succumbed in a relatively short time to intercurrent infections. Although it was not particularly noticed at the time, such deaths relieved the responsible members of the family and the physician from making explicit decisions about continuing treatment. Now, however, the question of how actively to treat the terminally or otherwise severely ill is among the most active for those interested in biomedical ethics. From the technical standpoint, the active treatment of infectious disease is only one of several interventions at issue; others include artificial feeding, artificial respiration, and various methods of supporting or substituting for the impaired circulation of the blood or excretion by the kidney. Since they all contribute positively to the extension of life in other circumstances, there is no question about the desirability of their further development. On the other hand, their very existence leads to questions about their proper use. Almost everyone who has studied the matter would concur that there are limits beyond which one should not go in employing life-extending technologies, but there is considerable difference of opinion as to the criteria for continuing or terminating treatments in particular cases. Perhaps the most important result so far of the active discussion is a new emphasis on the physician's responsibility for enhancing the quality of life, or at least maintaining its dignity, as well as for attempting its simple preservation or extension.

It is increasingly recognized that quality of life issues are not confined to the treatment of the terminally ill. Many treatments of prolonged chronic illness, which may properly be included among life-extending technologies, may involve time away from productive work, inconvenience, discomfort, pain, and serious disturbance of function. As the trade-offs become better understood, the general public better informed, and the physician more understanding of his responsibility, it is slowly becoming less rare for the physician and his patient to discuss quite frankly the course to follow. In some cases, this may involve some risk of shortening life in order to maximize comfort and productivity during the days that remain. Two common examples are the current treatment of hypertension and malignant disease. Many of the new drugs succeed in lowering blood pressure and prolonging life in return for a clear reduction in physical vigor, sexual potency, and emotional mood. As a leading textbook wryly remarks, such a result cannot be regarded as a therapeutic triumph. Similarly, very active treatment of malignant disease may prolong life for a few months or years at the cost of severe physical mutilation or chemical depression of function. No general solution can be suggested, and there is nothing to suggest slacking the search for new, more effective life-extending technologies in this area. What is needed is a more general awareness of the negative as well as the positive aspects of certain of them and a willingness to face squarely the inevitable trade-offs in individual cases.

Increasingly, the patient and his physician may find themselves making decisions that run counter to long-standing custom or even legal constraints. The prevailing tendency seems to be toward freeing the patient and his physician from former taboos and restraints regarding the acceptance or refusal of treatment and the obligation to preserve life at any price. Unfortunately, other trends severely interfere with the development of the requisite private, personal relationships betwen physician and patient. These involve the greater use of specialists who do not know the patient as a person, the growing reliance on legal restraints and malpractice laws, the tendency to submit the doctor-patient relationship to the scrutiny of quality review boards of various kinds, and the general tendency to make privacy a public issue. Each one of these trends, taken by itself, can find its appropriate defense. Taken altogether, however, they put obstacles in the way of the wisest use of life-extending technologies and impair the patient's freedom of choice.

Rather different questions regarding personal freedom arise from the growing realization of how much the individual person may be responsible for the preservation or extension of his own life. Curiously, the sense of responsibility for the rectitude and/or health of one's own life was probably more acute in former times than it is now when statistical validation is more convincing than it was then. As infectious diseases and various metabolic disorders have come increasingly under control, we are left with a group of disabilities that originate in or are influenced by what it is now fashionable to call "life-style." Most men who die between adolescence and early middle-age die by violence—suicide, homocide, and accidents (most of the latter due to improper operation of automobiles). These deaths raise significant questions of ethics and morals, but there is as yet little consensus regarding them. Suicide used to be considered among the most heinous of crimes, and the perpetrator's body was denied Chrstian burial and exposed to other indignities. This is no longer true in most countries though, in all but a few, assisting a suicide is a crime.

Ethically, suicide is still under a cloud, but there is a great deal

of individual variation. Many, perhaps most, people now regard as
entirely justified a suicide committed by a lonely old man facing a
painful terminal illness. The suicide of a young man with family and
professional commitments might be regarded, if not as a sin, at least
as a deplorable shirking of responsibility. The whole ethical situation is complicated by the modern tendency to regard suicide as
symptomatic of an illness rather than as a behavior over which the
individual has control, and therefore a responsibility. Indeed, in contrast to most other eras, contemporary thinking on ethics and morals
has concentrated on rights rather than responsibilities—on the obligation of various social institutions to the individual rather than that
of the individual to his society or to his immediate associates.

The question of individual responsibility increases in interest
and complexity as we pass from a consideration of overt, explicit
suicide to the more common, but less obvious, ways in which men
and women shorten their own life expectancies. Society is not indifferent to these behaviors and their results, but there is great uncertainty about what to do about them. Many states require motorcy-
lists to wear crash helmets, for example. A few foreign countries
have passed laws regarding the use of seat belts. The United States
is readying itself to require people to purchase, at considerable expense, automatic passive protectors such as the air bag. Several governments put a heavy tax on tobacco and alcohol. All these measures, with their varying degrees of coercion, are undertaken in part
to protect the individual against himself, and in part to protect society against the social costs of the self-destructive behavior in question. The history of this kind of legislation is notoriously unsatisfac-
tory. Many feel that it is wrong in principle and an invasion of
personal freedom or the natural right "to kill oneself in one's own
way." Whatever the philosophical position, there is a pragmatic recognition that laws regulating personal conduct do not work very
well.

In the past, self-destructive behavior may have been partially
controlled by the cultivation of personal codes enforced by group
pressure or religious sanction. Within the memory of those now living, English gentlemen always paid their gambling debts, devout
Methodists did not smoke, drink, or drive fast horses, and American
college students did not steal from one another. Now the informal
interpersonal understandings and intrapersonal promptings of con-

science that regulated social behavior have largely given way to an emphasis on rights and litigation. In any case, even though many deviations of behavior serve to shorten life expectancy, they seem to lie beyond the reach of medicine and public health as these professions are ordinarily understood.

Thus, much of what remains to be done to maximize life expectancy within the normal or natural life span involves matters of personal life-style, which cannot be treated or regulated from outside without invasions of privacy or personal freedom. Perhaps, however, it is worth pausing to note that not only do modern life-extending technologies raise value problems for society; changes in social and individual value systems raise problems for life-extending technologies. The question then arises as to what society can properly do to alter the individual's value frame. If society can be shown to have a responsibility for extending the lives of its citizens, and if at the same time it can be shown that much shortening of life is due primarily to the individual's own actions, what is society's proper role? Presumably there is little objection to discovering the facts and making them widely known, as the Surgeon General did in relation to cigarette smoking. Most governments in the past have also found it appropriate to engage in educational campaigns and, as we have seen, experiments have been attempted with regulatory legislation, but there is much controversy about both their propriety and effectiveness. Implicit in efforts to design a good society is the purpose of providing its citizens with health and life-preserving options. It seems obvious that much of the violence in our inner cities, and many self-destructive practices such as smoking dope, would at least be reduced if jobs and constructive recreation were available. Nevertheless, there will probably always be a substantial remnant of persons who will perversely opt for self-destructive ways of life, no matter now "perfect" their society might be. One is reminded here of Goethe's sardonic question, "What is so boring as a succession of beautiful days?"

Finally, we must consider the possibilities inherent in various informal and formal social mechanisms designed to influence individual behavior. Alcoholics Anonymous is the prototype of lay organizations that rely on group dynamics to effect changes. Classically, in Europe, but especially perhaps in England and this country, explicit religious conversion has been a powerful influence. All of these social mechanisms contain an element of coercion, and the balance between the individual and the common good is not always clear. In other times, governments have had no doubts about coupling the power of religion with the secular forces of law and order, but such practices have always been unconstitutional in the United States. Perhaps I have said enough to show that certain needed life-extending technologies raise problems of freedom and coercion that extend beyond the confines of medicine as normally understood and that can be solved, if at all, only within a much wider context.

A final complicating factor is the increasing financial responsibility of society for personal health care. Attention can no longer be focused exclusively on the individual and the conflict between his "right" to health services and his equally important right to be left alone. Questions of equity and justice will be an ultimate concern of those who are paying the costs. When everybody pays for everybody else's personal health services, either through taxes or insurance premiums, is it fair or equitable that those who conscientiously follow health protective precepts should be required to pay the costs of repairing the traumas and treating the illnesses of those who deliberately risk their lives? This question, which was more or less taboo among liberal thinkers even a few years ago, is now asked with increasing frequency by those who feel a responsibility for designing a workable national health scheme. Already, people in hazardous occupations may be forced to pay higher insurance premiums, and it seems likely that this principle of "assigned risk" will be extended in the hope of developing some approach to equity in a situation that is inherently inequitable.

Considerations of equity and justice also are involved in the development and application of very expensive life-extending technologies. The recent legislation providing special support for the treatment of patients with terminal kidney disease has triggered a great deal of public and professional discussion of some of the principles and practicalities involved. Although the report of the recent commission on biomedical research, and certain other publications, have held out the hope that basic research will ultimately provide us with cheap technological fixes for all the ills of man (such as, for example, penicillin for lobar pneumonia), other, perhaps more reflective authors point out that the cheap elimination of one disease simply makes way for other more expensive ones. At least for the foreseeable future, society would do well to prepare itself to cope with an increasing flow of ever more expensive medical technologies. It is not too early to begin drawing up guidelines for the application of such technologies in answer to the following kinds of questions. Does the "right" or the "social desirability" of a new technology vary with its cost effectiveness or does everyone have an absolute right to a therapy he or his physician feels may offer even a very low probability of improvement? Should the probable life expectancy of the individual to be treated make a difference? Should some estimate of social utility enter the picture?

Most recently, a new twist has been given to the problem; certain authors have asked whether the expense of cost effectiveness of a proposed new technology should be taken into account when requests for research and development are being considered. It has long been customary in estimating appropriations for military research to consider the ultimate cost effectiveness of the completed weapon system as a whole. This has not been customary in the funding of medical research and, as far as I know, the question of ultimate cost was only seriously raised for the first time by the committee that undertook a technology assessment of the artificial heart. In this case an attempt was made to estimate the cost of installing an individual heart and to multiply this estimated figure by an estimated number of eligible individuals. The final recommendation of this committee, however seems influenced not so much by this computation as by questions concerning the probable safety of the proposed nuclear power supply. The whole question of funding or limiting basic and applied research on the strength of predictions about cost-effectiveness in the narrow sense, and long-term social, psychological and moral side effects is in a relatively primitive state. Until very recently, most academicians have regarded freedom of inquiry as an absolute right initiated by the moral victory of Galileo over the Pope and firmly established by the rules and regulations regarding freedom of learning and teaching, which had accompanied the foundation of the Prussian universities in the beginning of the last century.

Interestingly enough, and obviously germane to our present discussion of life-extending technologies, recent inquiries into the nature of man's genetic structure have caused a respectable fraction of the academic community to consider the possibility that some things should not be inquired into. This possibility brings us naturally to a consideration of our second group of life-extending technologies, those that have as their primary object the extension of the normal life span. Although current discussions of this possibility are concerned primarily with extensions of say twenty-five to fifty years, there is no actual theoretical limit; in his recent book entitled *Prolongevity,* the respected science writer Alfred Rosenfeld talks unabashedly about immortality.

Clearly, technologies looking towards indefinite extension of the life span raise all the moral questions we discussed, but in a more acute form. In a word, if a moderate extension of life for a severely defective infant is moderately undesirable, an infinite extension of its life is infinitely questionable. But it is the problems peculiar to lengthening of the normal life span that should command our attention in this section. The first set of problems is social in the widest sense. First, and most obviously, if everyone lives to be much older than they are now, the population of the world will increase proportionately and the ratio of the various age classes will be seriously distorted. The same thing is true, in only a very limited sense, of the curve-squaring technologies previously discussed. We have actually already experienced in advanced countries most of the increase in population and change in distribution among age classes that is likely to occur from this source. In 1900, only 4.1 percent of the population was 65 or over. The figure in 1976 was 10.7. If everyone lived till 80 and there was no population growth, only about 19 percent would be above 65, but if everybody lived to be 130, half the population would be beyond what we now regard as the retirement age.

It is contended that many of the proposals for extending the life span would also extend the period of useful and enjoyable life so that everything would be stretched out equally. Even if this were true, there is no doubt that the stretching out process would cause a lot of stresses and strains in society, as retirement ages were forced up and younger individuals found it harder and harder to rise to positions of emminence and responsibility. Perhaps all these practical problems could be solved by good will and careful thought, but the stress on existing social institutions is sure to be much greater than those caused by any of the life-extending technologies that have been available so far.

Even if these difficulties could be overcome, however, we are still faced with interesting philosophical and biological questions. The philosophical question is perhaps most easily expressed from within a utilitarian framework. Granting that there must be some optimum population for the world, an increase in longevity simply means that there could be fewer people in a given time. This means that fewer people will have the opportunity to experience the joys and sorrows of life. If one applies the doctrine of diminishing returns, the total amount of happiness would appear to be reduced. Furthermore, even the enjoyments of old age might lose considerable of their piquancy if one knew they were likely to continue almost indefinitely. The days would no longer dwindle down to a precious few, but would stretch out into the infinite boredom of constantly diminishing returns. All these effects on the individual would in turn reduce the total amount of human happiness.

So much for the strictly utilitarian aspects. From the biological point of view, the situation is, if anything, even more questionable. Among biologists, the presumptive explanation for the species specificity of aging and death is closely related to the mechanism of evolution. The idea, in its simplest terms, is that one is programmed to live long enough to demonstrate fitness and then disappear to make room for a new model. Actually, of course, human biological evolution proceeds very slowly and human "fitness" cannot be described simply in terms of reproductive capacity. Even postmenopausal women and men (if there are such) have contributions to make to the survival and further development of the race. Nevertheless, the principle that the obsolete should ultimately make room for the new should apply to cultural as well as to biological evolution unless something quite remarkable and unforeseen is built into the newer life-extending technologies. The people whose lives are prolonged are likely on the average to prolong the various ideas and practices they and others of their generation have developed. Inevitably, the process of social evolution will be slowed down. Although it may not ever be given to human beings to say precisely what the point of living is, observation of the panoply of life as we see it would reveal change and the production of new models as occupying a very high place in the order of nature. The widespread introduction of life-span-extending technologies would inevitably reduce the possibility of change and do so simply, so far as one can see, for the selfish advantage of that tiny fraction of humanity that happened to be alive at the time the extending technologies became available. Although it is probably impossible to prove any ethical proposition beyond a peradventure, the wish to live more or less forever at the expense of the opportunity of an indefinite number of potential others to live at all, appears to be unjust on its face. Furthermore, if the biologist's belief in the importance of change and the encouragement of what might be termed new experiments in living has any validity at all, there is perhaps a kind of cosmic effrontery in wanting to live forever.

In addition to the social argument, which would seem compelling, it is worth considering the situation from the point of view of the individual whose life is to be extended. All of us know in a general way that we must die sometime, and virtually all of our life planning takes this into account in some way or another. It is commonly observed that many people consciously risk their lives in order that the recognition of death may emphasize for them the uniqueness and importance of life. Postponement of death to some unidentifiable point in the future might result in a life of increasing boredom, so that the temptation to incur deliberate risk would be constantly increased. Finally, the victim of immortality would find himself entirely preoccupied with deciding when and how to commit suicide. Not everyone is likely to feel this way, of course, but the probability that some will is high enough to require planners for immortality to plan for this further contingency.

Another set of considerations arises out of the fact that in most lives the balance of pain and pleasure is a somewhat precarious one. One of the consolations for the pain is the reflection that some things cannot be changed. What's done is done and we had better put up with it, or put it out of our minds. A reinforcement for this point of view is that, after all, life is short and does not provide many opportunities for correcting mistakes. A life of longer or infinite duration might take away this consolation; with so much time at our disposal we would have no excuse for not going back to fill the gap or correct the error. It is worth noting, also, although it would take a good deal of research to establish the point beyond a doubt, that most of the things people set their hearts on ultimately decline and pass away. It may be fortunate for most of us that we also decline and pass away before the houses we built, the families we raised, the looms we invented, the clipper ships we commanded, and the empires we were determined not to dissolve reach their peak and begin their inevitable decline.

One final speculation may be worth listing for future exploration, although it can be put forward only tentatively and largely on the basis of anecdotal and literary evidence at present. It has often been asserted that, in order to live at all, human beings need some structure of myth and illusion to give meaning to their lives. Many of these structures are religious in nature and depend for their validation on mystical insight into the existence of other, unseen beings who care about us and have made a place for us in their scheme of things. Other less imaginative solutions may serve the secular. The love of other human beings, the love of money, the fascinations of scientific curiosity, and the satisfaction of artistic creation, have all, at one time or another, made life worth living for some people. But also, at one time or another, most or all of the things people live by and for have been demonstrated by some skeptical philosopher to be largely illusory. It is also part of conventional wisdom that illusions tend to disappear over time. Old men, by and large and overlooking the deathbed confession, seem to have fewer illusions than young ones. There is thus a distinct possibility that prolongation of life will mean a steady decline in the number of illusions for a substantial, though admittedly unknown, fraction of the human race. We may have to face the paradox that the ultimate result of life-extension technologies is the recognition of the pointlessness of the entire exercise.

All this may simply add up to this: ever since man became a conscious, thinking, designing human being, he has molded his individual philosophy and his cultural institutions to the biological fact that we all must die. In a thousand different ways, conscious and deeply imbedded in the unconscious, men recognize the cyclical nature of their lives and the fact that all things have their seasons. Shakespeare may have overschematized things a bit with his seven ages of man, but the general idea is certainly one that dominates the entirety of human existence. Our fundamental ideas about the meaning of life are based on what we know and feel about death. So fundamental are these assumptions, convictions, and feelings that no research group could detach sufficiently to assess the psychological and social impact of any substantial lengthening of the normal life span, especially of infinite extension. All one can reasonably say at this time is that the impacts and readjustments would be profound and it might be wise to think about them before they happen.

This situation is all the more difficult because the love of life is so thoroughly built into us that at first glance it seems impossible for any substantial fraction of the human race to want anything else but its indefinite extension. Indeed, the momentum in that direction is so great that it would probably be impossible to slow it down to any significant degree. Until recently, the science of gerontology has languished, not because of lack of interest in living longer, but because the weight of opinion was against being able to do much about it. The recent uncovering of several promising leads has changed all that. Gerontologists are going about with smiling faces and appropriations are beginning to increase. Only now and then does one hear a voice like that of Robert Sinsheimer suggesting that aging should be put on a list of those things we should not try to know more about. The debate on whether we can save ourselves from ourselves simply by trading enforced ignorance for our tradition of free inquiry is only now beginning, but it seems unlikely that our problems will be solved in this way. It is much more probable in the long run that we will deal with potential immortality as we have dealt with the results of so many other researches that were "contrary to nature." In a word, we will have to find some way of deciding ourselves what used to be decided for us. When death is no longer inevitable, it may ultimately become desirable, and mankind will simply have to devise the machinery for deciding when it is best to die.

The transition from our present state to one of at least potential immortality is sure to be long and tortuous. We cannot foresee the nature of many of the immediate steps, let alone the ultimate goal. But it is not too early to consider the wrenching effects on many value assumptions that lie so deeply in us that we are scarcely conscious of them.

Related Books and Articles

Abrahamson, H. *The Origin of Death: Studies in African Mythology.* Uppsala, Sweden: Studia Ethnographica Upsaliensia, 1951.

Acton, Jan Paul. "Measuring the Monetary Value of Lifesaving Programs." *Law and Contemporary Problems* 40 (Autumn 1976): 46–72.

Asimov, Isaac. "The Coming Age of Age." *Prism,* 3 (January 1975): 52–56.

Bailey, Herbert. *CH₃, Will It Keep You Young Longer?* New York: Bantam, 1977.

Bailey, Richard M. "Economic and Social Costs of Death." *The Dying Patient.* Edited by Orville G. Brim et al. New York: Russell Sage Foundation, 1970.

Bakan, David. *Disease, Pain, and Sacrifice.* Chicago: University of Chicago Press, 1968.

Becker, Ernest. *The Denial of Death.* New York: The Free Press, 1973.

Benet, Sula. *How to Live to Be 100: The Life-Style of the People of the Caucasus.* New York: Dial Press, 1976.

Bjorksten, Johan. "The Crosslinkage Theory of Aging." *Finska Kemistsamfundet Meddelanden* 80 (1971): 23–38.

———. "Approaches and Prospects for the Control of Age-Dependent Deterioration." *Annals of the New York Academy of Sciences* 184 (June 1971): 95–102.

———. "The Crosslinkage Theory of Aging." *Journal of the American Geriatrics Society,* 16 (April 1968): 408–27.

Boeyink, David. "Pain and Suffering." *Journal of Religious Ethics* 2 (Spring 1974): 85–98.

Brandon, S.G.F. *The Judgment of the Dead, The Idea of Life After Death in the Major Religions.* New York: Charles Scribner's Sons, 1967.

Brim, Orville G. et al. *The Dying Patient.* New York: Russell Sage Foundation, 1970.

Brotman, H. "Life Expectancy: Comparisons of National Levels in 1900 and 1974 and Variations in State Levels, 1969–1971." *The Gerontologist* 17 (1977): 12–22.

Butler, Robert N. *Why Survive?—Being Old in America.* New York: Harper & Row, 1975.

Callahan, D. "On Defining Natural Death." *The Hastings Center Report* 7 (June 1977): 32–37.

———. "What Obligations Do We Have to Future Generations?" *American Ecclesiastical Review* 164 (April 1971): 265–80.

Callahan, Sidney, and Christiansen, Drew. "Ideal Old Age." *Soundings* 57 (Spring 1974): 1–16.

Caplan, Arthur L. "The 'Unnaturalness' of Aging and Its Implications for Medical Practice." *Man and Medicine.* In press.

Capron, A.M., and Kass, L.R. "A Statutory Definition of the Standards for Determining Human Death: An Appraisal and a Proposal." *University of Pennsylvania Law Review* 121 (November 1972): 87–118.

Choron, Jacques. *Death and Western Thought.* New York: Collier Books, 1973.

Comfort, Alex. *Ageing: The Biology of Senescence.* Revised Ed. New York: Holt, Rinehart & Winston, 1964.

———. "The Position of Aging Studies." *Mechanisms of Ageing and Development* 3 (March–June 1974): 1–31.

———. "The Biological Basis for Increasing Longevity." *Medical Opinion and Review* 6 (April 1970): 18–25.

———. "The Prevention of Ageing in Cells." *The Lancet* II: 7477 (17 December 1966): 1325–29.

———. "Longevity of Man and His Tissues." in *Man and His Future.* Boston: Little, Brown, 1963.

Cooper, Barbara S., and Rice, Dorothy P. "The Economic Cost of Illness Revisited." *Social Security Bulletin,* Department of

Health, Education, and Welfare. Pub. no. SSA 76–11703 (February 1976): 21–36.

Crane, Diana. *The Sanctity of Social Life: Physicians' Treatment of Critically-Ill Patients.* New York: Russell Sage Foundation, 1975.

Dubos, Rene. *The Mirage of Health.* New York: Harper & Row, 1959.

Ekerdt, D.J., Rose, C.L., Bosse, R., and Costa, P.T. "Longitudinal Change in Preferred Age of Retirement." *Journal of Occupational Psychology* 49 (1976): 161–69.

Ettinger, Robert C.W. *Man into Superman.* New York: St. Martin's Press, 1972.

Fabrega, Horatio, Jr. "Concepts of Disease: Logical Features and Social Implications." *Perspectives in Biology and Medicine* 15 (Summer 1972): 583–616.

Fuchs, Victor R. *Who Shall Live? Health, Economics, and Social Choice.* New York: Basic Books, 1974.

Golding, Martin. "Obligations to Future Generations." *The Monist* 56 (January 1972): 85–99.

Goldstein, Samuel. "Biological Aging: An Essentially Normal Process." *Journal of the American Medical Association* 230 (23 December 1974): 1651–52.

———. "The Biology of Aging." *The New England Journal of Medicine* 285 (November 1971): 1120–29.

Gordon, P. "Free Radicals and the Dying Process." *Theoretical Aspects of Aging.* Edited by M. Rockstein. New York: Academic Press, 1974.

Gruman, Gerald J. "A History of Ideas About the Prolongation of Life: The Evolution of Prolongevity Hypotheses to 1800." *Transactions of the American Philosophical Society* (December 1966).

Gubrium, Jaber F. *The Myth of the Golden Years: A Socio-Environmental Theory of Aging.* Springfield, Illinois: Charles C. Thomas, 1973.

Harman, Denham. "Free Radical Theory of Aging: Dietary Implications." *American Journal of Clinical Nutrition* 25 (August 1972): 839–843.

———. "Free Radical Theory of Aging: Effect of the Amount and

Degree of Unsaturation of Dietary Fat on Mortality Rate." *Journal of Gerontology* 26 (October 1971): 451–54.

———. "Prolongation of Life: Role of Free Radical Reactions in Aging." *Journal of the American Geriatrics Society* 17 (August 1969): 721–35.

———. "Prolongation of the Normal Life Span by Radiation Protection Chemicals." *Journal of Gerontology* 12 (1957): 257–63.

Harrington, Alan. *The Immortalist*. New York: Random House, 1969.

Harvard Medical School, Ad Hoc Committee of the Harvard Medical School to Examine the Definition of Brain Death. "A Definition of Irreversible Coma." *Journal of the American Medical Association* 205 (1968): 337–40.

Hausman, David B. "What is Natural?" *Perspectives in Biology and Medicine* 19 (Autumn 1975): 92–101.

Hayflick, L. "The Cell Biology of Human Aging." *New England Journal of Medicine* 295 (1976): 1302–8.

———. "Cell Biology of Aging." *BioScience* 25 (October 1975): 629–37.

———. "Current Theories of Biological Aging." *Federation Proceedings* 34 (January 1975): 9–13.

———. "The Strategy of Senescence." *The Gerontologist* 14 (February 1974): 37–45.

———. "The Biology of Human Aging." *American Journal of the Medical Sciences* 265 (1973): 432–45.

———. "Human Cells and Aging." *Scientific American* 218 (March 1968): 32–37.

Heinlein, Robert A. *Time Enough for Love*. New York: G.P. Putnam's Sons, 1973.

———. *Methuselah's Children*. New York: New American Library, 1968.

Hick, John H. *Death and Eternal Life*. New York: Harper & Row, 1976.

High, Dallas M. "Death: Its Conceptual Elusiveness." *Soundings* 55 (Winter 1972): 438–58.

Hoffer, William. "What Price is Right for Human Life?" *Prism* 2 (August 1974): 13–15, 54–55.

Holck, F., ed. *Death and Eastern Thought*. Nashville: Abingdon Press, 1977.

Hopkins, Edward W. "The Fountain of Youth." *Journal of the American Oriental Society* 26 (1905): 1–67.

Illich, Ivan. *Medical Nemesis.* New York: Bantam, 1976.

Institute of Society, Ethics and the Life Sciences, Task Force on Death and Dying. "Refinements in Criteria for the Determination of Death." *Journal of the American Medical Association* 221 (July 1972): 48–53.

Kalish, R.A. "Death and Dying in a Social Context." *Handbook of Aging and the Social Sciences.* Edited by R. Binstock and E. Shanas. New York: Van Nostrand Reinhold, 1976.

———. "Four Score and Ten." *The Gerontologist* 14 (1974): 129–35.

———, and Reynolds, D.K. *Death and Ethnicity: A Psychocultural Study.* Los Angeles: University of Southern California Press, 1976.

Klarman, Herbert E. "Application of Cost-Benefit Analysis to Health Systems Technology." *Technology and Health Care Systems in the 1980s,* Department of Health, Education, and Welfare. Pub. no. HRA 74-3011. Edited by Morris Collen. Washington, D.C.: U.S. Government Printing Office, 1973.

———. "Application of Cost-Benefit Analysis to the Health Services and the Special Case of Technological Innovation." *International Journal of Health Services* 4 (1974): 325–52.

———. "Present Status of Cost-Benefit Analysis in the Health Field." *American Journal of Public Health* 57 (November 1967): 1948–53.

Kohn, R.P. "Human Aging and Disease." *Journal of Clinical Diseases* 16 (1963): 5–21.

Kohn, Robert R. *Principles of Mammalian Aging.* Englewood Cliffs, N.J.: Prentice-Hall, 1971.

Kurtzman, Joel, and Gordon, Phillip, eds. *No More Dying: The Coming Conquest of Aging and the Extension of Human Life.* Los Angeles: J.P. Tarcher, 1976.

Layard, J. *Stone Men of Malakula.* London: Chalto and Windur, 1942.

Leaf, Alexander. *Youth in Old Age.* New York: McGraw-Hill, 1975.

———. "Every Day Is a Gift When You Are Over 100." *National Geographic* 143 (January 1973): 93–118.

Lieb, I. "The Image of Man in Medicine." *Journal of Medicine and*

Philosophy 1 (June 1976): 162–76.

Longmore, D., and Rehahn, M. "The Cumulative Cost of Death." *The Lancet* I: 7914 (3 May 1975): 1023–25.

Lorand, M.A. "Some Considerations on the Causes of Senility." *Clinical Practices in Social Biology* 57 (1904): 500–02.

Marsh, Michael. "Beyond Death: The Rebirth of Immortality." *The Hastings Center Report* 7 (October 1977): 40–42.

Marx, Jean L. "Aging Research (I): Cellular Theories of Senescence." *Science* 186 (20 December 1974): 1105–1107.

———. "Aging Research (II): Pacemakers for Aging." *Science* 186 (27 December 1974): 1196–97.

McCay, C. M. "Experimental Prolongation of the Life Span." *New York Academy of Medicine* 32 (1956): 91–101.

Medawar, Peter B. *Aging: An Unsolved Problem of Biology.* London: H. K. Lewis, 1952.

Medvedev, Zhores A. "Caucasus and Altay Longevity: A Biological or Social Problem?" *The Gerontologist* 14 (October 1974): 381–87.

Mushkin, Selma J. "Health as an Investment." *Journal of Political Economy* 70 (October 1962): 129–57.

National Council on Aging. *The Myth and Reality of Aging in America.* Washington, D.C.: National Council on Aging, 1975.

Neugarten, Bernice L. "The Future and the Young-Old." *The Gerontologist* 15 (1975): 4–9.

———, and Havighurst, Robert J., eds. *Extending the Human Life Span: Social Policy and Social Ethics.* Washington, D.C.: U.S. Government Printing Office, 1977.

Nozick, Robert. *Anarchy, State and Utopia.* New York: Basic Books, 1974.

Palmore, Erdman, and Jeffers, Frances C., eds. *Prediction of Life Span.* Lexington, Mass.: D.C. Heath Lexington Books, 1971.

Parsons, Talcott. "Definitions of Health and Illness in the Light of American Values and Social Structure." *Patients, Physicians and Illness.* Edited by E. Jaco. Glencoe, Ill.: Free Press, 1958.

———, Fox, R. C., and Kidz, V. M. "The 'Gift of Life' and Its Reciprocation." *Social Research* 39 (1972): 367–415.

———, and Lidz, V. M. "Death in American Society." *Essays in Self Destruction.* Edited by E. S. Schneidman. New York: Jason Aronson, 1967.

Pope Pius XII. *The Pope Speaks* 4 (1957): 393–95.

Ramsey, Paul. *The Patient as Person.* New Haven: Yale University Press, 1970.

Rawls, John. *A Theory of Justice.* Cambridge, Mass.: Harvard University Press, 1971.

Reichel, William. "The Biology of Aging." *Journal of the American Geriatrics Society* 14 (1966): 431–46.

Reynolds, F., and Reynolds, M., trans. *The Three Worlds of King Ruang.* Berkeley, Cal.: Berkeley Research Publications, forthcoming 1979.

————, and Waugh, E., eds. *Religious Encounters with Death: Studies in the History and Anthropology of Religion.* University Park, Penn.: The Pennsylvania State University Press, 1977.

Rice, Dorothy P. *Estimating the Cost of Illness.* Health Economics Series, no. 6. Washington, D.C.: U.S. Public Health Service, 1966.

————, and Cooper, Barbara S. "The Economic Value of Human Life." *American Journal of Public Health* 57 (November 1967): 1954–66.

Rieff, P. *The Triumph of the Therapeutic.* New York: Harper & Row, 1966.

Rockstein, Morris, ed. *Theoretical Aspects of Aging.* New York: Academic Press, 1974.

Rosenfeld, Albert. *Prolongevity.* New York: Alfred A. Knopf, 1976.

————. "The Death of Old Age?" *Nature/Science Annual.* New York: Time-Life Books, 1975.

Schelling, Thomas C. "The Life You Save May Be Your Own." *Problems in Public Expenditure Analysis.* Edited by Samuel B. Chase, Jr. Washington, D.C.: The Brookings Institution, 1968.

Segerberg, Osborn, Jr. *The Immortality Factor.* New York: E. P. Dutton, 1974.

Shaw, George Bernard. "Back to Methuselah." *Complete Plays with Prefaces,* vol. 2. New York: Dodd, Mead, 1963.

Sheldrake, A. R. "The Ageing, Growth and Death of Cells." *Nature* 250 (2 August 1974): 381–85.

Sherman, H. C. "Vitamin A in Relation to Aging and to Length of Life." *Proceedings of the National Academy of Science* 31 (1945): 107–16.

Shih-Yu, Ying. "Life and Immortality in Han, China." *Harvard*

Journal of Asiatic Studies 24 (1964–65): 80–122.

Smart, J. J. C., and Williams, Bernard. *Utilitarianism: For and Against*. Cambridge: Cambridge University Press, 1973.

Smith, John Maynard. "A Theory of Ageing." *Nature* 184 (26 September 1959): 956–57.

Stanford Research Institute. *Minimum Standards for Quality of Life,* U.S. Department of Commerce Pub. no. PB-244 808. Springfield, Vir.: National Technical Information Service, May 1975.

Steinfels, Peter, and Veatch, Robert M. *Death Inside Out: The Hastings Center Report*. New York: Harper & Row, 1975.

Strehler, Bernard L. "Aging at the Cellular Level." in *Clinical Geriatrics*. Edited by Isadore Rossman. Philadelphia: J. B. Lippincott, 1971.

Szilard, Leo. "On the Nature of the Aging Process." *Proceedings of the National Academy of Sciences* 45 (1959): 30–45.

———. "A Theory of Ageing." *Nature* 184 (26 September 1959): 957–58.

Taylor, Vincent. "How Much is Good Health Worth?" *Policy Sciences* 1 (1970): 49–72.

Vaisrub, Samuel. "Nature's Experiment in Unnatural Aging." *Journal of the American Medical Association* 226 (December 1973): 1565.

Vaupel, J. "Early Death: An American Tragedy." *Law and Contemporary Problems* 40 (Autumn 1976): 73–121.

Veatch, Robert M. *Death, Dying, and the Biological Revolution: Our Last Quest for Responsibility*. New Haven, Conn.: Yale University Press, 1976.

———. "The Medical Model: Its Nature and Problems." *Hastings Center Studies* 1 No. 3 (1973): 59–76.

———. "What is a 'Just' Health Care Delivery?" *Ethics and Health Policy*. Edited by Robert M. Veatch and Roy Branson. Cambridge, Mass.: Ballinger Press, 1976.

———. "The Whole-Brain-Oriented Concept of Death: An Outmoded Philosophical Formulation." *Journal of Thanatology* 3 (1975): 13–30.

Walford, Roy L. *The Immunologic Theory of Aging*. Baltimore: Williams & Wilkins, 1969.

———. "The Immunologic Theory of Aging: Current Status." *Federation Proceedings* (1973).

Williams, Bernard. "The Makropoulos Case: Reflections on the Tedium of Immortality." in *Problems of the Self.* Cambridge: Cambridge University Press, 1973.

Zeckhauser, Richard. "Procedures for Valuing Lives." *Public Policy* 23 (Fall 1975): 419–64.

———, and Shepard, Donald. "Where Now for Saving Lives?" *Law and Contemporary Problems* 40 (August 1976): 5–45.

Index

tryptophan-deficient, 10
vitamins and minerals, importance of, 10
Diethylaminoethyl moiety, in life-span extension, 19
Dimethylaminoethyl moiety, in life-span extension, 19
Disaggregated measure of valuing lives, 205
Disease, concepts of, 37–41
  aging as disease, 41–43, 184–94
  dualistic, 38, 40
  holistic, 38, 39, 41, 82
  iatrogenic (doctor-induced), 39, 40–41
  physical-organic, 38, 39
  value-laden, 39, 40, 41
Disease control and elimination
  effects on freedom, 235–36
  effects of life-extension technologies on, 92–93
Distribution of life-extension technologies
  according to theories of justice, 53–58
  claims to, 49–53
Divorce, effects of life extension on, 98–100
DMAE. *See* Dimethylaminoethyl
Dualistic concept of disease, 38
  choice of life-extension technologies with, 40
Dworkin, Gerald, 124
Dyck, Arthur, 126, 128–29, 131

Eating, restrictions on as assault on freedom, 232
Education, effects of life extension on, 109–11, 244, 245
Effort, as basis for distribution of life-extension technologies, 51
Egalitarian theory of justice, 55–56, 57–58, 204–5
  choice of life-extension technologies with, 56
Elderly, reacting to, with curve-squaring, 87–88, 98
Eliade, Mircea, 150
Emergentism (view of man), 44–45
Endurance position. *See* Autonomy (endurance) position
Engelhardt, H. Tristram, 41–42, 118,

125–26
Entitlement theory of justice, and choice of life-extension technologies, 56–57, 57–58
Entropic aging, 7
Environment, personal, mastery of, changes with aging, 89
Environmental control, effects on freedom of, 93, 238
Equality of all, as basis for distribution of life-extension technologies, 49–50
Erikson, Erik, 155, 241–46
Euthanasia. *See also* Right to die laws
  active, 126–28, 134–35, 250–51, 257–58
  beneficent. *See* active
  benemortasia. *See* passive
  effects of life-extension technologies on, 71–75, 248–67
  involuntary, 250
  passive, 128–29, 135–36, 250–51, 257–58
  present laws and recent developments, 70–71, 249–57
  voluntary, 250
Everone, Chadd, 10
Experimental vs. customary treatment, 259–60
Extraordinary care, 73, 259–60

Fabrega, H., 39
Family, effects of life-extension technologies on, 46, 94–104, 244–45
  childbearing and -rearing, 100–2
  homes and hospitals, 102–4
  inheritance, 96–98, 244
  intergenerational relations, 94–96, 244–45
  marriage, divorce, remarriage, 98–100
  women and careers, 100–2
Finances of health care, management of for just life extension, 37, 282–83. *See also* Aggregating measures of valuing lives
Fletcher, Joseph, 33
Fluoride, effects on freedom of use in water, 232, 264
Frank, Dr. Benjamin, 11
Frankl, Viktor, 111